Andrew Pacho

Lead Us To
A Place

~your spiritual journey

through

life's seasons

Lead Us To A Place

by Andrew Pacholyk MS L.Ac

Copyright © 2018

Editor: James Palacio

Cover design: Robert Collison

Front cover image: Shutterstock, artist: Ullithemrg

Back cover photo: Jeanne Atkin MS. L.Ac

All rights reserved. No part of this book may be reproduced or transmitted in any form or by any means, electronic or mechanical, including photocopying, recording, or by an information storage and retrieval system - except by a reviewer who may quote brief passages in a review to be printed in a magazine or newspaper or upon request to publish an excerpt or article.

The author of this book does not dispense medical advice or prescribe the use of any technique as a form of treatment for physical, emotional, or medical problems without the advice of a physician, either directly or indirectly. The intent of the author is only to offer information of a general nature to help you in your quest for emotional and spiritual well-being.

ISBN 978-0-692-12041-5
Library of Congress Control Number: 2018905713
Wellness Press, New York, NY

About the Author

Andrew Pacholyk, MS, L.Ac is a licensed acupuncturist and certified herbalist in the State of New York with a full time practice in New York City. Andrew specializes in rejuvenating therapies based in the ancient Chinese Medical approach to Endocrinology, Gynecology and Pain Management. His knowledge, expertise and clinical training has offered him the ability to experience and continually learn about the body and its energy system in health, as well as in disease.

Andrew is on the American Board of Integrative Holistic Medicine, American Board of Preventive Medicine, American Pregnancy Association and National Certification Commission for Acupuncture and Oriental Medicine.

Peacefulmind.com is the life work of Andrew Pacholyk MS, L.Ac. Peacefulmind.com focuses on a place for you to come, relax, and become a centered, more powerful human being. Discover more about Andrew, his practice and his life's work at http://www.peacefulmind.com

Andrew's articles on spirituality, health and wellness have been published all over the world in 30 languages. He is an ongoing contributor in such publications as Aromatherapy Times, Health Magazine and OM Times Magazine.

Andrew is the author of *The Crystal Astrologer Course* and *Chakracology Course*. His other healing studies include the *Color Elite Color Therapy Course, Complete Meditation,* and most popular *Crystal Medicine Course,* and *Crystal Light Crystal Therapy Course.*

Andrew is an educator. He has taught and certified over 100,000 students worldwide in these specific healing techniques.

Foreword

By Jean-Claude Van Itallie

"What a beautiful, moving and instructive book, a good read, a spiritual adventure, it seems, for writer and reader both.

In it, the knowledgeable healer Andrew Pacholyk becomes our personal guide, our genial host – caring, vulnerable, poetic, joyous and authoritative – to a world of spiritual self-help.

This is a delightful how-to book, chock-a-block with centuries old healing techniques for all the senses and from many traditions – pilgrimages, prayer, dance, meditation, crystals, and daily exercises.

It offers an organized way to look at the world at every age and in every season.

It is also a reference book of tools and techniques, a friend to turn to for precise information on how exactly to help yourself live more healthily and creatively.

Thank you to the author for his compassion and practical suggestions.

May we consult this book often and apply its techniques so as to make the world a better place for all."

Jean-Claude van Itallie ~ Playwright and founder/director Shantigar Foundation for Theater, Meditation, and Healing

Dedication

We are all on a journey. From the minute we leave the womb to the moment we reach the tomb. Our journey is really our own personal experience. It is what we choose to do with the time that we are given that can make our journey as enriching as it can be. I would like to dedicate this book to all those who seek to *look deeper* in their travels. To those who *dare to go beyond* the comfort of their front door and make their *dreams a reality*. To those who are *brave enough* to step forward and find the passion inside their heart, I applaud your *fortitude and raw guts* that make you want to be who you *really can be!*

Acknowledgements

No life is an independent light. We collectively "bump into" spiritual beings who inspire us, make impressions, make our lives better or simply show us kindness:

~ **to Mom**. Your unconditional love and eternal care has made me a better man. For every turn in life, you were there. You gave us everything, sacrificed everything and created a life most yearn for. I am proud of your strength, fortitude and blessings on every level. Thank you!

~ **to Dad**. I know you are with me, always. "I love you forever" too!

~ **to Steven**, no brother is as compassionate, interested and cares, more than you. What a blessing to have someone like you to go through life with. I am eternally grateful.

~ **to Tonito**, tu eres la luz más grande en mi vida y mi ángel guardián, eterno. Mi vida ha encontrado significado por tu culpa.

~ **to Katherine Pacholyk**, I am grateful for you. You are the love of my brother's life (and mine). You are an inspiration to me with your devoted work ethic, attention to details and the way you have transformed your life from corporate dynamo, beautiful bride, to wonderful mom. Thank you for being there.

~ **to my Alexa**, you are my angel. May you always grow in love, have compassion and understanding toward others and find the love in all things. I adore you.

~ **to Melody Stahovic**, you give me courage, appreciation and the greatest gift of all, love!

~ **to Irene Cassianos**, I will never forget the unyielding love and care you have shown your husband and family and for the kindness and generosity of spirit. Thank you for making me meals, every day I was in the hospital. That simple act of kindness will stay with me always. Thank you.

~ **to Jean-Claude van Itallie**, your pearls of wisdom and generosity have made me a better man. You have shown me how to be inventive, unapologetic for my desires in life and for helping me to find an even stronger connection to the Sacred spirit. Thank you for writing my forward!

~ **to James**, AKA Fiona St. James, what better way to go through life, than with someone who has your back, makes an effort to be your friend and teaches us how to be ourselves, every day. Besitios, siempre!

. ~ **to Antonio Santos,** our lives are a snap shot of each decade and I'm so glad you are always in the picture! Thank you for lifetimes of fun and laughs, the tools you gave me to be better and that, "I've got your back" feeling!

~ **to Sylvia Mendez**, gracias por cuidar de mi Tonito (y yo). Gracias por guiar nuestras vidas con un corazón abierto. Gracias por iluminar el mundo. Te amamos.

~ **to Shannon Foreman**, sometimes people come into our lives as if they were a memory from the past. You are an angel I recognize from another time and place. Your incredible power to heal is evident in all the clients who are attracted to you and all the love you give back in return! I am so grateful for you. You have enriched my life in ways, you may never know. Thank you!!

~ **to Myriam Oliveras**, you are a powerful light of heavenly love, trying to burst forth from your God given body! You have an immense amount of healing to offer others, and you do it, everyday! You came into my life, as we were supposed to meet. I am blessed to know you!

~**to John Langoni**, I am so grateful for your artistic and technical input, hard work and help on the creation of this book. I could not have done this without you!

~**to Robert Collison**, you are a master at your craft. Many many thanks for the amazing cover. I truly appreciate you!

~ **to my family, Stahovic, Tinti and ALL the Pacholyk clans**, we are bound together by the deepest connections: blood, love and gratitude.

~ **to Chris Jewell, Heidi and Ursula Whitman**, you are the sisters I never had and you hold the dearest place in my heart! Thank you.

~ **to Libby, Martha Jayne and Billy Barrett**, how they gonna keep us "down on the farm" after we've seen P.A.! We share some of the greatest childhood memories. I'll never forget. Thank you.

Lead Us To A Place

*"With gratitude and love I give each day and night for **life** I've lived.*

I give thanks and special praise for good and precious memories saved.

And now it's time for me to move into the next adventure, soon.

Lead us to a place where we,

can gain a better sense and see,

more love, more truth more grace toward thee,

and grant us more humility.

So with your help, I ask of you to teach me, guide me bring me to…

the place where I'm supposed to be with unencumbered effort, please."

~ Andrew Pacholyk MS L.Ac

Table of Contents

Chapter 1

A Brief Introduction

I am grateful that you have found this book. Thank you for taking the time to peruse my heart-felt expressions on healing.

Throughout my life I have had two major careers. One was dance, the other medicine. I have been blessed to be able to live the two most important things I have created in my life.

My first career was as a professional dancer for 20 years. I've been fortunate enough to travel the world, either with my dance career or by means of my own. I have been able to see some of the most amazing and sacred places on earth. In each location, I have learned more about the cultures, local traditions and even more about myself! As a dancer, I was able to express myself through movement, song and acting. I was able to use my body as an instrument to show others who I was and how I could relate to the world - through self-expression. It was also a way for me to bring joy to others. It was a glorious and rewarding career.

I discovered my second career after an accident happened to me. I suffered 2nd and 3rd degree burns over my left arm and both legs. This debilitated me, physically, for 7 months of my life and emotionally, for 7 years after. Lost, after the end of my dance career, I had no direction and no idea where to go next. I am grateful to my partner, who steered me in the right direction.

My second career became a gratifying choice in holistic medicine. Out of this, I started to create tools to help assist my patients along their journey... myself included. I worked hard for the opportunity to study with several great mentors along my path, each adding a piece to the puzzle about myself, as well as my inquisitive mind.

Through my acupuncture and metaphysical practice, I have been able to work with a lot of people. Some, simply come in to get well or for preventative measures, while a majority of others would come to me to unearth a deeper meaning or better understanding of "who" they are and "why" they are here. It is constantly fulfilling to me to be able to explore these questions with them.

My study of Chinese Medicine has been profound. Traditional Chinese Medicine (TCM) is the oldest, continually practiced, and professionally administered health care system in the world. It is a documented medical system spanning over 2,500 years based on comprehensive philosophies, rational theories, clinically tested and empirically verified by over 100 generations of highly educated practitioners.

Chinese Medicine is a total system of internal medicine which is comprised of a diagnostic procedure based on signs, symptoms and treatment styles including acupuncture, herbal medicine, exercise, diet and meditation. Its foundation is based on the principles of balance; the interdependent relationship of Yin and Yang. Through this balance, health is achieved and maintained.

The Chinese approach all forms of healing in a very poetic manner. It is through this paradigm of medicine, which allowed me to look at the seasons from a different perspective.

The start of each season is one of the best ways to remind ourselves that it is time to evaluate our health. Our moods and bodies change as the seasons change. Regulated by cycles of light and dark, climate changes and our circadian rhythm, we can focus on staying healthy with food, exercise, sleep and a smart seasonal detox.

From the Chinese medicine paradigm, people experience "seasons within them", as the body goes through passageways or doorways, to the next stage or cycle of life. In the Taoist tradition, this is considered the "heavenly gate" or "divine door." The way health is looked at through these systems of belief, express that the mind and body are as one, working together in a trifecta along with the spirit.

We must learn to cultivate our spirit. To be considered in good health, we can learn to quiet the mind and find harmony within the body. Only then, can we achieve harmony with the world and nature around us.

Experiences from My Mentors

Teachers and mentors play an important role in our journey through life. I have been fortunate enough to have several mentors who have left me with healing life lessons, lasting impressions and tools I still use today. Here is a brief synopsis and the teachings they have shared with me.

Perhaps the most profound mentors were my **parents, John and Andrena Pacholyk.** They took the time to teach us beneficial lessons each day. They nurtured and **taught with love. It was their greatest tool.** They would teach by example and give love along the way. Discipline was inevitable when my brother and I were very young and, in many ways, I think it instilled a strong work ethic in us both. My brother and I were highly involved in sports, music groups and many extra-curricular activities. They always taught us that **we could achieve anything we put our minds to.** That ultimate love and attention is why I honor my parents. For their lessons and discipline, I am truly and unconditionally grateful!

Steven Pacholyk is an esteemed and respected man. He also happens to be my brother. Growing up, it seemed that I was always the one protecting him, watching over him (and taunting him, of course). Now, as adults, it is completely opposite. **He is my guide and protector.** An impressive business man at age 8, Steven created an opportunity to supplement his allowance by selling ice cream to our neighbors down the road. Dad turned our little red wagon into an ice cream "truck" and Steven's entrepreneurial spirit was born. His love and devotion (and quite frankly, his reincarnated spirit) connecting him to Gettysburg and the Civil War, lead him to be the youngest National Park's Guide in Gettysburg history! Steven, you are my **guiding light.**

Diana Banks was my dance teacher in my early and formative years at college. She was my ballet and jazz teacher. She stood about 4 feet tall and was in her late 60's yet she was a powerhouse of energy, insight, and wisdom. **She taught by positive reinforcement.** She encouraged us every day to be the best that we could be. She would always bring out the best in each individual. She was able to read each person's weakness and strengths. She would then encourage our strengths as she gently modified our weak points. She would merely point out, in a very private way, what we needed to work harder at. Diana was an accomplished dancer, actress, and performer who shared with us her greatest **pearls of wisdom,** for which I am eternally grateful. She was an amazing woman.

Dr, Gloria Bonali was another dance teacher who taught choreography, modern dance, and jazz. She was equally amazing in her own special way. **Her teaching method was to encourage by rewarding you** when you did something right. She was sparing with the compliments, but when she did praise you, either with kind words, or by offering you a dance to choreograph, you knew you did something right. I am grateful for her encouragement of my career.

David Howard was my greatest ballet teacher in New York City. A master teacher for some of the most renowned ballerinas of our time, he was the head of his own company and school. Mr. Howard **taught by example.** He rarely gave compliments, yet there was something in his teachings that wanted you to do better. I believe it was my desire to "please the master" or show him that I understood what he was trying to convey. His method of the ballet was easy on the body. His teaching technique took the natural approach to working with the strengths you had and not forcing your weak points. He taught how to disguise these weaknesses by not bringing to much attention to them. For example, my strength as a dancer was through my expression from the waist up. I was not so much a technical dancer with a perfect turn out, so therefore he would help me to disguise the fact that my feet were not perfect and helped me to bring people's attention to my persona or how I would relate to the audience. He was a master of his craft. I am grateful the Universe led me to him.

Martha Graham was by far the toughest teacher I have ever had. She gave very little encouragement, was a strict teacher and used the teaching method of **making an example out of your weaknesses.** For instance, one day we were doing a floor exercise where we are seated on the floor with our legs bent, one in front and one behind. The exercise was a series of contractions from your center, which would slightly turn your body so that you were free to lift either the front or back leg off the floor. As I was going through the routine, Martha was not happy with the lack of distance I was unable to achieve with my knee coming off the floor. So, she proceeded to place a lighter under my knee so that the flame would allow my front knee to lift off the floor higher. As I struggled to contract and lift my knee higher I could smell the hairs burning on my leg as she continued to hold the flame there and lecture as to how the knee should be higher off the floor in the contraction. Although this was one of the most memorable incidents I took with me, it truly allowed me to 'turn a corner' in my dancing and made me even stronger and more accomplished. Though it was hard for me to handle at the time, the overall experience made me a greater dancer.

Deva Inglesia Germana was my great yoga teacher. **She taught by expression of the greatest good and would constantly move you out of your comfort zone.** What served you the best is what she brought out in you. She worked on developing the successes of your body and how to express it, not only in movement but also through words. She would teach us to know the same movement either by doing it, saying it in different ways or chanting it, in order to achieve the same end results. She was a disciplinarian who would physically manipulate your body into the proper postures in order to "feel what was the correct posture." Whether it felt bad or not, it was important to her that you knew what **'felt correct'**. She took my discipline as a yogi to a new level.

James Palacio AKA Fiona St. James, is my fearless and wonderful best friend. They say that people come into our lives for a reason. With James, I can give you 35 years' worth of reasons. **Friends have to make an effort to be friends.** James has truly been that person. Many of my dear "friends" have come and gone, but James and I have been through life's ups and downs and we have faced them like two troopers going off to win the battles and enjoy the spoils, together. Friendships are most likely taken for granted, but when someone actually works at being your friend, may they bless your life always. James, thank you!

Zachary Selig gave me great insight into the world of metaphysics. Through his sweeping teachings of the Chakra, the aura, crystals, the metaphysics of light, sea, and sky, and his knowledge shared as a painter, helped me to grasp great insight into a broad spectrum through his **"teaching by example."** He would share with me that **there is very little 'right or wrong'** rather just varying degrees of the truth. I was lucky enough to become his friend in the mid 90's in Miami Beach, where we were able to live freely and *'run about as children'* learning from the great gifts of nature, which Miami still gives. I learned from Zachary how color and light bring about energies that continue to enlighten his work as a world-renowned painter, Santero, author, designer, and metaphysician. For his teachings, I am truly grateful, for they allowed me to 'turn yet another corner' as I continue growing as a human being.

15

Dr. Carl Miller is one of my greatest teachers of medicine. He is a Gastroenterologist and internal medicine specialist, as well as the president of my graduate school and head of New York Presbyterian Hospital in New York. **He taught by allowing you to discover and explore ~ layer by layer.** He was famous for giving a packet of information, usually a list of words, and sending you on your way to discover each and every meaning. He would encourage you to use these words in context and in examples that were new, and then quiz you on this same information. Therefore, the effort you put into the work was the result you got out of it. If you didn't put much effort into the work that week, you would surely get a failing grade on the quiz. He taught me how **going back and reviewing what you've learned** over a course of a few lessons, really enforced what you retained (and what you did not). I use this method in all the courses I offer, today. Thanks to him, I become a specialist in my field of medicine.

Tonio Ruiz (Tonito) has been my mentor for over 30 years. He has a special teaching method of **combining love with subtle discipline.** He has given me some of my greatest lessons in humility, tolerance, self-respect, and learning how to love. He has given me a deeper comprehension of spirituality through understanding. He has shown me how to face my fears. He has given me support and unconditional love for most of my adult life. These are lessons we all continue to struggle with, yet Tonito has made them attainable through patience, understanding, and by **setting the example.** He taught me how **action speaks volumes, while words mean nothing!** Everyone's actions determine who they are, NOT what they *say they are* or what they're *going* to do. He has shown me that people's reactions come from their present or past circumstances and should not be taken personally. He makes you face what you're most afraid of by encouragement and understanding. Next to my parents, there has been no greater teacher than Tonito in my life. As a great psychic once told me, Tonito has been with me through many lives, most often in the same role. How blessed I have been to find someone to follow me throughout the ages.

Perhaps there have been those in your life who have been great teachers or have followed you through many incarnations. Look closely; you may be very surprised to still find these mentors in your life today.

Try This Practical Exercise

1. I encourage you to make a list of your mentors throughout your life.

2. Write out their names and who they were/are to you.

3. Express their teaching methods and how it helped to form who you are today.

4. What did you like about their teaching methods?

5. What did you dislike about their teaching methods?

6. Good or bad, did it ultimately help you to learn?

7. Think through your life. When I made this list, I realize I had more teachers than I thought I had. All of which made lasting impressions.

Chapter 2

Tools in this Book

Throughout this book, you will find me making references to the rhythms of time from different cultures. I often connect the passage or transition through the seasons by relating them to music, color, stones, aroma and much more. I consider the references from other countries and their cultural, spiritual and historical traditions to be amazing teaching tools of self-discovery. I have dropped some "gemstones" along the way for you to follow. These are little "pearls" I have created to help myself to understand a subject a little better. I hope you find them useful. I will relate life marker to our senses, as well as our physical and metaphysical processes for the purpose of looking a little deeper into "who WE are" and how we can access more of our own innate wisdom. I hope you enjoy this journey.

In this book, I make many references to energy. The energy around us and the energy within us. We are all vibrating, energetic beings that are constantly regulating - constantly fluctuating. This never stops, even after death. I also believe we still "resonate" energy after death, in the form of spirit.

This book does not preach religious dogma nor a one-sided view of faith. Rather, this book is a "window" to all faiths, religions and ancient beliefs that lead us to the same place... our spirituality. It is up to you to decide what you feel, speaks to you and gives you a chance to formulate your own belief system.

Positive affirmations

Life is built on positivity, one block at a time. The minute you open the window to fear and anxiety, the winds of worry whistle in and start to wreak havoc on your mind.

Affirmations that are positive, encouraging and keep you focusing forward, are the goals of using these "words of wonder."

The premise of a "mantra" was something I learn from my yoga mentor. She would often say, "use your mantra. It is the greatest weapon against self-doubt, insecurity, and fear."

A mantra or positive affirmations are words or one word or sound, repeated to assist with the concentration in meditation. You do not have to be meditating to repeat a mantra. It can be done anywhere and at any time.

~"I have time for everything, today."

~ "I am positive, happy and strong."

~ "I will get this job today."

~ "Just breathe."

Now it's your turn. "I am _____ "

"I can _____ "

"I promise_____ "

"Today I will realize _____ "

What is your word for today? "_____ "

Crystals

Stone and crystals have been a part of every faith, religious belief, and spiritual dogma since the beginning of time. They have been used as altars and temples, in churches and cathedrals. They show up in crowns of kings and queens, on the breastplate of Aaron, subscribed to the 12 tribes of Israel, and adorn the staffs, garments, and relics of popes and religious leaders in every period. Crystals have been used as a spiritual tool for centuries.

Crystals have been in my life since I was a little boy. From collecting them, gather them, and rockhounding, I have made a career out of selling rocks! **"Crystals are like friends."** When you first make a new friend, you naturally sum up who they are by what they like and dislike, associate with, and have an affinity towards. Crystals can be used as an adjunct therapy in any form of healing. Why? Because they work on many levels. They are beautiful to look at, great to meditate and relax with, and are soothing and comforting. Just like an old friend.

Working with Crystals

The meaning of crystals and stones have come from every culture and religion including the Mayan, Chinese, Indian, Greek, Roman, Celtic, Tibetans, and many more. Stones and crystals have been used as tools to look within. They have been used as remedies and objects of beauty to admire. Whether you see these gems as just pretty bobbles to look at or tools to a new awareness, I hope you find their stories engaging. These *stone stories* have been handed down through families and tribes, teachers and shaman, and are the traditions of many cultures. **All the metaphysical meanings of these stones come from these belief systems.**

*Create a medicine pouch. Put your crystals in a pouch and carry them with you. This is one of the most interesting and oldest remedies. Choose 2 - 4 crystals. These complementary stones are carried or worn on the person or placed in a certain area. They can be used for anything from meditation to emotional balance. Carry stone(s) in your pocket or purse.

*Crystal concoctions or elixirs are the recipes of the past. It is recommended to place clean stones or crystals into distilled water and place them in the morning sun through the day and into the night of a full moon for 24 hours. This allows the vibrant energy of sun and moon to reflect through the water and into the crystals, therefore charging the water with their vibrational force of light and color. Use the elixirs to anoint the pulse points of the neck, behind the ears, inside of wrists, or tops of feet.

*Crystal Hydrotherapy was used by the ancient Greek and Roman physicians for centuries. Hydrotherapy and crystals have a number of uses. Crystals or crystal salts with warm water will relax spasms; therefore, hydrotherapy has been useful in treating such conditions as muscular strains and sprains, muscular fatigue, and backache. If your crystal can tolerate water (see list), then bathing with the crystal is a way to work with your stones. Wearing crystals such as magnetic hematite, quartz, and copper are used for pain syndromes.

*Crystal Massage. Use your stone as a massage tool. Use some essential oils or massage lotion on the skin and use your stone to massage the areas, which feel painful, blocked or stuck. You will find this to be a great remedy.

*Meditate with your crystal. Place your crystal in your dominant hand or on the floor in front of you. Close your eyes and concentrate on the color of your stone. Slowly try to feel the crystal's magnetic pulse. Remember: "Energy follows thought." The imagery of visualization is very powerful. As you breathe, you may inhale and exhale through your centers of energy. This can bring awareness tof your own vitality. (See: Vital Energy)

*You may utilize the vibrational power of sound or music during your healing session. Stones may enhance a positive, reconnecting flow of energy, along with music and sound. This may allow you to bring up, recognize and clear emotional blocks. Mantras, sounds and music connect us to a Universal flow.

*By "laying of the stones" on your body, you can begin a healing transformation. In meditation, you may choose to visualize the corresponding color of each Chakra energy saturating and balancing every part of your body. On the following pages, are the Chakra centers and their corresponding colors, points, and locations. The crystals listed are suggestions for these energy areas.

* Lay the stones around your body in an "Aura net" either on the floor or on a mat or massage table. Lay within the circle of stones. This encourages an "energy net" to meditate within, dream upon or just relax in after a stressful day.

Cleansing your Stone or Crystal

Method One: Cleanse your crystal by smudging it with sweetgrass, sage, cedar, or incense. Light the herb, then blow out the flame. Pass the crystal several times through the wafting smoke.

Method Two: If a particular crystal should not be placed in water, (see list) simply cleanse your crystals by placing them in a bowl of flower petals.

Method Three: Water can cleanse your crystal. Clear away dirt, grime, and fingerprints by running them under room temperature or lukewarm water. Soak your crystals in water with the petals of flowers such as rose, honeysuckle, or orange blossoms for up to 24 hours.

Method Four: Some crystals CAN be cleansed in sea salt water. Add one teaspoon of sea salt in a glass bowl with 4 ounces of room temperature to lukewarm water. Stir and dissolve the sea salt. Place the crystals in the water. Make sure the crystals are covered. Let them bathe in the water for 24 hours. This is a wonderful way to rejuvenate your crystals. It washes away the negative charge it has absorbed over time. (Note: Some crystals should NOT be washed/cleansed in salt water/sun for it changes their physical properties, (not their metaphysical properties.) They are listed below):

Not to be cleansed in Salt Water:

*Alabaster *Calcite *Carnelian *Hematite *Labradorite (Spectrolite) *Lepidolite *Lodestone *Moldavite *Opal *Turquoise *Ulexite

*Use caution only with the softer Mica and crystalline stones

These stones may fade in sunlight:

*Amethyst *Celestite *Opal *Turquoise*

Method Five: Soaking the crystals in a solution of 1 quart of warm water, one tablespoon of sea salt OR a quarter cup of apple cider vinegar for 20 minutes to half an hour, is a quick clearing technique that is not too drastic and quite thorough. A similar solution with distilled vinegar actually seems to work well with just a quick dip in the water. Dry your stone thoroughly.

Method Six: Some stones, such as lodestone, magnetite, metals, or magnetic stones can be cleansed in alcohol, brandy, or cologne.

Method Seven: Crystal clusters make great chargers and can also cleanse any crystal just by placing it on top of the cluster for 24 hours.

Method Eight: Use a dry cloth to simply wipe off dust, oil, and fingerprints. Massage a stone with essential oil. Essential oils are the true plant essence and work like the smudging/smoke method. You can then, dry off the stone and polish it with a cloth.

Tips for Charging Stones

After cleansing a stone, it is a good idea to energize it again. Somewhat like recharging a battery. Placing it on or within an energy source is a good way to do this.

*Charge and energize your crystals by placing them under the light of a full moon for up to 24 hours. (up to two nights of a full moon)

*Some crystals love to be charged and energized in the sun. Allow them to sit in the daylight for up to 24 hours. (up to two days of sunlight).

*Charge your crystals by burying them in the earth or pot of soil (make sure you mark where you buried them!), for up to 24 hours.

*Place your crystal to be charged in a bowl of tumbled hematite stones or tumbled quartz crystal for up to 24 hours.

Activating your Stone or Crystal

Hold your stone or crystal in your dominant hand. Hold it up and level with your heart or Heart Chakra and project toward your crystal a thought pattern of unconditional love. This simple act, the act of stating it to be so, (intention) will establish an electromagnetic connection between you and your crystal. Now you are ready to do your healing work.

Essential Oils

Essential oils are the true nectar of fruits and plants. Essential oils are the actual essence or spirit of nature's gifts. They are extracted from the flowers and herbs by way of either cold-pressing as with citrus fruits or by steam distillation as with plants and flowers.

These pure oil extracts have therapeutic properties to be used in many different forms of healing and health. Recalling a certain scent from a specific memory or special time in your life is a transforming experience.

Using essential oils

Essential oils are used in a variety of ways. You can inhale them directly from the bottle. You can use them for skin care, hair care, and body care, as well as, for many beauty purposes such as personal hygiene, aromatherapy baths, or a foot massage. Use them to give and receive aromatherapy massages. Inhale aromatherapy oil blends to relieve congestion, clear your head and make breathing easier. You can also make wonderful fragrances with essential oils.

Aromatherapy can help prevent or ease an assortment of ailments. Essential oils can boost the immune system. You can treat aches, pains, and injuries with essential oils. Aromatherapy can help reduce stress, lift depression, and restore emotional well-being. You can disperse essential oils through the air in your home or office to increase productivity or alter moods.

Essential oils can be utilized in hundreds of different ways. You can create massage blends, inhalants, rubs, compresses, diffuser blends, or perfume blends. Choose the form which fits into your lifestyle and suits you best.

How to Create Your Recipe Blends

*Bath Blend: Add 15-20 drops of essential oils to a bathtub already filled with warm water. Disperse the oil in the warm water with your hand. Soak in the bath for up to twenty minutes. Repeat as needed, then cleanse your tub.

*Massage Blend: Add 10-15 drops of a chosen essential oil to 4 ounces of a carrier based oil such as sunflower, safflower, jojoba, or canola oil. Pour a quarter size drop into the palm of your hand and bring your palms together. Disperse the oil over the area you want to massage and rub in a circular, clockwise motion. Gently massage the area for 10-20 minutes or over the entire body for a total body massage.

*Diffuser Blend: Place 8-10 drops of essential oil in a diffuser bowl filled with water. Most diffusers use a tea candle. As the candle warms the bowl, the aroma from the blend diffuses into the air. This blend can also be placed in any lamp ring or automatic diffuser.

*Inhalant Blend: You may blend several essential oils together or use one particular oil. Simply uncap the bottle and place it up to one nostril. Close the other nostril with your finger as you inhale deeply. Switch nostrils and inhale once more. Be sure to close the opposite nostril as you inhale. Try not to touch the bottle to the skin for the area under the nose is very sensitive and the oil may slightly burn or irritate the area. Repeat as often as needed.

*Rub Blend: In 1 tablespoon of carrier base oil, add 8-10 drops essential oil. Massage the rub into appropriate areas for 5-10 minutes. Repeat as needed.

*Compress Blend: Blend 5 -10 drops essential oil in a quart of cold water. Saturate a cloth with the water/blend mixture and apply to the affected area for at least 10 minutes. Repeat treatment often.

*Perfume Blend: Blending 2 to 3 essential oils together in jojoba or sunflower oil can make a lovely perfume. Dab this delicate, concentrated mixture on your pulse points of the sides of the neck, inside of the wrists, or tops of the feet. Remember the rule: Less is more.

Essential Oil Guidelines

Essential oils are classified as either top, middle, or base notes. These single notes have a general rule of thumb:

*Top notes: are the fastest acting and quickest to evaporate. Lasting 3-24 hrs.

*Middle notes: are the moderately volatile, affect metabolism, and body functions. Last 2-3 days.

*Base notes: are slower to evaporate, the most sedative and relaxing oils. Last up to approximately one week.

*Essential oils are very concentrated. Their safe use requires they be treated with care and respect. The user should be knowledgeable about their properties and actions before use. Most personal applications require drops rather than ounces.

*Keep oils out of reach of children and away from pets. Please do not ingest by mouth. Because of the potency of certain essential oils, proceed carefully and with guidance from a trained aromatherapist if any of the following situations exist: pregnancy, high blood pressure, epilepsy, open wounds, diabetes, rashes, neurological disorders, or if taking prescription medications or homeopathic remedies.

*Most undiluted pure essential oils are not applied directly to the skin. For application to the skin, dilute in a pure carrier oil, such as almond, grapeseed, or jojoba. For full-body and foot baths, dilute the oils in water. Special care is advised when using essential oils, which heighten skin sensitivity to ultraviolet light. These oils include angelica, verbena, and citrus oils such as bergamot, bitter orange, lemon, and lime. Avoid exposure to ultraviolet rays for a minimum of four hours following application of photosensitive essential oils.

*Check Peacefulmind.com for specific precautions about each essential oil. Essential oils have different levels of potency. The more potent the oil, the smaller the quantity used. Sage, fennel, hyssop, and wintergreen are relatively more potent than most oils; rose, lavender and chamomile are relatively mild. Most essential oils are safe and nontoxic when proper dilution recommendations are followed. When in doubt, seek guidance from a professional aromatherapist or medical professional.

*Essential oils are not meant to be use when treating certain medical conditions. For conditions lasting more than a week, and/or with fever or other unusual symptoms, proper diagnosis and treatment from a licensed medical practitioner is necessary.

*Essential oils are very concentrated, so it's important to handle them with care. Please read these cautions carefully:

*Always read and follow all label warnings and cautions.

*Keep oils tightly closed and out of the reach of children.

*Never consume undiluted oils. Cook only with those oils approved for food use. These oils are certified as GRAS (Generally Recognized As Safe) by the FDA.

*Don't use undiluted oils on your skin. (Dilute with vegetable oils.)

*Skin test oils before using. Dilute a small amount and apply to the skin on your inner arm. Do not use if redness or irritation occurs.

*Keep oils away from eyes and mucous membranes. Stop using oil immediately if redness, burning, itching, or irritation occur. Wash the area, thoroughly.

*Avoid use of these oils during pregnancy: bitter almond, basil, clary sage, clove bud, hyssop, sweet fennel, juniper berry, marjoram, myrrh, peppermint, rose, rosemary, sage, thyme, and wintergreen.

*These oils may irritate those with extra sensitive skin: allspice, bitter almond, basil, cinnamon leaf, cinnamon bark, clove bud, sweet fennel, fir needle, lemon, lemongrass, melissa, peppermint, tea tree, wintergreen.

*Angelica and all citrus oils make the skin more sensitive to ultraviolet light. Do not go out into the sun with these oils on your skin.

*Sweet fennel, hyssop, rosemary, and sage should not be used by anyone with a history of epilepsy.

*People with high blood pressure should avoid hyssop, rosemary, sage, and thyme.

***

Meditation

Meditation is a time-honored art of finding stillness. Meditation helps us live a healthier, less stressful life. The physical and psychological benefits are wonderful. Meditation calms the sympathetic nervous system and lowers stress hormones, such as cortisol. "Peace is a practice". The more you continue a meditation practice, the greater the benefits offered you. Prayer falls under this category. For what is prayer, but the asking, confirming, and receiving of wishes we meditate upon.

Meditation Basics

This is ALL you will ever need. This is for the person who has NEVER meditated before AND it is for the expert meditator. WHY? Because all meditation starts with the root of intention.

"No matter what the tree, they all grow from one seed, which takes root and branches out"

Therefore, know this:

Meditation is like the lotus tree or flower. Rich with many, many layers, leaves, or petals. It blossoms to be a vibrant plant or flower, but at its core, it is the same, basic principle, ~ the seed you plant.

1. The Seed: Your intention: the reason you do this
2. Air to grow: Your breath: in order to reach the roots
3. Food to grow: Your thoughts: how you choose to nourish the seed
4. Water to grow: Your ability to flow and let go: how you magnetize your purpose to bring it back

Now, **forget everything** you know about meditation.

~ Sit in a comfortable position. Whatever that position is. No right or wrong. The idea is to be at ease, yet aware. It is important to sense the space around you with an image of the top of your head pulling upwards, while your sitting bones feel grounded and pulling you downward.

~Close your eyes.

The Seed

~State your intention or purpose for meditating TODAY. You can say it out loud, if that connects you to your reason.

Today, in this moment, I am meditating for:

_____

(hint: keep it simple, yet focused) For example, instead of meditating for world peace, meditate on something that may be an easier challenge to start with. Meditate on peace in your corner of the world or in your immediate location) such as peace in your household, or peace in your mind. (We will get to world peace later.)

Air to Grow

With your eyes remained closed, breathe.

Now, you are going to breathe with intention. You are going to take breaths with purpose. Each breath is now offered to your intention (or the reason you are meditating today.)

Breath is considered the "air, which circulates." Breath reaches all the way down to the root of the seed (in order to sprout the intention) as breath reaches all the way out to the branches, as intention (the seed) grows.

You have this amazing ability to do this. As you focus on the inhale...draw your breath down to the root of your lungs (seed-intention). As you focus on the exhale...expel the breath out to the branches of your fingers and toes.

Breathe in a manner that comes naturally to you. Do not overthink this. There are many forms and techniques for breathing. but, for the purpose of this meditation, it is important not to become overly critical of details. This should form as a natural, easy process of taking in and letting out. Taking in and letting out.

Food to Grow

Your thoughts are how you CHOOSE to nourish the seed

Like your body, you can choose to eat food that is good for your body and soul or you can choose food, which clogs your heart, congests your lungs and makes you ill.

Your thoughts are no different. Your thoughts can empower your mind and soul or they can destroy your self-esteem, disempower your actions, and create doubt, pain, or panic.

Bring to mind 3 thoughts to EMPOWER your intention

1._____
2. _____
3._____

Because we are human, doubt, insecurity, and uncontrolled thoughts will seep into your mind. Rather than fighting them, let them in, but do not let them dwell there. This is where the free-will of meditation takes over. (Remember, there will always be a struggle between the EGO self and the TRUE self) Your free-will allows you to make a choice between good (true self) or bad (ego self).
Whenever I am teaching this technique, this is what I hear next, *"well, it's easier said, than done."* My reply is, "this is why you are already resisting." With a statement like this, you are already showing (not only to me but to the Universe) that you have already (shown your weakest side, resisted, given up,) let doubt take over.

Bring BACK to mind 3 thoughts to EMPOWER your intention

1._____
2. _____
3._____

Nourish with the good food of thought and blessings. With each inhale, feed your intention some good thought. With each exhale, release or expel anything, which does not belong there.

Water to grow

Your ability to *let flow and let go* is how you magnetize your purpose and actually watch, as the Universe brings it back to you, 10 times stronger. Water moves intention (thoughts) to flow. This is the flow you need to release and let go. Your wish will boomerang back to you, with magnetic attraction, but only if you are willing to truly release it.

At the end of your meditation, it is the last important step to release or let go your intention. It is the "giving away", which shows the Universe that you are not holding on, wanting or trying to control the outcome. It reveals that you are able to show STRENGTH in your conviction, TRUST in another force, with a BLESSING to go forward.

Letting go is probably one of the hardest things in life for us to do. Yet, if you really let go of something (an intention, material things, a loved one), you will find that their purpose serves the greater good (yourself, others, and the true reason.)

Holding on shows how tight our grip is around something (someone). Letting go shows us our ability to share, honor, appreciate what we have/had.

This shows you harmony with something larger than yourself. You will be better able to serve others if you have a healthy mind to support it. If you receive greater knowledge, you are better able to understand the reasoning behind the action.

NOW, open your eyes.

Movement/Dance/Yoga

With movement/dance/yoga, I had the golden opportunity and made the choice in my life, to dance professionally for 20 years. It was my first and most glorious career. It took me all over the world. Through this rare, difficult, rewarding, and very fleeting career, it granted me some of the greatest joys in my life!

We were born to move. No matter what form you do it in, moving is an essential part of our lives from the day we are born throughout the seasons of our lives and into old age. Movement keeps the muscles flexible and the bones suppler within their framework. Movement can be as simple as stretching in the morning or as graceful as the disciplined dancer. No matter what form you choose to do, move as much as you are able, every day.

Exercise is what your body instinctively wants to do, especially under stress: the fight or flight response, and it works. It burns off some of the stress chemicals which tension produces. When a muscle is worked to its capacity (muscle failure) then it is a relaxed muscle. Regular exercise builds stamina that can help anyone battle stress. Even something as casual as a walk around the block can help you burn off some of the tension (and calories) that you carry around. What motivates you? What is it that moves you or makes you want to get up? Use what motivates you. Find purpose. No more excuses. You'd be surprised what you could do, if you put one foot in front of the other…

How to Get Exercise in Your Life

You can increase the amount of exercise you get each week by 10 or 15 minutes. Your goal in 4 weeks' time is to have raised your limit.

*Walk, instead of driving everywhere.

*Take the stairs at the office, not the elevator.

*Bike to anywhere.

*Stretch while you relax. Walk the treadmill while watching a favorite TV program. Peddle away on a stationary bike while you're talking on the phone or waiting for the washing machine to finish.

*When your children want to play, participate with them.

*Get up from the sofa to change the channel.

*Consider parking your car a further distance from your destination.

*Listen to music and dance your way through housecleaning.

*Start slow – a few minutes at first. Then, pick up the pace and go longer.

*Workout clothes are not necessary but wear good walking shoes.

*You may not always get a day of exercise in. Avoid the guilt and pick up where you left off.

*Even if you miss a few days, you won't lose all the benefits you've gained.

*Be flexible. Do what you can, when you can.

*Find a partner. Take the stairs at the office, walk around the park or run errands, as you chat away the time with a partner.

*Instead of building your life around exercise, build exercise around your life.

The most important way to get exercise into your life is to SCHEDULE it into your day. You schedule appointments, dinner, meetings…. exercise (as a priority) should be no different. Keep moving!

Music

Music is the expression of the soul. MUSIC HEALS. There is nothing more fulfilling than incorporating music into your life. Music can delight all the senses and inspire every fiber of our being. Music has the power to soothe and relax, bring us comfort and embrace joy. It can lift our feet and hearts right off the ground and transport us to a special place, all our own. Music is our common energy. Add music to your life, every day. What does your musical life consist of?

Create A Musical Playlist

Throughout this book, I have created playlists around some of life's greatest moments, emotions and events. I would like you to do the same. Maybe you already have songs you have created into playlists that boost your mood, help you through your exercise routine, or that you play on a rainy day. If you don't, I encourage you to start a list.

Start with a subject: love, work, play, exercise or a mood you are in. Make a list of 5 or 10 songs that help or inspire you. Take a look at the playlists in this book. Learn about the power of **entrainment**. This handy "tool" can change your mood, lift your spirits or bring great inspiration. Music is a magic medium. Use it to find the spirituality, drive, or motivation in your life. Keep it close. Play it often.

Poetry/Writing/Journaling

Poetry is a relatively new tool for me, but like music, it is the rhythm of words without a song. Its impact can move us, especially if we can relate to the subject matter. From forms of poetry such as ABC and Carpe diem style to Haiku and Verse, the arranging of words for rhyme or reason can have a powerful impact on our spirit.

Sometimes, we just need to express ourselves in a way we cannot seem to do in any other medium. Some people paint, some dance, some sing…. others find healing through words.

I encourage you to pick up a pen and start writing words. Create phrases that give you hope or express a dream. They may not make sense at first, but they don't have to. Get these words out on paper. My foray into writing and poetry started through a personal journey I was writing about. From there, I explored expressing myself through a style of rhythm in words. It almost feels like writing a song or expressing a feeling I cannot seem to get out of my head, any other way.

My friend and editor, James Palacio, wrote his entire book, based on his daily journaling. Find a nice notebook or journal to write in and start writing down thoughts, dreams, and even conflicts.

Each time you write in your journal, date the page. Write a positive affirmation on the top of the page, for each day. If it is a dream journal, write down key symbols, images, colors, and keywords that mean something to you! Remember, words, like magic, have power. Positive, reinforcing words give strength. Negative, condescending words breakdown everything you have built up. Through words, happiness and joy can be served, but the wrong words in the heat of the moment can destroy and undermine all love and trust that you have created. Choose your words, carefully. Start writing!

Visualization

Visualization is an extraordinary treat for the mind. It is our will to see within our mind's eye, all that we can achieve. By putting your mind to the task, we "train the brain" to act out what we can visualize. We guide the imagery to show us how we want to use it or utilize it. We are only limited by our imagination. Dream big!

Your imagination can be a very powerful tool to help you release tension, cope with stress and calm anxiety. You can use visualization to harness the energy of your imagination and all it takes is setting a little time aside to work on mastering it. The great gift of this tool is that it can be done anywhere. Most people do this when they are meditating or before going to bed, but your guidance can be done anywhere or any time. Whenever you need this tool, take it out of your "tool belt" and use it.

Guided imagery takes this process one step further by guiding the images toward a specific life-enhancing goal, such as relaxing, healing, promoting personal growth, exploring alternative answers, clarifying values, stimulating creativity, or managing stress.

Skill, Not Magic

Research is beginning to document the significant power of our mental processes to positively affect our well-being. Yet guided imagery is not magic. It is a skill that you should practice. A skill you should practice a lot.

Your mind's eye is one of the most potent tools you have for triggering relaxation and promoting changes in attitude, perspective, or feelings. The effectiveness of guided imagery is grounded in the mind/body connection. As far as your body is concerned, sensory images have nearly the same impact as actual sensory experiences. Your body reacts physiologically to the imagined smell of baking bread in the same way it would to walk into a bakery. Mentally anticipating a fearful event can be just as frightening (or even more) than the event itself.

Guided imagery offers an opportunity to harness the natural power of your imagination to work for physical and mental health. It is a skill which can grow more useful with regular routine.

Always Begin with Relaxation

When your body and mind are in a state of active relaxation, it is the best preparation for guided imagery. You will find that relaxation is essential to guided imagery, for when the mind is free of burden, it is much easier for us to relax. Relaxation keeps the mind open, in order to stimulate the imagination and enhance guided imagery.

The benefits of guided imagery are immeasurable. What you do experience, first hand, is what you feel afterward. Once you have gained the ability to relax in a way that is soothing and natural for you, then you are more able to activate visual, mental, emotional, physical, and even spiritual associations at will.

Some people use guided imagery every day as part of a regular relaxation or meditation ritual. Others may use imagery only occasionally for specific needs such as healing after a surgery, recovering from a divorce, generating new ideas for a project, or coping with a particularly stressful day.

Ultimately, if you integrate guided imagery into your life, you will probably feel greater self-empowerment and move your life in a positive direction.

Our Senses

Our senses, (all 6 of them) have a direct or indirect effect on our body, mind and spirit. If we are left without one of them, our body does an amazing job at making the remaining ones more acute so that we gain insight from another perspective. For those who have all of their senses, I encourage you to not take them for granted, as they are powerful tools in healing. Experience your senses right now: What do you feel beneath you? What do you see in front of you? What are you hearing around you? What scents are you picking up? What do you desire to taste right now? What is your intuitive hunch telling you?

By simply making yourself aware of these senses, can change the way you understand something, learn to comprehend an issue, or participate in the immediate world around you. Each sense is a gift we should never deny and it should be in our conscious thought whenever coping with a problem, appreciating a moment, or acquiring ways to understand something better.

Signs and Symbols

Sacred symbols are the language of the Universe. They are symbols recognized throughout the world as a way of conveying or communicating a message. They represent a meaning without necessarily conveying any words. Like symbols in societies and in our dreams, they express to us a definition, purpose and often reason they are in our lives or make their presence known in times when we need them most!

Signs and symbols are something I recommend you be more aware at recognizing. Finding spirituality can be gained by a unique lesson located. A lesson we reach out for when life hits us in the face (such as a health issue or the loss of a loved one) or it can be a subtle brush, that is profound. Pay attention. Spiritual awakenings or "shifts in spirit" happen all around us. What we pass off as coincidence, is actually our "spiritual sense" vying for our attention.

Entire cultures are based on signs and symbols that hold relevance, meaning, and interpretations, which can distinguish between a raise of a hand to a wave of a hand. Symbols are not just images, but an entire encyclopedia of language found in signs from religion, art, science, politics, and literature. They define our knowledge, based around such things as our own identities and the ways we express ourselves.

~ Gain perspective from something that is familiar.

~ Learn to acknowledge the subtle signs that get your attention.

~ Expand your reference of signs and symbolism by understanding the meaning of archetypes. Archetypes enable you to gain a greater amount of information about your world and those in it.

~ Notice how these apply to your life in the moment or what they could mean to your future.

~ Signs and symbols that show up in your life may stimulate a thought or feeling. This subtle "nudge" or "reminder" can be profound if we are paying attention.

Vital Energy

We are all energetic beings. Our life force, Qi, Prana, or vital energy is talked about in many Eastern paradigms such as Chinese Medicine, Celtic, Vedic, Tibetan, as well as Ayurvedic Medicine.

We often think of energy when we are either raring to go or feel exhausted. But, energy is a subtle dance between many aspects in our lives. There are the activities which energize us or the surroundings that drain us. Have you ever been in an environment that seems to "take" your energy? Have you been in a situation that gives you motivation or energy to move?

Have you ever been around a person who feels like an "energy vampire" draining you of every breath? How about being near someone you just can't get enough of their "en-light-en-ment?" These are all subtle degrees in which we can feel and sense energy around and within us.

Like the acupuncture points along the meridian lines found in Chinese medicine or the marma points in Ayurvedic medicine, the **Chakra Energies or "wheels of light"** are invisible energy centers within the body. These energy centers seem to map out along our body from the tip of the coccyx bone to the crown of the head (and upward).

These energy areas follow the major nerve plexus or nerve ganglia within the body and can be used to help balance our emotions, bring physical stability, and help us to understand our higher purpose or awareness. They were first talked about in the Vedas, a large body of knowledgeable texts, originating in ancient Indian around 1100 BC.

In his book, *Radical Healing*, author Rudolph Ballentine, MD makes reference to the Chakra:

"The Chakra are stations along the central axis of your being. Each one is a point at which energy can be expressed in a certain set of actions, attitudes and emotions. The Chakra are a map of the soul which you must move along for healing to happen."

Here, you will find a list of each of the seven major Chakra centers that relate to the most important aspects of the mind, body, and spirit. When reading about these energy centers, place your hand over each area.

The Root/Base Chakra:

Location: Base of the spine
Color: Red/Black
Element: Earth
Sense: Smell
Musical Keynote: Middle C (vocalized as an "ooh" sound)
Associated Gland: Adrenal, the spinal column, bones, teeth, and nails. This includes the blood, building process of cells, the colon, and rectal area
Gemstones: Red or Black Agate, Bloodstone, Hematite, Red Coral, Red Garnet, Ruby, Black Obsidian, Black Tourmaline and Onyx
Herbs: Cedar, Clove, Pepper, Vetiver
Essential Oils: Frankincense, Myrrh, Patchouli, Rosewood, Thyme
Qualities and/or Functions: Survival, power to achieve goals, vitality, grounding, material security, stability, stillness, courage
In A Word: Evolution
Verb: I have

Muladhara: 1st Chakra (Base or Root Chakra): This center is related to the earth, our physical identity, and orientation towards self-preservation. This Chakra forms our foundation. It represents our survival instincts, our sense of feeling grounded and a connection to our physical bodies. It is how we relate to those around us. Ideally, this Chakra brings us health, prosperity, security, and dynamic presence.

The color used for this area is red or black and it is the color which energizes this region. When this Chakra is balanced, you feel in good health and connected with your surroundings. It is used to ground your essence, feel comfortable, and protected. This Chakra gives you determination, a feeling of being "rooted," and assists in our survival mode.
When this area is not balanced, we can become overbearing and egotistical. To help center this Chakra, consider eating red food, or using color in the form of candles, clothes, or lights around you. The symbol of this Chakra is the Square.

Life development: The Root Chakra is a representation of our growth pattern from conception to age one. This is the most significant time for physical growth of a baby as far as internal development and their need to survive. This is their time of dependency for food, warmth and shelter. This is the period that helps us to become anchored into the physical word.

The Sacral/Spleen Chakra:

Location: Below the navel
Color: Orange
Element: Water
Sense: Taste
Musical Keynote: D above middle C (vocalized as the "o" in "home")
Associated Organs/Systems: Reproductive organs, kidneys, bladder
Gemstones: Carnelian, Orange Calcite, Moonstone, Blood Citrine, Jasper
Herbs: Damiana, Gardenia, Sandalwood, Ylang-Ylang
Essential Oils: Benzoin, Cardamom, Clary Sage, Elemi, Fennel, Sandalwood
Qualities and/or Functions: Primal feelings, awe, enthusiasm, open to others, personal creativity
In A Word: Fertility
Verb: I feel

Svadhisthana: 2nd Chakra (Spleen or Sexual Chakra): This center is associated with water, our emotional identity, and orientation towards self-gratification. This center is related to ourselves and our sexual identity. It connects us to others through feeling, desire, sensation, and movement. Ideally, this Chakra brings us fluidity and grace, depth of emotion, sexual fulfillment, and the ability to accept change.

The color used for this area is orange and it is the color which energizes this region. It stimulates our creativity, vitality, and sexual expression. When this Chakra is balanced, it initiates adaptability and flexibility. This Chakra is connected to procreation and bringing in new life. When it is out of balance, it causes one to manifest fear more easily, sexual imbalances, and unsettled emotions.

To help activate this Chakra, introduce more orange foods, wear orange clothing and stimulate the olfactory nerves with the scents of sweet flowers or citrus. The symbol of this chakra is the Circle.

Life development: The Sacral Spleen Chakra is a representation of growth from six months to age two. This is the period of pleasure and self-gratification. It is a period of self-discovery and the beginnings of separation from the mother and developing child.

The Solar Plexus Chakra:

Location: Above the navel, but below the chest, within the solar plexus
Color: Yellow
Element: Fire
Sense: Sight
Musical Keynote: E (vocalized as the "o" sound in "top")
Associated Organs/Systems: Pancreas, liver, stomach, spleen, gall bladder, autonomic nervous system, lower back, muscles
Gemstones: Amber, Citrine, Infinite, Tiger's Eye, Sapphire, Serpentine
Herbs: Bergamot, Carnation, Lavender, Rosemary
Essential Oils: Bergamot, Cardamom, Hyssop, Juniper, Lemon, Rosemary
Qualities and/or Functions: Personal power, social identity, self-control, energy, will, peace, radiance, joy, inner harmony, vitality, and inner strength
In A Word: Empowerment
Verb: I can

Manipura: 3rd Chakra (Solar Plexus Chakra): This center is associated with fire, our ego identity, and orientation towards our self-definition. This Chakra is known as the power center. It rules our personal power, will, autonomy, and our metabolism. Encouraging us to move forward.

The color used for this area is yellow and it is the color which energizes this region. Yellow is very good for getting in touch with your power and to build confidence. Intuition is believed to begin in this area. Although, the Third Eye Chakra is most associated with intuition, the "spark" is what is felt in our solar plexus. This is our "gut" feeling.

When balanced, this Chakra gives us strength, provides the ability to hold energy for personal power, and emotional control. It brings spontaneity and non-dominating power. This is the primary center of our free will. When unbalanced, it produces rage and destructive behavior. To help activate this Chakra, consider sun bathing, drinking electrolytes, or introduce more yellow foods, lighting or clothing. The symbol of this Chakra is the Triangle.

Life development: The Solar Plexus Chakra is a representation of growth from approximately 18 months to age three. The "terrible twos" are where a proper balance of freedom and discipline are important. Poor disciplinary habits create an overbearing, egotistical child. Excess control can cause overbearing and demanding children who expect too much.

The Heart Chakra:

Location: The center of the chest
Color: Green/Pink
Element: Air
Sense: Touch
Musical Keynote: F (vocalized "ah")
Associated Gland: Thymus, controls the heart, blood circulation, immune system, lower lungs, rib cage, skin, upper back.
Gemstones: Emerald, Jade, Rhodonite, Rhodochrosite, Rose Quartz, Ruby, Kunzite, and Watermelon Tourmaline.
Herbs: Marjoram, Geranium, Jasmine, Lavender, Rose, Ylang Ylang
Essential Oils: Geranium, Jasmine, Lavender, Rose, Ylang Ylang
Qualities and/or Functions: Unconditional love, harmony, forgiveness, healing, compassion, personal transformation, sharing, devotion, selflessness
In A Word: Compassion
Verb: I love

Anahata: 4th Chakra (Heart Chakra): is associated with air, represents our social identity, and orientation towards self-acceptance. This energy is in the middle of the Chakra system of seven. It is related to love and is the integrator of opposites in the psyche: mind/body, male/female, persona/shadow, ego/unity. A healthy Heart Chakra allows us to love deeply, feel compassion, find a deep sense of peace, and a feeling of being balanced.

The color used for this area is green or pink and it is the colors that energize this region. This energy center deals with physical healing, balance, harmony, and compassion. The Heart Chakra is the center of our emotional balance and is most important in all facets of love. When it is balanced, you trust in others, take risks, love and feel loved, unconditionally.

To help activate this Chakra, eat lots of greens, surround yourself in nature, and be open to new experiences. Wear a touch of pink to identify with your compassion. The symbol of this Chakra is the Crescent.

Life development: The Heart Chakra is a representation of growth from age three to approximately age seven. The child learns about relationships with others outside the immediate family (the outside world). Relating, will build good self-esteem and self-acceptance.

The Throat Chakra:

Location: the throat area
Color: blue
Element: Ether
Sense: Sound
Musical Keynote: G (vocalized "eh")
Associated Glands: Thyroid, controls the jaw, neck, throat, voice, airways, upper lungs, arms
Gemstones: Aquamarine, Chalcedony, Turquoise, Blue Quartz, Kyanite, Angelite, Blue Obsidian, Apatite, Azurite, Lapis Lazuli, Sodalite
Herbs: Basil, Chamomile, Cypress, Eucalyptus, Frankincense, Sage
Essential Oils: Benzoin, Basil, Chamomile, Cypress, Eucalyptus, Frankincense, Hyssop, Linden Blossom, Peppermint, Rosewood, Sage
Qualities and/or Functions: Creative self-expression, communication, inspiration, wisdom, confidence, integrity, truth, freedom, independence
In A Word: Communication
Verb: I speak

Visuddhi: 5th Chakra (Throat Chakra): is associated with sound, our creative identity, and orientation towards self-expression. We experience the world symbolically through vibration, such as language, speaking and listening. The color blue helps with this balance. This chakra deals with taking in and releasing out.

If this center is balanced we are able to communicate openly, as well as express what we do or do not want, in a diplomatic manner. When this center is unbalanced, we tend to talk without stopping, speak without listening, dominate conversations, or just the opposite, the inability to express ourselves. To help activate this Chakra, wear blue, introduce blue foods into your diet, or utilize more blue light into your surroundings. The symbol of this chakra is the Star.

Life development: The Throat Chakra - represents the growth from age seven to twelve years of age. This is the time to develop self-expression. With the feeling of being supported, it gives us the security to voice our message and be at peace with ourselves. Disruptive, abrasive, and boisterous behavior tends to be the product of underdeveloped, lower Chakras and can improve by working on improving the centers below the Throat Chakra.

The Third Eye Chakra:

Location: Middle of the forehead
Color: Indigo
Element: Light
Musical Keynote: A (vocalized "ee")
Associated Glands: Pituitary, controls the endocrine system, the left-brain hemisphere, the left eye, nose, ears, sinuses, and parts of the nervous system
Gemstones: Amethyst, Azurite, Lepidolite, Iolite, Lapis, Sodalite
Herbs: Jasmine, Mint, Mugwort, Star Anise
Essential Oils: Anise, Angelica, Hyacinth, Jasmine, Juniper, Lemon, Pine
Qualities and/or Functions: Inner vision, intuition, clairvoyance, insight, perception, imagination, concentration, peace of mind, projection of will, manifestation
In A Word: Perception
Verb: I see

Ajna: 6th Chakra (Third Eye Chakra): is associated with light, our archetypal identity, and orientation towards self-reflection. This Chakra is related to the act of seeing, both physically and intuitively. As such, it opens our psychic faculties and our understanding of who we are. When balanced, it allows us to see the "big picture.". It helps us to experience spiritual wisdom and enlightenment. It is the center of physical and spiritual understanding. This is where we receive information that we "feel" from our gut or Solar Plexus Chakra and are then able to "see and express" simply what we interpret.

When unbalanced, we tend to lose sight of our intuition, and the ability to perceive those things beyond our own physical manifestation.

The color to energize this Chakra is indigo, a combination of red and blue. It deals with clairvoyance and mental activity. To help activate this Chakra, add dark purple or dark blue accents of color through clothing, foods, and lighting. The symbol of this Chakra is the Pyramid.

Life development: The Third Eye Chakra represents the growth from age twelve to twenty. This adolescent time develops proper discernment and perception. This allows for greater insight. Greater insight shows us how to evaluate the action of others and their belief systems.

The Crown Chakra:

Location: the top of the head
Color: Violet or white
Element: Thought
Musical Keynote: B (vocalized "ohm")
Associated Glands: Pineal, controls cerebrum, right brain hemisphere, right eye, central nervous system
Gemstones: Amethyst, Clear Quartz, Diamond, Iolite, Selenite, Herkimer Diamond, Kundalini Quartz, Tiger's Eye.
Herbs: Frankincense, Lotus, Neroli, Rose, Myrrh, Spruce
Essential Oils: Frankincense, Myrrh, Neroli, Rose, Pine
Qualities and/or Functions: Perfection, integration, unity with the divine, wisdom and purpose, Universal consciousness, understanding, enlightenment
In A Word: Divinity
Verb: I know

Sahasrara: 7th Chakra (Crown Chakra): is associated with conscious thought, Universal identity, and orientation towards self-knowledge. The Crown Chakra relates to Universal consciousness as pure awareness. It is our connection to the greater world unseen. When balanced, this Chakra opens us up to receiving knowledge, wisdom, understanding, spiritual connection, enlightenment, and bliss.

When this Chakra is out of balance, there is a lack of belief, lack of trust, and poor sense of boundaries. There is a feeling of not having a purpose in life.

The colors used for this area are violet or white and are the colors that energizes this region. This energy center represents all that is divine. The white/violet light is truth and clarity. The symbol of this Chakra is the Lotus.

Life development: The Crown Chakra represents growth and activity from the age of twenty. This is the time when an adult is most likely to begin reacting fully to the world around them. If the adult chooses to continue to develop his mind by asking more in-depth life questions, they can bring in new found mysteries to be unlocked. This is the beginning of self-discovery, unabridged exploration, and a spark for the curiosity of life.

A Word About This Energy

Throughout this book, I make references to these energy centers. As you see, they relate to colors, elements, music, functions, and glands within the body. They resonate with such tools as herbs, oils, crystals, sound, and meditation.

The color system (over the centuries) has been likened to the colors of the rainbow. ROY G. BIV (red, orange, yellow, green, blue, indigo, violet). Red is the lowest and longest frequency in the light spectrum, while violet is the highest and shortest frequency of light in the visible spectrum.

When we are drawn to, or attracted by a certain color, consider looking at that particular Chakra center and its associations. Take notice as to its meaning and what the color signifies in relationship to the other items in the list. You will find that they are probably traits you should pay attention to, need more of, or could use to help connect to your higher self.

For example, need more energy? Consider wearing red. Have some foods in the red-orange spectrum like tomatoes, peppers, strawberries, or watermelon. Meditate within the red-light spectrum. Carry a red stone such as ruby or jasper or meditate with that stone.

These areas of energy are check points. They each happen to align with a major nerve center along the body, so if physical issues come up, bring your attention to that center. How is it related? What are you finding to be the relationship to your issue? Many times, gentle massage of this center can help. Have an herbal tea with one or two of the associated herbs or use one of the oils as a massage oil or inhalant blend. Look at the emotions tied to this area. Do you see a connection?

Consider looking at these centers as pools of light. They have an intense center that softens outward from the middle and "bleeds" or blends into the next color. These centers transition from one into another. They do not have cut and dried borders but transform into the next area. Like life, everything changes from one moment to the next, just as light can cross over from one color to another, seamlessly becoming the next color. It is the spaces in between that are most interesting. Be sure to explore these transitions, as well.

Chapter 3

What Is Our Spiritual Quest?

Throughout my career as a health and wellness practitioner, patients would often ask me this question. What is my spiritual path? The question has many layers and is hard to sum up in a paragraph. The topic has been debated for centuries by scholars and clergymen. What I have come to realize, is that our spiritual journey is a culmination of little experiences we gather along the way. These are experiences or lessons we learn. They are like bricks in a wall or threads in a quilt we bring together to construct or weave a better understanding of God.

In his wonderful book, *Seven Steps to Self-Healing,* Dr. Edward Taub described spirituality as our deepest healing resource. "To recognize a power that is greater than our own" is to recognize our spirituality.

When we are spiritual, we consciously strive to live with awareness, love, faith, and devotion. Our spiritual health is comprised of:

"a condition marked by a diminished sense of fear and the daily experience of unconditional love, joy, gratitude, and a personal relationship with your God (or an awareness of an inner source of infinite power and compassion.) Our spirit also comes through social health – and consists of a strong, positive connection to others in community, family, and intimacy with one or more people. Often, we mistake religion for being spirituality. But, as a scholar once said, "**religion is only the bridge to spirituality.**"

My own spiritual quest started as a Catholic altar boy. My love and devotion to the Virgin Mary as a child, became even more devote as I grew older. Disappointed by many of the man-made doctrines put out by the Catholic church, (that seemed to change again and again, almost yearly), I searched to supplement my spiritual quest by looking at the doctrines from other religions. My spiritual enlightenment is now stronger than ever. I take with me the best of many spiritual teachings, through the following tenants:

~ heaven is within us, first.

~ Do unto others as you would have them do unto you.

~ Generosity, charity and kindness will open an individual up to unbounded blessings.

~ You reap what you sow.

~ Follow the spirit of the scriptures, not the words. Look behind them to the thought they indicate.

~ Whatever name man chooses, Nature, Being, The Absolute, there is but one God.

~ Do no harm.

~ Forgiveness and goodness are man's two greatest spiritual needs.

~ Judge not, least ye be judged.

~ Honor and respect your elders.

What brings us closer to our spiritual selves? I believe that **finding spirituality, actually starts from within us.** I have seen countless people who go to church, synagogue or temple, yet do not seem to take away from this experience, a spiritual understanding, let alone apply it to their daily lives.

By choosing to look at ourselves a little deeper, it may explain WHY we are not finding what we are looking for elsewhere or why we may be unhappy. We often seek answers elsewhere, first, before checking in with ourselves. Self-awareness, self-love, and self-examination give us clues as to what we seek, what we need, and how we can actually go about discovering this. If we pay more attention.

Spirituality can be found anywhere. You can experience it in a church or temple, in the beauty of nature, in a yoga, dance or exercise class, or in the darkest, most unlikely places. Spirituality is a state of mind. It is an experience that brings you closer to the realization of life's truths. It can be found when facing fear, enjoying simplicities or contemplation from within.

Below, you will find a spiritual truth, referred to as the *Golden Rule*. You will see a similar concept throughout each of the World's religions, no matter how varied in beliefs they may be, otherwise.

The Golden Rule

~ You shall love your neighbor as yourself. – JUDAISM: Leviticus 19.18

~ Treat others as thou wouldst be treated by thyself. – SIKHISM: Adi Grandth

~ Desire not for anyone the things that ye would not desire for yourselves. – BAH FAITH: Gleanings 66

~ That nature is only good when it shall not do unto another whatever is not good for its own self. – ZOROASTRIANISM: Dadistan-i-Dinik

~ All things whatsoever ye would that men should do to you, do ye even so to them: for this is the law and the prophets. – CHRISTIANITY: Matthew 7.12

~ Not one of you is a believer until he loves for his brother what he loves for himself. – ISLAM: Forty Hadith of an-Nawawi

~ Hurt not others with that which pains yourself. – BUDDHISM: Udana 5.13

~ Regard your Neighbor's gain as your own gain and your neighbor's loss as your own loss. – TAOISM:T'ai Shang Kan Ying P'ien

~ Never do to others what would pain thyself. – HINDUISM: Panchatantra 3.104

~ Do not do to others what you do not want them to do to you. – CONFUCIONISM: Analects 15.23

Remember, spiritual lessons are encrusted in our daily life experiences as jewels or gemstones. They are made available to everyone who wishes to pay attention and listen.

I have had many spiritual teachers in my life and all have contributed to my knowledge and understanding. But my greatest "ah-ha" moments seemed to come from looking within myself for a deeper interpretation that I could learn and accept.

Spirituality comes when you are ready to look at it. In truth, our connection to spirit comes by way of looking inward. Yet subtle clues can come from external sources that intrigue us or connect to our emotions.

Nature holds the secrets to so many lessons in spirituality. Not only does our connection to spirit express itself through nature, it is the fundamental building blocks of life's answers. The elements are a perfect example of how they mimic our emotions. For example, a balanced fire element can cook our food or an angry fire can scorch thousands of acres. Calm water can nourish our bodies or rushing water can carve paths out of stone. Air together with water can create a terrible hurricane, while heat can warm the earth in order to grow rich in harvest. We see the same behavior within us. Balancing them, allows us to better comprehend ourselves. This opens a greater door to trust and seeing the bigger picture around us.... that which we cannot control, see or understand. This is spirituality.

The seasons grow in curiosity and peak in full fruition, as they then sustain and finally transition into the next interval. This too, mirrors our spiritual journey. This series of cyclical advancements culminate into a process, like stepping through another door. Our spirituality is constantly revolving through transitions.

Being spiritual is knowing ourselves. It is our beliefs that bring us closer to a spiritual life. It is our trust that allows us to put our "faith" in a power greater than our own. It is our quest to understand our purpose in this life and what may be the meaning behind it. I was once told that we all have a purpose in life and it is part of our spiritual journey to uncover it.

The Universe has natural laws that it follows. For a world without law is a world with complete chaos. Nature has spiritual laws. When these laws are broken, mischief, mayhem, and manic behavior pursue. Therefore, the act of obeying, allows for a disciplined life. The act of following a disciplined life, allows you better understanding of who you are and how you can achieve your goals. A commitment (of any kind) needs a disciplined life to help you fulfill it. At the heart of any successful person, is self-discipline.

Finding spirituality starts from the exact point you are RIGHT NOW. We must learn to cultivate our spirit. To be considered in good health, we can learn to quiet the mind and find harmony within the body. Only then, can we achieve harmony with the world and nature around us.

Chapter 4

Seasons of Our Lives

The seasons are also a mirror to our lives. These "seasons" come to pass in a cycle that is divided into 4 sections or life stages. Metaphysically, life is divided into windows or markers, such as the directions, times of day, and seasons in the year. These "cycles" will then repeat themselves in a never-ending circle of life. We celebrate life in these poetic cycles, as does every other culture in the world.

The "Rhythm" of Time

We are controlled by the seasons and the rising and setting of the sun. This powerful energy source dictates all we do on earth. From seasonal allergies to "seasons of our lives" we follow the flow of nature and our own circadian rhythm. Our hearts beat to the tempo of the seasons and follow the cycles of light and dark from how we work to how we harvest. How we sleep to how we rise. Throughout history, we have culturally examined these cycles and lived our lives by them.

Vedic Life Cycles

Within the Vedic texts (Samhitas) there are 4 metric texts (mantra). In particular, the Rig-Veda (mantra) offers up a reference to the *"cakra"*. Since the texts are rich in symbolism and figurative understanding, these metaphors, which related to the "Chakra", not only refer to the 7 sacred rivers, which run through India, they also refer to the cycle of the seven subtle bodies of energy. The Chakra centers have 7 larger, distinct areas focusing on emotion, function, form, and the human energy fields. They also relate to a series of milestones in our growth cycle. Each Chakra represents a time when certain skills develop and life transitions represent a developmental stage.

Science of Life

The Ayurvedic paradigm of medicine works with the elements, dosha, and seasons for better living. The "Science of Life" is considered the art of living in harmony with nature. In Ayurvedic philosophy, people, their health, and the Universe are all thought to be related. It is believed that health problems can result when these relationships are out of balance. Much like the Chinese and Tibetan medicine paradigms, better health is realized once our mind, body, and spiritual selves come into better alignment or balance.

Celtic Tree of Life

The Celtic Calendar is a compilation of pre-Christian Celtic systems of timekeeping, with the Gaulish Coligny calendar, used by Celtic countries to define the beginning and length of the days, weeks, months, seasons, quarter days, and festivals. The year was divided with the arrival of the darkness, in October at *Samhain* and the arrival of the light half of the year starting in May at *Beltane*. These original holidays were later adopted by the church, combined into other traditions, or made into new ones. Celebrated all over the world and in different cultures, these holidays are the same, as we know them today, only they go by different names including Halloween, Easter, Candlemas and May Day, to name a few.

Astrological Seasons

The Greeks and Romans gave us the basic principles of Astronomy and Astrology depicting the grand cycle of life as the stars moved through the sun and the zodiac in one year's time. When we look at the rhytmn of the sun, we can see the vibrational dance on a daily basis. The zodiac signs are a window of time within a 12-month cycle and each sign resembles a life marker.

Chinese Organ Cycle

Our circadian rhythm is our internal, daily biological clock. This clock can be influenced by many different elements, such as light and darkness, time of day, and temperature. In Traditional Chinese Medicine, the clock shows us how our energy moves through the 12 meridians over a period of 24 hours, spending two hours at maximal levels in each organ In general, when treating a patient in accordance with this biorhythm, the best time to treat an excess of energy is at or shortly before the time of greatest activity, while the best time to treat depleted energy is following the peak times.

Season of the Indian

The Native American traditions sometimes represent the stages of life through the Medicine Wheel. This cross within a circle indicates the four directions. The symbolism represents east – birth, childhood; south – youth, growing up; west – aging, mature adulthood; north – wisdom, death. The stages of life are a cycle, where, like the seasons, death gives rise to rebirth and is a renewal of the life impulse.

Feng Shui Cycles

The lunar calendar has a sixty-year cycle. In Chinese Astrology, the five basic elements of Metal, Water, Wood, Fire and Earth, make up all matter, which are combined with the twelve animal signs of Rat, Oxen, Tiger, Rabbit, Dragon, Snake, Horse, Sheep/Goat, Monkey, Rooster, Dog and Boar/Pig to form the sixty-year cycle.

Lunar Cycles

When we look at the cycles of the moon, we can see the waxing and waning of life on a daily basis. This revolution has great power over the tides of our emotions. The 28-day cycle represents the complete manifestation of energy from start to finish. The cycles of the moon ebb and flow as natural rhythms around our lives. We can learn to find empowerment within this flow in order to manifest what we want in life.

And then, you have your birthday.

Gemstone:

It's YOUR Day!

"we grow each day as time goes by,
from week to week, to months that fly,
away as we approach the climb,
from when we're born, that special time.
Our day of birth should be profound,
for its the day when we came round
~ to show the world just who we are,
and leave a mark that reaches far~
and wide we stretch our arms out long,
to find our purpose and be strong

~Andrew Pacholyk MS. L.Ac

The "Life" Markers

Our life seasons have a beginning and end. We know them as life and death. Between these two absolutes are windows or markers, such as the directions, times of day, and seasons in the year. These "cycles" will then repeat themselves in a never-ending circle of life! The time of each season is cordoned off into seemingly unrelated relationships (with nature, with others, with ourselves), yet there is a connection or on-going cycle that appears as markers, again and again.

These occurrences can be seen as a pattern when you look at them over time. This has also been something Chinese Medicine has taught me. As the practitioner does not tend to look at the signs and symptoms of a problem rather, they look at the patterns that take place.

We also tend to see our lives through milestones. These are often life-changing events that lend themselves to our own personal growth. Birthdays, anniversaries, children, the life and death of those close to us. We also associate a variety of sensory perceptions to these milestones, commonly called "the senses": hearing, vision, taste, smell and touch. It is these senses which I find the most powerful, as they have the greatest recall to our memories, no matter where we are.

It is this sensory perception, which I focus on in this book. The power of "recall" is amazing. You can be somewhere that you are not familiar with and suddenly smell a "memory" that can literally take you back to a very specific moment, time of day, person or event.

Use All Your Senses

The power of our senses can be harnessed as an unbelievable tool that you can use to your life's advantage! Eating well, living in a healthy manner that works for you and working in a clutter free environment are essential for living well.

Visual Esthetics

Seeing is a special sense. Rhodopsin in the rods of the eyes are activated by a photon of light > light activates a G protein called "Transducin" > Transducin activates phosphodiesterase > phosphodiesterase hydrolyzes many molecules of cyclic GMP > hyrdrolyzation of cyclic GMP causes gates in the cell to close cutting off the flow of sodium ion causing an action potential > the action potential travels through many layers of retina through the optic nerve > to the cerebral cortex where it is interpreted as **vision**.

Feng Shui (pronounced Fung Shway) is the ancient Chinese art of placement to enhance the flow of "vital life energy" known as Qi. Practitioners believe that rooms, buildings and all environments can be arranged and decorated in a way that maximizes the flow of Qi, resulting in improvements to health and happiness of those who live in that environment.

Feng Shui is the esthetics of life. Although you may not be familiar with Feng Shui, when you walk into a room or home that is full of disorderly chaos, you can sense the discourse when you see a place full of clutter, as opposed to walking into a room with no clutter, open space and a room that just seems to have "good flow". You can sense this and are very aware of the contrast. Visual Esthetics is the organization our brain keeps. Our eyes are attracted to visual esthetics and beauty. Feng Shui is the ancient practice of arranging a physical environment to maximize personal harmony and success.

Therapy of Aroma

Scent holds a special place in our brain. When stimulated by a smell, our olfactory nerve takes control. The power of our senses can be harnessed as an unbelievable tool that we can use to our life's advantage! Once the Olfactory receptors identify an aroma > nerve cells relay this information directly to the Limbic system of the brain. > Here, aromas can trigger memories and influence behavior. > Additionally, the Limbic system works in conjunction with the pituitary gland and the > Hypothalamus region of the brain to regulate the hormonal activities > and triggering the production of hormones that govern appetite, body temperature, insulin production, overall metabolism, stress levels, sex drive, and conscious thought and reactions > direct to the Limbic system.

Aromatherapy is the practice of using naturally distilled essences of plants to promote the health and well-being of your body, mind, and emotions. This essence, called essential oils, can restore balance and harmony to your body and to your life. Essential oils of plant, fruit, and flower essences are created to center and enhance the body and mind in order to help us in preventative measures, as well as, an effective cure for many illnesses. Scents can induce an amazing power as they influence our moods. Our sense of smell is the most direct path to our emotions. This is the principle behind the ancient art of aromatherapy.

Sound Psychology

Hearing is a unique sense. Sound waves hit the tympanic membrane > the tympanic membrane vibrates and moves the ossicles of the ear (the incus, malleus and stapes) > which transmits the sound to the basilar membrane > this vibration causes the stereocilia hairs to move > causing an action potential which travels to the cerebral cortex > which translates into what we hear.

Music is a magical medium and works as a very powerful tool. Music is one of these senses like smell, which can transport us right back to a certain time, milestone or life marker, automatically transforming our spirit. Music subtly bypasses the intellectual stimulus in the brain and moves directly to our subconscious. Music can delight all our senses and inspire every fiber of our being. Music has the power to soothe and relax, bring us comfort and embracing joy! There is music for every mood and for every occasion.

Nutritional Sense

Taste is desired. The repeated use of a particular taste is acquired. We learn how to like or dislike food through an experience unlike any other of the senses. The gustatory cells > clustered in **taste** buds on the tongue mouth and throat > react to food or drink > where they mix with saliva > surface cells send information to nearby nerve buds >, relaying messages to the brain. This is how we taste.

Diets are associated with cultural behaviors, world locations and availability of certain foods. Both the Indian and Chinese paradigms of medicine classify the balance of nutrition according to taste. The five tastes are bitter, salty, sweet, sour, and pungent. When eating each of the five tastes, this often constitutes a balanced meal. Each taste works to nourish a specific organ system and each taste is correlated with a season and a temperature such as hot, warm, cold, cool and neutral. The combination of tastes can strengthen the body, whereas an excess of one particular taste can weaken it. For instance, too much sugar weakens the spleen and stomach and leads to digestive weakness. Therefore, eating a balance of the five tastes, eating frequently and with smaller portions, leads to good nutritional sense.

Tactile Learning

Touch is a powerful tool. Our touch is profound. It is healing, connecting, comforting, and soothing. Our sense of touch can make all the difference in how we learn. Studies in neurophysiology have shown that physical experience creates especially strong, neural pathways in the brain. When we participate in tactile/kinesthetic activity, the two hemispheres of the brain are simultaneously engaged. This type of learning experience helps assure that new information will be retained in long-term memory.

Our tactile system is activated through receptors in the skin > our senses give us information about size, shape, texture, and temperature > our kinesthetic system is activated through movement with receptors located in the tendons and muscles > the kinesthetic system recognizes the movement through memory receptors in the brain.

We learn through this touch. We each have a preferred method of learning and comprehending and this includes either auditory, visual, or tactile/kinesthetic.

The best learning tool seems to be that, which we physically do, as we may not always remember what we have heard or seen, but we all seem to recall an action. A relevant Chinese proverb refers to this as: *"I hear and I forget; I see and I remember; I do and I understand."* Touch and kinesthetic memory enhance everyone's sense of awareness and learning.

Our Innate Sense

Intuition has long been considered the 6th sense. Intuition is believed to begin in the area of Solar Plexus. Although the Third Eye is most associated with intuition, the "spark" is what is felt in the area of our solar plexus. This is the biggest nerve center in our body, connected to almost all the organs. The solar plexus is often where we consider our "gut" feeling to come from.

We are all born with intuition. Our connection to it is strongest as children. Probably because as children, we are not encumbered with care or responsibility and simply enjoy the clear conscious thoughts that we entertain in our brains. The older we become, the more layers we take on, smothering that open consciousness and awareness we innately used as children.

What is often called the sixth sense, intuition can be defined as "the ability to sense or know immediately without reasoning". We all have hunches, gut feelings, or intuitive insight. The feeling one gets when first hearing about something or someone, or the first impression when we meet someone new...these are all simply our intuition. Intuition is often considered the ability to synthesize and deduce from all of our accumulated unconscious experiences.

Therefore, we "know" much more than we realize. It is also through the perception of our (other) five senses, which, allows us to "tune in" to our intuition. Those who pay attention can find intuition a useful tool in their lives.

The Interconnectedness of All Things

In Chinese Medicine we have a theory most people have heard about and that is Yin and Yang. Yin and yang are two words we frequently hear in connection with balance. Yin is generally thought of as being feminine, while yang is considered masculine, but there is much more to this. Yin is also related to the earth, moon, darkness, shade, rest, space, west and north.

Yang on the other hand, is related to light, sun, brightness, heaven, time, south, east and left. In ancient times, when the daily cycle of night and day were noted, it was thought that day corresponded to yang and yin corresponded to night. Yin and Yang are looked at in four distinct ways.

Yin and Yang are in: **Opposition**: in relation/relative to each other.

Interdependent: you cannot have one without the other.

Mutual Consumption: control and balance one another.

Inter-transformation: one transforms into the other at its Zenith.

Yin and Yang exist in everything in the Universe in relationship to each other. The duality of the Universe and the world around us is expressed in the "Tai Chi," symbol, as a circle created by a light and a dark side, positioned end to end with one small circle of yin in yang and yang in yin. This is the presence of its complement. This has been accepted for several thousand years in Chinese philosophy, but the acknowledgment that every male has a feminine aspect, and every female has a male side, is new to the Western mind and medicine.

Together, yin and yang comprise a whole, and yet there is an element of each in the other. But sometimes, we have too much yang, and other times, we have too much yin. It is up to us to find and maintain the balance between the two in our physical, mental, emotional, spiritual, sexual and intellectual selves. Achieving this balance helps us become grounded or centered.

Energy medicine is based on this belief that the human body is composed of energy fields. When the energy is properly distributed and circulating freely, the body is healthy. When out of balance, imbalances or abnormal amounts of energy are believed to indicate an excess or deficiency.

Energy Cycles

The cycles in nature (seasons) are a prime example of a cycle of energy. When working with the energy of natural cycles, you are likely to get better results. Discover how cycles define our lives.

In their book, *The Secret Language of Birthdays,* authors Gary Goldschneider and Joost Elffers. breakdown the four functions of life into four cycles of life. Their correlation between the natural seasons and the seasons of our lives, explains the equivalence between our functions, moods and behaviors throughout these major life markers.

Life Cycle 1 - Intuition	Life Cycle 2 - Feeling	Life Cycle 3 - Sensation	Life Cycle 4 - Thought
An open sense of willingness. Represents Spring, intuition, zodiac signs of Aries, Taurus, Gemini and is our 1st quadrant of development from birth to 21. This suggests the following types of consciousness and experiences: action of all kinds; decisions; determining; controlling; accomplishing; implementing; working; fore-brain; deep sleep and attention.	Introduction to the self. Represents Summer, love, zodiac signs of Cancer, Leo, Virgo and is our 2nd quadrant of development from age 21 to 42. This suggests the following: love; emotions effects; drives; fun; intensity; enthusiasm; imagination; strength; joy, laughter; playfulness; right brain; impulses; and dreams.	Awareness of life's perception. Represents Fall, new knowledge of prosperity, zodiac signs of Libra, Scorpio, Sagittarius and is our 3rd quadrant of development from age 42 to 63. This suggests that sensing means perception; observation; our 6th senses; unprocessed information; consciousness; sensuality; left brain; sense of consciousness.	The coming of age of life's lessons. It represents Winter, knowledge gained, zodiac signs of Capricorn, Aquarius, Pisces and is our 4th quadrant of development from age 63 and onward. This suggests that thought represents: reason; logical thinking; analytical; order; connect; deliberation and reflection.

Spring - Intuition	Summer - Feeling	Fall - Sensation	Winter - Thought
Priorities of life Beauty, Cleansing, Creativity, Intuition, Sex	**Priorities of life** Luck, Love Confidence, Happiness, Success, Money Strength	**Priorities of life** Divination, Forgive, Intent, Journeys, Knowledge, Prosperity	**Priorities of life** Peace, Protection, Self-Balance, Self-Healing, Self-Power
Personal Growth Create Healthy Beliefs	**Personal Growth** Yoga Exercise	**Personal Growth** Gratitude, Spirituality	**Personal Growth** Understand Death
Element: Air	**Element**: Fire	**Element**: Earth	**Element**: Water
Musical Landscape Spring songs Songs of Air Desert Melodies	**Musical Landscape** Songs of Love, Luck, Fairytale, Wedding songs	**Musical Landscape** Fall Moods, Memorium	**Musical Landscape** Songs of Winter, Angels
Seasonal Landscape Desert	**Seasonal Landscape** Sea	**Seasonal Landscape** Mountain	**Seasonal Landscape** Valley
Mineral Kingdom Desert Stones Top 10 Stones	**Mineral Kingdom** Sea Stones Top 10 Stones	**Mineral Kingdom** Shaman Stones Top 10 Stones	**Mineral Kingdom** Top 10 Stones Moon Stones
Food for Thought Spring food	**Food for Thought** Summer foods	**Food for Thought** Fall foods	**Food for Thought** Winter foods
Essential Oils Top oils for Spring	**Essential Oils** Top oils for Summer	**Essential Oils** Top oils for Fall	**Essential Oils** Top oils for Winter
Cycle Celebrations Imbolc Ostara	**Cycle Celebrations** Beltane Litha	**Cycle Celebrations** Lammas Mabon	**Cycle Celebrations** Samhain Yule
Seasons of the Sun East Sunrise Sun Salutation Solar Meditation	**Seasons of the Sun** South Solstice Ritual Sensational Sunsets	**Seasons of the Moon** West Moonrise Twilight New Moon Meditation	**Seasons of the Moon** North Moonset Total Eclipse Full Moon Meditation

This second chart, is my interpretation of these incredible cycles in our lives. In each "quadrant" of life, there tends to be issues that we focus more on and spend most of our time involved with. These are the natural emotions, feelings, thoughts, and sensations we all experience on our journey through life.

I have related "personal growth' markers along the way, which tend to line up with our way of thinking as the seasons turn. You may also be aware that these "seasons" have another meaning. They represent the physical seasons that come and go each year, but also make reference to the timeline of our life cycle or "life seasons".

Of course, the four seasons transpire every year while each transition makes us think about the priorities, landscapes, elements, scents, and celebrations we experience within each one.

This too, mirrors the evolution of our life span, broken down into groupings or seasons we express through our own life time. They are turning points in how we grow – mentally, physically, and spiritually.

I have added references, which have brought me more awareness in *my life*. These references are tools for growth and self-awareness. I will attempt to stimulate all your senses and bring you closer to knowing yourself. Knowing more about *"the self"*, for me, was the key to my gained spirituality, humanity, and the conscious awareness of how "the little things in life, can create big changes." The divine "spark" is within us all. It is simply a matter of getting in touch with this sense of divinity.

I have used tools within nature, such as elements, minerals, foods, herbs, plants, flowers, landscapes, and celestial bodies in order to bring more awareness to the cycles and their spiritual connections.

I have intertwined different religious dogma, music, poetry, movement, and meditations for guiding you to a better understanding.

I have introduced the earliest "cycle celebrations" from ancient times that have transformed into what we now know as the major holidays and transitions we embrace.

So, now I ask, that you follow this path, with an open-mind, an enlightened heart, and the desire to understand just how much of a spiritual being you really are.

Chapter 5

Spring

Spring represents birth, renewal, and rebirth. Spring is our life's beginning or introduction. Within our life cycle, Spring is associated with our first quadrant of development from birth through our 20's.

Our teens and 20's is our time of self-discovery. It is the vibrant, raw energy of an uncut diamond or impulsive expression of a wire of electricity that has been cut and is flailing in the air. In our teens and 20's we have an open sense of willingness to explore, an immature sense of boundaries, and a raw sense of intuition. We often fly with abandon, run without care, and do it now, pay for it later.

Gemstone:
The Promise of New Beginnings

~ *"At last the season, Spring awakes,*
to honor all from Winter's break.
To offer up more green, more light,
with equal parts of day and night...
You offer us a brand-new turn,
and find new ways that we can learn,
about the promise that you've made,
to make anew each day, each day.
Again, I'm grateful for this time,
when life begins to sing and shine.
away from winter's frigid touch,
and grant us all more love and such!"

~ Andrew Pacholyk MS. L.Ac

The season of Spring is much like this. It has been celebrated over the centuries as the beginning of the rebirth period. This season is one of the most embraced and most significant of the season changes, for it denotes the start of new life, regeneration of nature, creativity, and the renewal of the spirit.

With the new promise of Spring, the reset button has been pushed and we are now given another chance to change what we did not like last year. As the moon resets its cycle each 28-29 days, the new moon represents the beginning of the swing of the pendulum of time as does the promise of sunrise. Like any other cycle, it allows another opportunity for growth. Spring's willingness and raw emotions not only mirror the early years of our lives when we notice everything but expresses our need to burst forth and explore everything - without care, reason, or awareness. This reflects the intuitive thought of 'doing' and not thinking too much about it. Although raw and unrefined, it is the action of 'doing', which represents Spring. When conscious mind, meets conscious thought, we are living in the moment, or in the NOW. This awareness encourages our act of accomplishment and drive. It stimulates our impulsive need to move fast and move forward.

Consciousness and Awareness

Limited views and opinions are stifling. They detach us from reality, decrease our awareness and shut down our mind. We all have a limited view of some areas in our lives. Gaining a broader perspective is self-awareness. Being able to open up your mind and allow for the free flow of thoughts and ideas can be liberating. Spring can give us this feeling and opportunity to do so.

Welcoming a new opinion or way of doing something can bring new meaning to your life. If you release these closed thoughts and make room for a different opinion, you may be surprised at the outcome.

Striving to meet difficult goals has pushed us to stretch the horizons of what we think is possible. We share the ways in which obstacles and challenges have made us stronger and given us confidence to continue setting goals and dreams in our adventures, our business, and in our day to day lives.

This is conscious living. To start living in consciousness, we must start to experience the fourfold principle of intuition, feeling, sensation and thought.

"The routine without meaning is the empty life"
~ Edward J. Lavin

How meaningless is a life without goals? Become conscious of your goals. Get in touch with the life your desire. You are the one who can make this happen. Only you. Become aware of how you can make this happen.

Change your perspective. Change the way you look at something. Give it a fresh, new outlook. If you feel oppressed or beaten, held back or disorganized, rise up! Look past the blocks you feel are in front of you. My mentor, Zachary always use to say, "it's time to flip the switch."

Gemstone:
An O' To Spring

"I've waited through the Winter's freeze,
for some type of warmer breeze,
to Spring upon us, all at once,
and take away that awful crunch,
of snow that lurks beneath my boots.
It's time to let a change take root.
But now it's rain that beats me down,
and wind that whips us all around.
I see how much it mirrors life,
and realize we all have strife.
So no more struggles, let it go,
I must "allow", and let it flow.
O' Spring, I will ~ honor the new...
transitions make us stronger too."

~ Andrew Pacholyk MS. L.Ac

Gemstone:
The Priorities of Life Mantra

"Each day we are given, is an opportunity to learn to live to capacity. A peaceful mind comes from letting ourselves know that everything, I mean everything, will be all right in our lives. The priorities in our lives should always be self-healing, self-balance and self-power, first!

Allow yourself to see beauty in the everyday and to be beautiful. Believe in your happiness. It is always within you. Express your creativity. It is the outlet of the soul. Believe in the power of divination. The Universe has a plan for us; work with it, not against it. Be ever forgiving, we are all here to learn life's lessons. You make your own luck, success and prosperity. Trust your intuition. It is your truth.

We must love ourselves, so that we may love others, even more. We are sexual beings. Our "sexual-esteem" allows us to honor it in a satisfying and enjoyable way. The confidence in ourselves and our abilities, is an important part of our well-being. Our well-being comes from opening our mind, listening and taking action with the knowledge we acquire.

We are deserving. Everything is ours for the asking. Just ask. We are protected. Protection always comes by letting go of the fear inside ourselves. Through our intention and beliefs, we can cleanse our mind of negativity. Your individual journey is your own. There are no obstacles outside of us!"

~ Andrew Pacholyk MS L.Ac

The Priorities of Life

In each aspect of our lives, there are certain "priorities" we find important and tend to focus more on. This is often based on our age or need to fit in, our self-discovery, or need to be recognized.

Our priorities of life are the cornerstones we use to define ourselves. They help us to better understand who we are. Sometimes, these "priorities" are not priorities at all, yet when they come up, they force us to recognize ourselves, out of need or circumstance.

Throughout this book, you will find these priorities, according to the seasons of our lives and when they seem to be most appropriate along our journey. I encourage you to look at each priority, as a friend. A friend who wants to make you a better person and empower you throughout your life!

Beauty

In the "Spring" of our life cycle, beauty can be very important. We all want to be beautiful. Please understand **that we are all beautiful!**

Beauty encompasses a whole range of characteristics. There are many things, which make us beautiful. Of course, symmetry is the most obvious.

Taking good care of yourself **physically, mentally/emotionally, and spiritually all have a way of making us more attractive.**

Even though you may not have been born with great symmetry, do not despair. There are many ways to create it. There are ways to create symmetry with makeup. Makeup shouldn't be used as a tool to replace your own natural beauty. Makeup should be used to enhance your face's best features and to hide the features you dislike.

Symmetry can be altered with physical exercise and weight training. This can change the look and proportions of your body to better improve your symmetry. Diet can also change our proportions. The perfectly symmetrical body is often described as the X shape. The top of the X represents broad shoulders, wide upper back, narrowing into a small waist. The bottom half of the X represents proportional legs which widen out from the hips. Although, we can't change our height, we can change our proportions.

Gemstone:

My Beauty

*"I honor who I am, alive,
my soul can speak with gifts,
divine.
With self-esteem and don't forget,
I shine with inner radiance.
To bring about my one, true self,
and glow with greater
confidence"*

~Andrew Pacholyk, MS L.Ac

There is nothing more beautiful than a confident person. Confidence oozes beauty and attraction. We may not have been born a model, but we can learn to make ourselves beautiful.

It is our right to be a confident and assured person. It is our greatest gift and is often the one thing we find most elusive. Our beauty mirrors our confidence levels. Of course, confidence levels constantly change. Especially when we are out of our comfort zone. We tend to only be aware of our lack of confidence when we are placed in an awkward situation. Here are 10 tips for creating and keeping confidence and beauty around for the long haul.

1.Visualization and guided imagery: Picturing yourself as the person who is confident, successful and admired can be a very powerful tool. Energy follows thought. When you program your thoughts to reflect your wishes, you tend to put your energy into making it so. The mind can be the most helpful tool in the way we desire to live our lives and be who we want to be. If you can believe it, you can achieve it.

2. Music: Music is the great motivator. Music empowers our spirit and can give us the confidence to grow, realize who we are and even give us strength when we need it most. Music as a confidence tool is as individual as we are. Find the music that gives you passion for life. The passion to grow, as a budding flower, into the person you wish to become. Let music inspire you, lift you up and help find your voice. Music works on the Entrainment Theory. The beat of the music aligns with our heart and body rhythm. Slower music gives us time for reflection, inspiration, and introspection. Faster music moves us, motivates us, and pushes us forward. Use music to create more confidence in your life.

3. Positive affirmations: These are words or statements that we say to ourselves or out loud to train the mind into positive thinking. "I am a strong and confident person." I will walk with my chin up and be proud today." Saying it out loud, affirms the truth. Saying it to a mirror is also a great tool, for it makes us look at ourselves in a re-affirming way.

4. Learn to love yourself more: This is a lesson we can always use and should constantly be working on. Who doesn't need to love themselves more? Love yourself more by talking to yourself in a positive, self-affirming, and loving way. Give yourself a confident pat on the back. Treat yourself well by taking care of yourself. Learn that belittling and berating yourself is not only done through words but through our actions, as well.

5. Take care of your physical appearance: When we take care of ourselves, we empower ourselves. Learn how to care for yourself by eating right, exercising, getting good, quality sleep, and have meaningful social interactions with others. Get a haircut, take care of your skin, find a style that you like to dress in and which makes you feel good about yourself.

6. Give a boost to your self-esteem: We all need a good kick in our self-esteem now and then. It is to be expected. When we are down, the first thing we do is doubt who we are and what we are doing. Self-esteem issues are different for different people. Although you may feel great about yourself in one area of your life, you may be extremely down on yourself in another. Welcome to the world. We can all seek to improve ourselves. It is time you became committed to truly loving and appreciating yourself and who you are.

7. Learn who YOU are: Learning how to love and respect yourself for the unique individual you are, can be the best confidence builder. No two individuals are alike. Cloning to one type of a look, a certain way of thinking or doing what everyone else is doing, will never give you confidence. Only a mask to hide behind. Celebrating our individualism is not only greatly liberating but it is secretly what everyone wishes for. Learn to be yourself and honor who YOU are!

8. Conquer your fears: Fear can hold us back, stop us in our tracts, and not allow us to live our lives to the fullest. One of the greatest obstacles in living a fuller more confident life is the fear of failure. The fear of not being good enough. There is no perfection in the world. There is only the ability to reach for and gain the most balance we can achieve at one time. This is all anyone can ask for.

9. Reset your belief system: Lack of confidence is often due to the fact that we have such deeply ingrained conditioning of self-hate and loathing that we do not know how to appreciate ourselves or enjoy our lives. By taking a look at our belief system, we can often see what is holding us back, what is creating blocks in moving forward, and the reasons behind our lack of love for ourselves. Are you at a cross roads due to the fact that your beliefs are negative, self-destructive, or evasive? You can change these beliefs.

10. Appreciate the gift of life: Those who truly do not appreciate their lives are missing out on it. We all have problems. We all have situations we would rather not deal with. We all have bad times. By concentrating your thoughts on these negative problems, you run the risk of getting caught up in the swell of spiraling emotions. These thought patterns pull you down like a whirlpool making it even more difficult to get up and get out. Learn to appreciate what you DO have. Be thankful. There are always those who are worse off than you are. When you work from a place of appreciation, it is easier to build a better life from there. Without a doubt, you can gain confidence by loving and accepting the gifts life has afforded you, no matter how small.

"As I change my inner attitudes, my outer experiences begin to mirror the change." ~ unknown

Cleansing

The cleansing and renewal of life, is the manifesto for Spring. Clearing out what no longer serves you, is your introduction to the turn of this season. Cleansing and clearing gives us the opportunity to let go and renew our spirit for the start of a new beginning.

Cleansing is the washing away of that, which is unclean. When talking about cleansing in holistic medicine, there are three main areas in our lives, which need to be addressed…cleansing the body, the mind, and the spirit.

Cleansing the body is done to keep our physical machine in optimum health. We are born into a body with physical limitations that begins aging the day we are brought into this world.

We can learn to use the body's own healing mechanisms to trigger change. There are many ways to bring about corporeal awareness and change.

Cleansing the mind is done to bring awareness to all that causes us limitations in thinking. The overthinking that is rooted in fear and deters us from living wholeheartedly, can be one of our biggest detriments.

We can learn to free our minds from this imprisonment and create a focused and well-balanced mind set.

Cleansing the spirit is brought about by learning to accept a Universal power that is greater than ourselves. It is the ability to look at those beliefs which do not serve us any longer and the possibility to honor those beliefs that do.

Gemstone:
Cleansing

"O sacred light, a wash me in,
your blessed glow, release my sins.
I'm free of negativity,
let go the shadow binding me.
O' cleanse my body, spirit ~ pure,
and let me know I'm reassured."

~Andrew Pacholyk, MS L.Ac

The Power of Placement

Feng Shui (pronounced Fung Shway) is the ancient Chinese "art of placement" used to enhance the flow of "vital life energy" known as Qi. Practitioners believe that rooms, buildings and all environments can be arranged and decorated in a way that maximizes the flow of Qi. This results in improvements to health and happiness of those who live in that environment. Although the translation of Feng Shui basically means "wind and water ," its scope and breath are much deeper than this.

The best way to start bringing the principles of Feng Shui into your life, are by clearing out the clutter within your environment. Clutter blocks the free flow of Qi. Clutter blocks this energy both in your physical space and within your mental space. Are you feeling "foggy" lately? Are you not able to get motivated? Do you feel like you are "stuck?"? Look around you. Perhaps it is because you have piles of papers, there - or stacks of bills, here. Maybe your front door is blocked or your windows are cloudy and dirty. This not only effects our way of thinking, it effects the way we feel. Learn to take back the control in your life, right now! It's time for some Spring cleaning.

"Allow thing in your life, which make your heart sing, feed your soul or nourish you on a daily basis" ~ Lao Tze

Decluttering Your Life

Clearing out space is the first step in freeing yourself from the burdens that surround you.

The first lesson is to start small.

Start with your desk, a closet, or one room. It is easy to become overwhelmed when you start decluttering a space. Do not allow it. If you only pay attention to the task in front of you, you will find it much easier.

1. I love to clear the space of everything. Take a look at the empty space. Ahhh… Remember when this last occurred? How do you feel in this space now?

2. Take a look at the items you removed. One by one, look over each and every item. Do you absolutely love it? How does it serve you? Is there an emotional attachment to it? Is it a good emotion or a bad one?

3. Items with bad emotions connected to them or items you do not absolutely love, no longer serve you. Consider getting rid of them now.

4. The items that you do love, you love for good reason. How well does it serve you or play a particular purpose? If you save it, find a great place for it, where it will do the most good.

5. Make a pile, box, or space for all the items you do not want. You can separate them into smaller piles to give away, gift them, or sell them. Throw out the items you wish to discard ASAP. There is an amazing feeling that occurs when we detach or let go of something we no longer need.

6. **Note on giving or gifting items**: charities such as the Salvation Army, shelters, or churches are usually very happy to take items you wish to give away. They usually prefer clothes to be cleaned or dry cleaned. The items you decide to gift to someone should be something very special and for whom you feel would really love the item or benefit from it. Do not just gift it to get rid of it. It is better to just throw it out if you cannot find an appropriate outlet for it.

7. The power of letting go offers the possibility of two types of peace: peace of mind – the potential healing of old emotional connections, wounds, or clearer consciousness. Then there is peace with others – the possibility of new, more gratifying relationships in the future.

8. It takes no strength to let go. . . only courage. Life either expands or contracts in direct proportion to your courage to let go.

By giving this fear up to the Universe to handle, you are essentially allowing yourself to let go and release this fear. In turn, it strips away any kind of meaning or significance it may have upon you. By letting go, this allows us to move to the next level in our lives or the next natural process. Often times, this is a fear in itself. The fear of "what will happen when I DO move to my next stage in life?" Feeling protected always comes by letting go of this fear.

Creativity

Living is an act of creativity. Not just being an artist, writer, painter but the sheer act of living is a creative force that we often do not acknowledge.

Living consciously and with awareness is an act of even deeper creativity. On many levels, creativity is an inner process. What you dream, imagine, and then give physical form to, is the transition from inner insight to an outer process.

This is what you create. Making a dream or an idea a reality. Creativity is often used to refer to the process of creating new ideas, actions, or approaches. Innovation is the process of both generating and applying such creative ideas in some specific context.

Although it may seem that creativity can sometimes come out of nowhere, in truth, it comes from a deep well of self-acquired knowledge, both conscious and unconscious.

Gemstone:
Creative Spark

"Stimulate my heart and mind,

So I can bring forth work divine.

I spin, and write and draw and paint,

Divine flow through as I create,

My masterpiece for all to see,

And share with those who are in need."

~Andrew Pacholyk, MS L.Ac

Building Blocks of Creativity

Creativity comes from combining our knowledge in new ways. That is why the creative process (although primarily a right brain/frontal lobe function) also emerges from our own unique knowledge and how we weave it together.

1. Often, in any situation, we must take quiet time to be with ourselves in order to observe and define an idea. What is it I want to create? Get specific. Define your goal. Write it down. Give it parameters. Start with one image, idea, or objective. What am I going to do to get from point A to point B? Allow the answers to come to you in your quiet time.

2. Carry a notebook or use an app on your phone. Have it with you to jot down a thought or phrase that comes to mind. Creativity can happen at any time. So, when the moment strikes, you have the opportunity to record the thought or creative genius.

3. Brainstorming: is a great technique used in generating creative ideas. Very effective when done with others, it's a stimulating way to get fresh ideas from different minds. Start by suggesting a topic or goal. "What healing product is needed in our spa?" "Which technique should we market for the holidays?" This is the foundation from which you and your group can start building ideas. With one suggestion, start building on top of that.

4. Association with Words: These are words or statements that can be said or written in order to stimulate the mind into digging deeper into our well of knowledge. Associating words in a brainstorm session, can open up a whole new path. This method takes a list of words and then builds an association between other key words on the list. Once an original word has been chosen, the next person will find a word they associate with it. The next person must then do the same with the previous word. Word association can be done on your own, as well. Open a book or dictionary and randomly choose a word. Then begin formulating associated words or ideas using this key word. You'll be amazed how well this works.

5. Thought Journaling: As you have probably experienced in the past, sometimes the harder you try to be creative, the least creative you are. Perhaps, not trying too hard is one way to tap into the subconscious. I find that journaling thoughts can be an insightful approach to listening to what your fore brain has to say.

Try suggesting a topic to yourself before bed. This is one way to "sleep on it." In the morning, recall your dreams. Even if they are images or colors or words.... jot them down first thing in the morning upon waking. Then go back to it later. See if something comes of it.

6. Wander: Take a trip. Walk around the block, through your neighborhood, or through a park. Head to the sea, the hills, or a mountain trail. There is a concept (and herbal formula) in Chinese medicine referred to as the *Free and Easy Wanderer*. Walking or simply wandering often allows us to clear our head and free our minds. This allows for the free flow of movement, creativity, and vital energy or Qi. It is extremely therapeutic.

7. Incorporate Mind Games: Some of the best ways to engage your brain is by using your memory functions. Individuals who are always learning something new about the world, or maintaining a playful spirit, will find creativity to flow easier than those who do not. Challenge your mind and memory function. By exercising your brain, it provides inspiration and fills your mind with information that allows you to make creative connections easily.

8. Avoid Doing Drugs: Drugs cloud your mind, impair judgement, and diffuses motor function. People on drugs think they are creative. To everyone else, they seem like people on drugs.

9. Educate Yourself: Learn as much as you can about everything possible. Fill your brain with inspiration, excitement, and passions that interest you. Understand how to incorporate the information you learn into your own creative spin.

10. Take Everything One Day at A Time: Sometimes situations can become overwhelming when looking at the big picture. Again, take your quiet time to observe the moment. Do some soul searching. Allow yourself to take all the time and space that you need to grasp your creative genius. Trust the Universe. It is within you.

"Creativity requires the courage to let go of certainties." – Erich Fromm

Intention

Intention is everything. Focus. Attention. What is often considered living in the NOW, intention can be defined as "a determination to think or act in a certain way."

Intention is a tool that can be used to bring about change. With clear intent, we formulate a greater deliberateness in order to achieve the end result.

Creating and setting your intention is the basis of all goals. Without this "map" it is hard to really know what you are trying to achieve.

Your intention is a laser focused approach to defining a goal. When your intention is defined, you then have the purpose and reasoning behind setting your particular objective.

<u>Gemstone:</u>
Intention

"Ring high, ring true, vibrations sing.
Like plucking on a tight bow string.
To focus on the here and now,
let higher energies, allowed...
a place for sanctity and peace,
where intention will increase."

~ Andrew Pacholyk MS L.Ac

The Map of Intention

When you break down the process of what true intention really is, you will find a process that unfolds before you. Like any map, you set your destination and follow where it leads. By applying this process, you create your intention. Here is how you map out your intentions:

1. Have purpose: Your reason behind your intention is purpose. Having a purpose infers a more determined path.

_____

2. Design your intent: This suggests a more careful, laid out and calculated plan of action. What, when, why where, how.

_____

3. Improve your aim: By improving your aim, you add to your implications or targeted effort directed toward attaining your intention.

_____

4. Gain your objective: Create a clear objective by aiming for something tangible and immediately attainable. _____

5. Reach your goal: The goal is the result of your intention, put into action and attaining it by persistence and un-wavering focus. _____

The Power of Intention

Finding focus is a welcomed clarity in order to bring awareness to our lives. How many people do you know who lead an almost incomplete and unexamined life? Art of any kind is the ability to tune in and make it your own. The attaining of your goal through intention is one of the most rewarding and self-gratifying accomplishments we can do for ourselves. And guess what? You deserve every single bit of it.

Tuning in to any energy is the ability to quiet the mind, allowing your inner self, or intention, to perceive truth. By practicing this art, we develop sensitivity toward inner information and the ability to condition our mind to listen on a much subtler level. This developing can give us the ability to sense energy and actually perceive our intention on an even more subconscious plane.

Techniques are vast and varied, all of which, can be used in calming and clearing the mind, therefore, achieving clearer perception. Include some of the following:

1. Clear intention is a result of meditation: Meditation is a time-honored technique that can take you into infinite dimensions of consciousness. It is a simple effort that becomes effortless as we do it more and more. One major principle to meditation is the ability to completely quiet your mind. By quieting our mind, it can allow us a clearer picture of what we really intend.

2. Become more mindful: Mindfulness is the act of being fully aware of what happens in each moment. Try living in the NOW. Be present. Honor each moment you are given. Acknowledge each task you take.

3. Energy follows thought. As you think of your intention, you are made aware of it. As you are made aware of it, you are able to bring it to fruition by asserting your energy. When you program thought to be positive, your intention will be positive. The outcome is inevitable. Especially when you see it as such.

4. Moving is the action to your motivation. There is a mountain of proof that movement is the best thing for mind, body, and spirit. Moving helps with depression, increases our cardiovascular system, moves energy (Qi) and blood, stimulates the brain, increases hormone production, and takes us from one place to the next. Use movement as a tool to move intention forward.

5. Intention reverberates. When we throw a stone in a calm lake, we can see how the ripples start at the center point, where we dropped the stone (our intention) and move outward from that point. When we specify our intention, it moves out through the Universe as do the ripples in the lake.

6. Intention is a reflection of many values. Our values are a direct reflection of our beliefs. When we have strong, sensible values, your beliefs reflect it. These same beliefs are an expression of our experiences. Most often, people who have relatively good or tolerable experiences have a better outlook on their beliefs.

7. Make Room for Change: Make it a nourishing, self-respecting place for change to take place in your mind. In the same way, create a life affirming, positive path to reach your goal. Make no excuses. Procrastination is the bi-product of feeling unworthy. Self-worth leads us in the right direction.

8. A lack of awareness + not being grounded + being unfamiliar = FEAR: Become familiar with what your intention is. Once you are familiar with the reasons why your intention is important, this takes the fear out of the equation. Getting familiar with the information you did not know or understand, can clear a path for reaching your goal. Take initiative and responsibility in seeing your true goal through to completion. This all begins with the intent. Once you are familiar, there is less fear and you become more grounded in your approach.

9. Make Every Effort: to do something each day that brings your intentions closer to your goal. You will choose to do this because you now understand why you want to reach this goal. When the fear behind it is gone, you will find the effort it takes to achieve your goal much easier. When you love and respect yourself more, you realize that you deserve to make that effort.

10. The Honoring of Ourselves: This is something we tend to lose sight of, especially as we grow older. Honoring everyone else first, (husband, wife, children, family, friends, colleagues) is the path we so often go down, before we take care of our own needs. It is like building a bridge without a foundation. The roots of a tree must be strong, in order to hold up the rest of its branches as it grows. So too, must you be. This is not a selfish act. When you feel stable, balanced, and nurtured (from yourself), the world around you, appears more in control.

11."**Excuse, instead of action**" seems to be the norm, instead of the exception. It seems so much easier to put off till tomorrow, what you could do today. Intention will help with this. By setting your intention, you have already agreed to the first step of your plan.

12. **Action is the by-product of intention**. You can have all the best intentions in the world, but, if you do not act upon that intention, it is, as if you never made it in the first place. Your action is your follow through. It is the realization of that intent. It is the sole purpose of your intention in the first place. When you state your intention, you must be ready to act on it.

Sex

In the "Spring" of our lives, sex is the journey of self-discovery. It is the "fumbling your way" through the intimacies and understandings of your body, along with that of another. Spring is truly the introduction to this powerful force that satisfies and intrigues us, baffles, and confuses us.

Our sexual health is one of the most important elements of our whole being and natural existence. Yet, one that is often shunned, ignored, or found to be downright "dirty." My yoga mentor once said, **"You should look at EVERY person as a sexual being."**

Tantra uses the energies of the body and sometimes the sexual energies, to transcend worldly attachments. Pleasure teaches us how to connect. It assists us in learning to feel more love, greater touch, and emotional healing.

Sacred sexuality goes beyond this to teach us about the deeper inner realms of our psyche and provides us with true understanding, connection, and compassion. Through passionate, sensual awareness you can increase the quality of your sexual life.

Gemstone:

Sex

"It is my will that I connect,

exploring levels that will affect

the way in which I see myself

in order just to be myself

with pleasure deep to satisfy

and rejoice in unions I define."

~ Andrew Pacholyk MS, L.Ac

~ Sex builds families and rips apart empires.

~ It is a tool for change and a weapon of destruction.

~ It is mundane or it is taboo.

~ It is traded and bartered, stolen and offered.

~ Sex is the common denominator between us all.

Top 20 Sacred Sexual Secrets

Sex is one of the greatest enjoyments we create in our head! Sex is mental. It is the result of a powerful mind, organizing and creating scenarios that are our deepest enjoyment. Often, when played out with a partner in real time, it may not be as amazing as we tend to image it to be. Unless, we leave our expectations behind.

In my fertility practice, I constantly have patients asking about ways to bring about or keep the "spark" alive in their relationship. I think the best keywords I can come up with are:

*Communication *Awareness *Respect

Here are my top 20 sacred sexual secrets for **any relationship**:

1. Be In The Moment: Most people miss what is going on for them in the moment. Be present for the fun.

2. Make Conditions Right: Turn off the TV, power down your phone, get focused, feel rested and take advantage of the desire.

3. Cultivate Sexual Mindfulness: Be playful, attentive, erotic and be involved in the sensory moment.

4. Create A Sensual Atmosphere: Utilize the power of light, the scent of aromatherapy, the magic of incense and the mood making sound of music.

5. Entice with Natural Aphrodisiacs: Nature holds the key with sensual foods, which have a "reputation" such as oysters, cocoa and juicy fruits.

6. Open Your Mind: Expectations can kill the moment! Try things that empower, enlighten and return you to the magic of youthful energy.

7. Let Go of Fears: Inhibitions are useless and block who you really aspire to be. This is really the time to complete who you are. The more you let go of your fears, the more highly aroused and more deeply impacted you will be by the sexual experience.

8. Be In Tune With Your Surroundings: Feel each sensation, your breathing, your environment, your sounds, your motions. When you are with a partner, be conscious.

9. Experience The Power of Color: Use color therapy by incorporating candles of color, lingerie, lighting or fabric in order to bring color into your environment.

10. Use Your Chakra Energies: Explore how this central energy system helps to keep us more grounded, in tune to carnal instincts, while the spiritual aspects or our sexual experience is more mental. The heart energy is at the center of this scenario, balancing the lower and upper portions.

11. Rev Up Your Kundalini: This major life force energy is an ancient system originating from India. It helps the student awaken and emerge from their spiritual nature, as this energy rises up through our bodies.

12. Give Up Control: Allow for the give and take of each other's lead. The giving up of power can be just as arousing.

13. Flow with The Rhythm: Entrainment is the tendency of two oscillating bodies to lock into phase, so that they vibrate in harmony.

14. Take Your Time: Only by exploring the erotic landscape, savoring all of the body's hot spots, can we find a road to ultimate fulfillment.

15. Express Your Joys: If it works, let your partner know. Being vocal about your pleasure may help entice your partner. If it's not, show them where it can.

16. To Release or Not To Release: Whether you're a believer in the great release of energy or simply transmuting this sexual force through other channels, there is always pleasure through a Sacred Union.

17. Reach New Heights: Rediscover the deep interrelationship between sexuality and spirituality.

18. Sex Is the Common Denominator: Sex is the energetic healer of our mind, body, and spirit and it is shared by everyone.

19. Honor Pleasure As A Divine Gift: Sex is the most honest aspect of the Universal creative life force, which electrifies every stage of our life.

20. Cultivate Pure Ecstasy: The goal of your Tantric practice is to bring high states of sexual arousal while remaining completely relaxed.

Personal Growth

Within each *season* of our lives, we have elements which we are drawn to, often because of our age and our mind set. Personal growth tools are those which help us find our way in life. They are our hobbies and interests, careers or jobs, ideas or concepts we are attracted to.

Hopefully, throughout your life, you will continue to find these interests. They are the interests that can turn into careers or take our lives down a completely different path. A path we could have never imagined.

The key to making personal interests work, is to be open to them. It helps to be curious about life. For this is the spark which can catapult our dreams into desires and desires into reality.

What are your personal growth interests? What are some of the hobbies or ideas that you act upon? Have they given you great joy? How about an interest that turned into a career?

Even our own ideas or hobbies can be stifled or blocked as we grow and this is often due to our belief system. Fear and the idea of falling, failing, or being ridiculed, are usually some of the reasons why people do not follow their dreams.

Belief in Ourselves

Our belief system is made up of a set of core values, which we tend to base everything we do, say, or believe in. To start our journey in life, we create a set of beliefs, which define us. As part of our healing process, we must evaluate our beliefs.

With the ability to believe, you can accomplish nearly anything. The more you believe in yourself, the more you will definitely accomplish. When we face situations that are near physical or mental impossibilities, then it is our belief system, or belief in ourselves, that determines IF it is possible.

Our body and minds are stronger and more complex than most people think. We are capable of much more. People place too many limits on what they can do. Learning to believe in yourself and your abilities is a hard job that never ends. Although, it does get easier with time. You need to start pushing yourself. Attempt things that are just outside your ability. You have to believe you can go past your limits. By putting in the time and effort you WILL succeed.

As you succeed, your confidence will grow. The trick to this is, every time you reach what you believe is your limit, remind yourself that you can do more.

Always assume that you can do more than you already have accomplished. One of the best things about expanding your limits, is that things that used to be impossible, can now be a part of your everyday life. By building the belief in your ability, you can accomplish anything in life. Try it.

*Our outlook on life tells us exactly where we are going.

* Our belief system is one of the major factors that can get us through situations or can cause our life to crumble around us. I do believe that there is a lot of innate goodness and balancing our minds do, subconsciously, to get us through hard times. The other portion of this is how we "program" ourselves to deal with any given situation.

* Our self-confidence and self-love are often the key to opening and strengthening this portion of our thoughts which in turn emanates from ourselves.

* Energy follows thought. Program thought to be positive and your energy will reflect it.

* Really appreciating what we DO have as opposed to what we would like to have, sometimes makes a significant difference. This is always an important element in healing that is often neglected.

Creating A Healthy Belief System

A belief system that serves us well, is a belief in unlimited abundance. Having a deserving and humble nature with room to understand, helps us to serve the common good. Sometimes, it is necessary to reinvent our belief system and redefine our values so that we can see clearer and be more able to achieve a fulfilling life that we desire. Consider these suggestions for creating a healthy belief system that serves you:

1. Start by allowing abundance into your life: There are no limits except for those we impose on ourselves. Believing you cannot have what you want in your life, is a self-destructive and disparaging idea that you create.

2. Use the words "unlimited possibilities." This is your mantra. I have, I desire, I believe in.... unlimited possibilities. Abundance is a long lasting, enduring enjoyment of life. It is being in love with living. You must learn to see every possibility as a path to a new adventure.

3. Understand that you are deserving: No, it is not your "karma", not your "lot in life", not "what you deserve" ... we are ALL deserving. You deserve all that the Universe is offering. These are unlimited possibilities.

4. Improve your self-esteem: We can all seek to improve ourselves. It is time you became committed to truly loving and appreciating yourself and who you are. Take a minute to look at your individualism. Honor who you are. Honor what it took to get you there. Chin up, chest out, and get moving.

5. Extinguish feelings of self-hate arising out of guilt: Is it possible that your guilty feelings are excessive? Your self-hate is reactionary? Who are you really punishing? Re-evaluate your situation. Stop self-punishment. It serves only to wear you down. Start forgiving yourself....and others.

6. Look at your negative beliefs: What is standing in your way? Is it issues around love, money, health? Take a look at these issues on an individual basis. Remove the question from the situation. Does it really have value? What is the true connection between you and this belief?

7. Are you generally happy? If so, make a list of 5 things that bring you happiness. If you believe you are not, make a list of 5 things that do not. Evaluate these 5 items of unhappiness. Each has a solution that you are going to solve.

8. Perhaps there is a current belief that no longer serves you. Have the courage and the strength to seek the truth. Allow yourself to let go of an old, hurtful, or useless idea or concept that does you no good. Allow yourself and let it go.

9. Search for meaning by reading and reflecting. The search itself will help restore a degree of purpose and sense of existence.

10. Some important values about your belief system include giving, sharing, accepting compliments, and recognizing new beginnings.

If we can give, unconditionally ~ we are happy. If we can share, unequivocally ~ we are at peace. If we can accept a compliment, gracefully ~ we are humbled. If we can recognize new beginnings, gladly, we are open.

***

Gemstone:
In Your Belief

"We tend to believe what we feel is right, and sometimes it is true,

but if we believe all we see and hear, then we really never knew...

how wide the range of truth can be, or different points of view...

If we'd believe with an open heart, then often things feel new.

We can often block these words that we may just have heard,

because our minds are simply closed, then all the lines are blurred,

inside our minds, because one fact has altered every thought

and cascades down our reasoning, so, this is what we bought.

Just how our first impressions lie, or judgments, they construe...

the reality, for what it is, it's sometimes hard to chew.

So, hear the honest truth be told, and listen with your heart,

A sound and healthy belief can come, when YOUR heart plays a part.

~ Andrew Pacholyk MS. L.Ac

Spring's Element: Air

Throughout the centuries, the elements have come to be associated with each season. The elements are the forces of nature that express their energies on earth, in the Universe, and within us. They are the fundamental building blocks of many paradigms from every culture and the building blocks for life on earth.

Air is one of the four classic elements from ancient Greek philosophy, science, and astrology. In astrology, there are four classical elements.

In the *Spring of our lives*, our personalities tend to match that of the element, air. We are gentle and tornadic, we can be cool or rage like an uncontrollable hurricane. Air has no boundaries and can float or flutter. It follows the path of least resistance and pushes past limitations we would often think twice about in later years. The paradigms of other cultures have recognized this fact.

In the Feng Shui and Chinese paradigms, there are 5 elements. Spring is associated with Wood, followed by Fire (Summer), Earth (late Summer), Metal (Fall), and Water (Winter). As in Chinese Medicine there is a fifth season and that is late Summer (falling between Summer and early Fall). Each element has certain characteristics, emotional, interpersonal and physical manifestations.

The Ayurvedic paradigm also has 5 elements. Spring is associated with Water, followed by Fire (Summer), Air (Fall), Ether (Winter) and Earth (late Winter and early Spring).

In some schools of thought, the element Air, is associated with the Fall season.

For the sake of this book, I have gone with the most notable and most recognized four classic elements of air, fire, earth, water.

Air represents the breath of life. It is an exchange of electrons or flow of energy. Air is our primary nutrient. Survival without it is measured in minutes. Breath is sustaining. It is so important, that we do it without thinking.

Your breathing is the voice of your spirit. It's depth, smoothness, sound and rate reflect your mood. The "cosmic breath", the Hindus speak of, is called "prana". It is also the energetic life force the Chinese refer to as "Qi" energy.

The Air Signs of the zodiac are Gemini, Libra, and Aquarius. They are curious, have initiative, are original, are generally well disciplined and are quick thinkers. The Air signs have a mental nature and are keen witted. They rationalize by thinking things out rather than being influenced by emotional or physical factors.

The Air signs possess the virtue of knowledge. This does not mean they are more intelligent than anyone else but are generally well rounded and informed.

They are good communicators. Most have a good grasp of the language and generally know a little something about everything. They have good personalities and are easy to get to know.

Each element has its own "personality" with positive and negative traits, correlating time, season, planets, directions and so on.

Air represents our mental activity such as intellect and the ability to reason. Air has an association with our memory, thoughts, knowledge and comprehension. It also rules new beginnings, friendship, clarity and positive expression. The Air personality is very good at making decisions and carrying them through.

We gain spirituality through the exploration of ourselves. Air or wind has often been associated with the intangible, illusiveness of spirituality. Powerful and ever-changing or gentle and peaceful, spirituality holds different ideas for different people. Ultimately, I believe, if you feel spiritual or sense the empowerment associated with it, you are on a path to self-realization, self-love and self-acceptance.

Utilize the element of air to lead you to a new place in your life. Go with the flow and access different ideas and concepts that come your way. Consider examining new ideas more closely. Be open to the possibility that everything (like the wind) can change. This can be either for the good or not so good, but the ideology of "air" helps us learn how to handle whatever comes out way.

Air

March 21 to June 21

(Spring equinox to the eve of summer solstice)

Abilities: Mind, brain, intellect, logical thought, curiosity, travel, youth, light, energy, computers, machines, impersonal, detached, mental powers, visions, psychic power, wisdom, learning, imagination, ideas, beliefs, theory.

Stones: Yellow topaz, citrine, mica, pumice, aventurine, clear quartz, lepidolite, blue lace agate, celestite, angelite, angel aura.

Plants: Acacia, bergamot, clover, dandelion, lavender, lemongrass, mint, mistletoe, pine, anise, broom, eyebright, hops, meadowsweet, sweetgrass, slippery elm.

Direction: East

Season: Spring (Autumn in the Southern Hemisphere)

Colors: Blue, White, Yellow.

Cycle Celebrations: Imbolc, Ostara (Spring Equinox)

Number 5

Time: Dawn

Zodiac: Gemini, Libra, Aquarius

Planets: Mercury, Jupiter

Angel: Michael

Sense: Smell

Time of life: Childhood

Gemstone:
Air

"The lift and lilt of gentle breeze,
can show its other face, you see,
when wind begins to whip and blow,
from hurricane to icy snow,
that hits OR smoothly rushes by,
these personalities a stride,
we just accept and let it pass,
this ever changing, rich air mass."

~Andrew Pacholyk MS L.Ac

Musical Landscape

Music has always played a major role in my life. Ever since those early days of piano lessons with Mrs. Uri or playing trumpet in classical and jazz bands, music has made a statement. I always remember the holidays or special occasions when my mom, Andrena, would regale us with wonderful pieces of music such as Malaguena or her own special version of Silver Bells. I have had the pleasure of singing in small and large choral groups from All-state to my own singing quartet group, Free and Easy, as well as, being a charter member of the infamous gospel choir, The Voices of Unity. Music continues to give me life changing moments and memories and I am forever grateful for this art and therapy.

Whether we know it or not, our lives are mapped out by the important moments we encounter. And most often, there is a song associated with it. Quite often, when we hear a familiar tune, it can take us back to the exact time and place, along with the experience that went with it! This "musical landscape" is the map of our lives.

From celebrations and ceremonies to proclamations and processions. Music marks the empirical reference we associated with time and place. Music is a magical medium that has always been a metaphor for our spirit.

The "tao" or "path" of music is the way. The way we hear music, our approach to making music, our understanding of the rhythm and rhymes of music are the conditions in which we understand its message. This is known as vibrational tuning or vibrational medicine, which validates that everything in the Universe is in a state of vibration and the frequency at which an object or person most naturally vibrates is called **resonance**.

In his book, *The Tao of Music: Sound Psychology*, brilliant author, John M. Ortiz was the first to introduce me to the ***theory of entrainment***. Dr. Ortiz is a licensed psychologist, psycho-educational consultant and speaker and founding director of the Asperger's Syndrome Institute in Philadelphia. He has over 25 years of clinical experience in various educational and mental health settings and his work with music therapy has been profound.

Entrainment Theory tells us that there is a rhythm to life. From the beat of our hearts to the beat of the streets, everything around us is set to its own timing. There is a natural tendency in nature towards harmony. When something is not in sync, has dissonance or discord, we know it and can sense or feel it. When our energies are in sync, this resonance is very apparent. This is the theory or entrainment.

Musically, entrainment involves the "merging with, or synchronizing to, the pulse of the music." This principle is related to the isomorphic principle which states that one's mood should be matched to the mood of the music and then gradually moved into the desired direction. The principle of entrainment is Universal. Appearing in chemistry, pharmacology, biology, medicine, psychology, sociology, astronomy, architecture, and more. An example of entrainment is seen in medicine. When two individual, pulsing heart muscle cells are brought close together, they begin pulsing in synchronicity. Another example of the entrainment effect is women who live in the same household, often find that their menstrual cycles will coincide. The entrainment process is quite evident in music. Entrainment in music, has the potential to (1) resonate with the listener's feelings, (2) transform negativity into positivity, and (3) promote a state of liveliness or serenity. Certain sounds, in specific sequence can help bring the listener from one emotion to another. *Entrainment is the tendency of two oscillating bodies to lock into phase, so that they vibrate in harmony.*

Musical Playlists for Life's Journeys

Create Your Entrainment Music

Create your own soundtracks to your life!

First, find several songs, about 10-15 minutes' worth, which match your "present" mood (anxiety, stress, depression, joy, contentment...).

Second, find several other musical selections, 10-15 minutes, which are between your present internal state and the state you wish to achieve.

Third, find several songs, about 10-15 minutes' worth, which match the desired mood state you wish to finally achieve (joy, relaxation, communication...)

Create a playlist with this music. You will notice that if you start out anxious, stressed, or fearful, your first choices in music will express these chaotic emotions. The second group of music will feel less chaotic and more soothing. The third group of songs will reflect a sound of happiness, relaxation, and a peaceful mind. This process, used in music therapy, is exactly what happens with the entrainment process.

Gemstone:
Spring Songs

"Like breath of fresh and fragrant air,

the songs of Spring are everywhere.

To brighten up and fill our days,

with new beginnings ~ come our way.

When creativeness abounds,

with motivation to be found..."

~ Andrew Pacholyk MS L.Ac

Andrew's Spring Empowering Play List

I thought it would be a wonderful gift to share the songs of Spring that make up my consciousness. These melodies cross several eras and genre, yet they ring true for me as the seasonal mind set and the amazing way Spring can be expressed in song.

1. Optimistic Voices, MGM Studio Orchestra
2. Little April Shower, Disney Chorus
3. April in Paris, Dinah Shore
4. Waters of March, Basia
5. All The Things You Are, Helen Forrest
6. Getting To Know You, Deborah Kerr
7. Songs Without Words, Spring Song in A Major, Allegro grazioso
8. Echo of Spring, Chuck Wilson
9. The Song Is You, Keely Smith
10. It Might As Well Be Spring, Astrud Gilberto
11. 99 Most Essential Spring Classics, Various Artists
12. Spring Awakening, Dan Gibson
13. Come Fly With Me, Frank Sinatra
14. Color My World, Petula Clark
15. Defying Gravity, Idina Menzel, Kristin Chenoweth
16. Seasons Of Love, Rent Soundtrack
17. The Alkemyst, Dos Hombres
18. History Repeating, Shirley Bassey
19. Feelin' (Love To Infinity Remix), Gloria Estefan
20. Every Breath, Janice Robinson
21. Waltz of the Flowers, Tchaikovsky's Nutcracker Suite

Music Associated with Air

The desert expresses its beauty through the rising and setting sun, painting the desert floor and sky with a multitude of fascinating colors. The air is dry, yet crisp and gives me a sense of empowerment as I associate it through music. On my visit to the desert, I was reminded, through the silence, how air (and wind) represent flexibility. Flexibility is one way to experience life through many prisms. These songs cross several eras, and genre yet they ring true for me as they encourage movement, represent freedom and the amazing way Air can be expressed in song. I call this list:

The Flow of Energy Playlist

1. Air on a G String, Royal Philharmonic Orchestra
2. Whole New World (Aladdin's Theme), Peabo Bryson
3. Flying Theme from E.T., John Williams
4. Summer Breeze, Seals & Croft
5. Hurricane, River House
6. Medley: Fur Elise/Windmills/Floating, Mike Strickland
7. The Flying Sequence, Superman, John Williams
8. Main Title, The Towering Inferno, John Williams
9. Up, Up And Away, The Fifth Dimension
10. Everybody's Free (General Electric Edit), Rozalla
11. I Giorni, Ludovico Einaudi
12. Walking in the Air, Chloe Agnew
13. Air and Simple Gifts, Yo-Yo Ma
14. No Air, Jordan Sparks
15. Floating On Air, 351 Lake Shore Drive
16. Love Is In The Air (Ballroom Mix), John Paul Young
17. The Air That I Breathe, Kd Lang
18. Sailing, Christopher Cross
19. Wind Beneath My Wings, Bette Midler
20. Desert Breeze, Desert Wind

Create Your Musical Playlist

1. List 5 songs that remind you of Spring

2. List 5 songs that remind you of Air

Seasonal Landscape: Desert

Desert climates around the world have a powerful and charismatic persona! My allure towards the desert has grown over the years as I discover more and more their illustrious beauty, as well as their treasures.

The desert holds on to secrets and then releases them centuries later, for a new generation to unearth and discover its Sacred past. The desert is a unique environment. From extreme temperature to extreme ways of life, it offers us a broad picture of the fullest spectrum of life itself.

Like Spring, it shows us the possibilities of promise, with equal opportunities of darkness and light. It teaches us how life can be harsh at times, but yet, how it can also be filled with the nourishment an oasis can offer.

From storms of sand to blistering heat, or air that is crisp with sunsets of inspiration, the desert teaches us how to listen. Silence can be a great tool for looking within and releasing the chatter from outside.

The desert represents our bare essence. It is our spiritual senses stripped down to the sparse and widening space that affords our mind an empty landscape in which to ponder our exposed selves. Within this opportunity we may see what it is we truly need in life in order to survive. It may also show us what we really need to thrive.

The desert opens us up to possibilities we may not have seen before we realized just how simple life *could be.*

The desert expresses its beauty through the rising and setting sun, painting the desert floor and sky with a multitude of fascinating colors. The air is dry, yet crisp and gives us a sense of empowerment as we can associate it through movement, artistry, poetry, or music.

I have had the opportunity to visit some of the world's greatest deserts and through these travels I have found music that tells the stories the natural surroundings can offer. "This oasis of musicality", are melodies that cross different times and genres in music yet ring so true in their accuracy.

I call this playlist:

Andrew's Desert Melodies

1. Desert Symphony, Del Rio
2. Overture (From "The Desert Song"), Constantine Callinicos
3. Sunrise at Sindhu, Desert Dwellers
4. Crystal Desert, Fiona Joy Hawkins
5. Sahara Sunset, Karunesh
6. Walking Through the Desert Near Palpa, The Smiling Buddhas
7. Navajo Skip Dance Song, Fernando Cellicion
8. Painted Desert, Grand Canyon Suite
9. Palm Desert, Ray Kelley Band
10. Las Vegas, Underground Lovers
11. Midnight In The Desert, Crystal Gayle
12. Desert Sand, Inc. Palms Down
13. Praise To The Desert, Tchaikovsky Symphony Orchestra
14. Desert Air, Gary Burton
15. Sonoran Desert Holiday, US Air Force Air
16. Desert Serenity, Karim Azedia
17. Tunisia: Winds from the Desert), Layali de Tunis
18. Desert Grooves 2, Various Artists
19. Desert Wind, Radiophonic
20. Desert Rose, Sting

The Mineral Kingdom

Crystals are profound gifts and a great integrative therapy that can be used in conjunction with any other form of health care for personal pleasure, meditation, stress relief, and healing. I have always been attracted to crystals ever since I was a little boy.

My interest never waned and as an adult, I have turned this hobby into a good living by collecting, offering and selling stones and crystals to all those who find the same awe and amazement with these shimmering beauties.

I have had the opportunity to visit some of the world's greatest deserts in search of rocks. As a rock hound, I have gathered a wonderful collection of some of the most powerful and energetic stones on the planet. Here are some of my favorites and the stone's "stories" to go along with them.

Desert Rose: This is a beautiful variety of gypsum that forms in the shapes of rose buds. This crystalline structure "blossoms" in the spaces between large sand particles. Its unique flower-like structure is selenite crystal and gains it reputation from being discovered in the desert and most often found below the water table. Metaphysically, Desert Rose is helpful in releasing old belief systems and useful in strengthening affirmations with a heartfelt intention. Also called the selenite rose, it is historically used for grounding scattered energy or energy that is spent pondering old ideas.

Sedona Vortex Stone: Famous for its energy centers or vortex, Sedona has become a magnet for those seeking powerful enlightenment and a spiritual connection. These amazing stones pulse with energy! These stones are most often located near famous vortex centers in Sedona such as Cathedral Rock Vortex, Boynton Canyon Vortex, Red Rock Crossing Vortex, Chapel of the Holy Cross and Bell Rock Vortex, to name a few. These vortexes, have their own energetic connections, but in general, they share a compassionate, nurturing, nature that engulfs you when you work with these stones. Cathedral Rock Vortex is famous for sacred Native ceremonies of the heart, as well as weddings. Bell Rock Vortex suggests a grand scale of spiritual energy, while Chapel of the Holy Cross shares a sacred presence with a nurturing attraction. The warm, red stones have a feeling of reverence and heavenly respect, offering peace, solace and a feeling of unity to the vortex.

Moqui Balls: This is a sacred stone from the Navajo Sandstone formations. They are made of iron and sandstone. According to native traditions, these stones offer insight, as they are able to sharpen the eye of its owner, bringing knowledge of what is natural and right. They bring inner peace and harmony to those who embrace them. Said to be used to contact spiritual beings, they are used for visions and sacred journeys. They act as a protector when placed in one's environment. They synthesis male/female duality, liberate one's nature and help us to recognize ourselves better. Used to realign our energy centers, they can release energy blockage, stimulate our vital energy and offer a feeling of being grounded, centered, and balanced.

San Andreas Fault Stone: The San Andreas fault is a crack in the Earth's crust in California, some 684 miles long. Recently, I was lucky enough to visit the Southern Segment of the infamous San Andreas Fault on a recent visit to Palm Springs. This earth line crosses the Coachella Valley from the Chocolate Mountains in the southeast corner and along the centerline of the Little San Bernardinos. The fault traverses California's Coachella Valley on the east side. Because of this fault, the Valley has many hot springs. The Santa Rosa Mountains to the West are part of the Lake Elsinore Fault zone. The results of a prehistoric "earth slide" reveal rocks from the Precambrian, Tertiary and Quaternary formations bringing forth stones from the earth's inner sanctum. Geological researchers have been able to find significant amounts of the mineral serpentine, granite, shale, and sandstone. These earth stones are grounding, especially during times of upheaval in our lives. Considered a "guardian stone", it embodies the elemental powers of fire and earth, molding together material that brings security, guarded protection, and steadfastness. This stone can literally change your life's "landscape" and offer you a whole new picture or perspective on something that may have been lying just beneath the surface. A great stone to encourage new beginnings.

Barite Rose: These very unique stones are an aggregate of barite (barium sulfate) crystals and sand, whose iron content gives it a reddish hue. The barite crystals form a circular array of flat plates, giving the rock a shape similar to a rose blossom. Rose rocks appear either as a single rose bloom or as clusters of blooms. The "rose rock" was selected as the official state rock of Oklahoma in 1968. These stones are rarer than diamonds due to the fact they only formed in a small area 250 million years ago from a sea eroding barite deposits. American Indian legend tells that spirits of Indian warriors returned to carve the Barite rose. It provides a strong and delicate connection to the spirit world and assists one on the path toward the journey and the goal. It can help relax the nervous system through meditation. In addition to dreaming and spiritual journeys, they offer a good solution for relationship loyalty, addiction and cleansing.

Atacama Desert Halite: The Atacama Desert of northern Chile is the driest desert on Earth in which, aridity not only forms the halite deposits but has also preserved them, almost unaltered. These deposits are largely composed of Ca sulfate and halite. This special white salt is only waiting for the moment to have its inherent stored energy and its bio-photon content set free, by adding water to it. Place some healing salt in a hot bath. Heat magnifies the natural healing properties of this salt. The salt will dissipate slowly, prolonging your enjoyment.

Black Obsidian: Obsidian is actually natural glass that is formed when hot lava is submerged in water. This is a strong grounding stone and is known as "the protector". It is said to "mirror one's soul". This stone brings about objectivity, dis-attachment and is grounding. Hawaiian tribes believe they reduce fantasy and escapism. Believed to absorb and dissolve anger, criticism, fear, and therefore, are protective stones. This unusual black stone absorbs darkness and converts it to white light energy. It is a warm and friendly stone, which is used at the Root Chakra, encouraging one's survival instincts and self-awareness.

Thundereggs: These stones are rough spheres usually containing centers of chalcedony in the form of agate, jasper or opal. These stones usually look like ordinary rocks on the outside, but when sliced in half and polished, they often reveal a star-like pattern or other intricate patterns and colors. A thunderegg is a nodule-like, geological structure and is just one of the forms that agate, jasper or opal can assume. It is believed that if they are powerful enough to contain and hold the energies of a volcanic eruption, then they could also store the energies of humans, making them ideal for healing or protective amulets.

Arizona Meteorites are magnetic and magical. The meteorites that have iron in them are actually attracted to magnets. Magnetic meteorites attract and repel energies and are used for sedation. It acts as a grounding stone. It assists in telepathy, meditation, and visualization. They can provide stability and balance including balancing the intellect and our emotional state. It brings a centering perspective and trust within your own intuition.

Gemstone:
Desert Oasis

"Against the winds and sands of time, stand ancient lands of God's design.
Where sacred tools of nature come, to those who seek the rising sun,
so listen now and find your peace, where light and sky will never cease..."

~ Andrew Pacholyk, MS L.Ac

Top 10 Crystals for Spring

This season is bursting forth in color, creativity, and spirituality. Spring is bubbling over with the fresh smell of cut grass, the blooming of multi-colored flowers, and fresh garden sprouts. Crystals echo the colors and energy of the season. I list some of my best gems for creativity, Feng Shui, detoxing, cleansing, and clearing energy, along with stones of spiritual significance.

Moss Agate: This stone connects one to nature. Moss agate containing inclusions of minerals that look like moss or foliage. They are most used for improving ego and self-esteem, emotional balance, and strengthening positive, personality traits. They allow us to see all the beauty one's eyes touch. Agates are grounding stones and one of the oldest good luck stones in history. They help obtain a better physical/emotional balance. They work to raise consciousness and build self-confidence. This stone was historically used to enable the person wearing it to choose their friends carefully. Agate is known to bring prosperity. It has been given to children as a protection stone. This stone helps us to have patience and allows for inner peace. Use agate as a gazing tool for divination and meditation. Agate balances emotions and brings insight to any situation. Agate is a fertility stone used for centuries as a great stone for Spring.

Amazonite: Assists in courage of personal expression, giving us the power to say the words we're afraid to speak. This green stone is instrumental in distilling the raw information used for personal expression. Good for anyone involved in the arts. It was believed to enhance masculine qualities. Utilize Amazonite in order to encourage the pursuit of your unique path in life. Amazonite is used to disperse negative energy. This gentle, friendly, soothing stone is used at the Throat, Heart, and Solar Plexus Chakra. This is a great stone for communication, confidence, and leadership. Reduces self-damaging behavior, increases self-respect, grace, and communication.

Aventurine: Heals emotional pain/fear/imbalance by dissolving blocks in the Heart Chakra. Used for encouraging Universal love, truth, and prosperity. Green is the color of healing and has a concentrated ability to dissolve emotional blockages. Aventurine helps to balance our thoughts and is one of the best stones to wear or carry during stressful periods. It can also be used in crystal layouts when stress is internalized in the solar plexus area.

Chrysocolla: Calms the mind so thoughts flow freely. This is a good stone for those who find their thinking processes to be intellectually sound but lacking emotional quality. Excellent for the Heart Chakra; this stone flushes and heals emotional heart blocks (loss, hurt, guilt, fear...) Used for allowing flexibility, self-forgiveness, peace of mind, and patience. Helps keep one in spiritual light, love, and healing, daily. Used on the Throat Chakra, it helps us express feelings, verbal, and artistic creativity. Helps one feel more comfortable speaking the truth. Brings personal confidence. Historically used by musicians, perhaps because of its reputation for having healing properties for throat and lungs.

Hawk's Eye: This stone, also called Falcon's Eye, helps us to gain perspective, to see (and face) situations fully. Hawk's Eye is the stone of vision, insight, and psychic awareness. It allows us to see the overview clearly and unflinchingly, as from a hawk's eyes. This stone is often used to balance pessimistic behavior and therefore, dissolves negative energy and the thought patterns associated with it. This "all seeing stone" allows perspective on any situation and it can help gently attune the Third Eye. Known to enhance psychic abilities such as clairvoyance. It helps us to look at an emotional block that may be buried deep in our psyche. This versatile stone can be used to heal earth energy and helps us to become grounded when used at the Root Chakra. This stone should be used for those who want to blame others for their problems and are not able to look at their problems directly.

Kyanite: is considered the "Earth Stone" due to its soothing earth tone colors, as well as its grounding and tranquil nature. The healing benefits depend on the color it's found in. Blue Kyanite is most effective when placed on the Throat Chakra in order to open the throat for communication and self-expression. On the Third Eye Chakra, it enhances psychic images, foresight, consciousness and meditation. Kyanite is used to answer questions, especially in imagery, such as in vision, dreams or written interpretations. It brings out our natural ability to manifest things into reality via thoughts and visualization. Black Kyanite is best used for grounding and balance at the Root Chakra. This is where it gets its "Mother Earth" reputation.

Lepidolite: This is the stone of rebirth. Useful for transitions in life. Helpful in times of stress and coping with death therefore, creating calm and relaxation. Lepidolite is used to help ease the transition from addiction. In tribal lore, this stone brings hope, relief, gentleness, self-love, patience, self-forgiveness, unworried sleep, mental/emotional balance and well-being. This stone is particularly good for students as it is helpful for studying, learning, manifesting, change and awareness. This stone is used for self-criticism. When we become down on ourselves, lepidolite allows us to see who we really are and the potential that lies within us. To enjoy the benefits from this stone, meditate with it on a daily basis.

Malachite: This stone has a steady pulsing electromagnetic energy due to its high copper content. On the Third Eye Chakra, this stone stimulates physical and psychic vision, along with concentration. On the Heart and Solar Plexus Chakra, it is a powerful healer. Releases and draws out pain, inflammation, depression and anger, as it heals emotional blocks. Protects well by powerfully cleaning the auric field, rapidly absorbing undesirable energies, including computer, TV, and other radiations.

Quartz: This stone is thought to amplify both body energy and thoughts. It can assist in the creation of power, clarity of thinking, meditation, cleansing, clearing the aura, spiritual development and healing. Clear quartz is considered the "stone of power" and is a dedicated healing stone. Pure white light passes through it easily, leaving all the colors of the spectrum unaltered, giving substance to the argument that clear quartz crystals can help balance all the elements needed to make us whole and fulfilled. It will unblock specific areas blocked from transmitting or receiving the flow of energy throughout the body.

Tourmaline: is a powerful, electromagnetic, striated gem. According to Indian legend, tourmaline strengthens body and spirit, as it transmutes lower frequency (thought) energy to a higher frequency of (light) spirit into the physical plane. Therefore, it can actually balance all the Chakra centers. Tourmaline radiates light protection for its wearer. This stone clears higher frequencies, effectively as it forms a protective shield all over the body (Aura). Tourmaline is a rod of power. I equate this crystal to that of the spinal column. It makes us stand up for ourselves, promoting confidence, self-realization, inspiration, tolerance and compassion. Therefore, it is one of my favorite crystals for alleviating fear. It banishes the victim mentality.

Food for Thought: Eating for Spring

Every culture looks at food as a healing remedy or medicine. It is also viewed as a form of spiritual nourishment. To keep in harmony with nature, foods for Spring should promote a healthy detox from the heavier foods we ate during the winter months. Our food choices should be lighter and boost our metabolism. Reprogramming the way we eat, can help us to lose weight, balance blood sugar levels, and keep our bodies running at optimum health.

When eating along with the seasons, there are two elements that should be taken into account. The "nature" of the food and the "flavor" of the food. The nature of the food refers to the food's innate temperature ie: cold, hot, warm, cool, or neutral. Eating a moderate amount of all flavors including sweet, salty, pungent, bitter, and sour, can help to keep your body balanced and regulated.

Sour taste is attributed to the liver and gall bladder, therefore, adding some sour foods in your diet during Spring can improve the liver's function. Consider apple, apricot, grape, grapefruit, hawthorn fruit, kumquat, loquat, mandarin orange, mango, olive, peach, pineapple, plum, raspberry, small red or adzuki bean, strawberry, tangerine, tomato, and vinegar.

To help tonify the liver, concentrate on eating chlorophyll rich foods such as spirulina, chlorella, barley grass, wheatgrass and Klamath blue green algae. Other green foods that are beneficial are kale, parsley, and collard greens.

Apple cider vinegar is beneficial as it's bitter/sour taste has a detoxifying effect on the liver. Also consider lemon, lime, or grapefruit juice in place of vinegar. Other bitter foods that can be used for detoxification purposes include rye, romaine lettuce, asparagus, amaranth, and quinoa.

Consider eating these foods for Spring:

1. Fruits and nuts: apples, dates, lychees, walnuts, peanuts, chestnuts.

2. Cereals, grains, and legumes: brown rice, corn, millet, oatmeal, sorghum, soybeans, black gram, adzuki bean, red kidney bean, broad bean.

3. Meat, poultry and fish: chicken, turkey, shrimp, carp, eel, chicken eggs.

4. Vegetables, seaweeds, potatoes, onions, carrots, chives, scallions, radishes, daikon, broccoli, asparagus, lettuce, cooked spinach, coriander, cauliflower, garlic, leeks, eggplants, Chinese cabbage, yams, sweet potatoes, celery, common mushrooms, shiitake mushrooms.

5. Herbs, spices, condiments, oils such as perilla leaf, peppermint, dandelion, honeysuckle flower, basil, parsley, wolfberry (gou gi berries), fleece-flower root, licorice, astragalus, rhubarb, ginger, pepper, honey, sesame oil.

Essential Oils for Spring

Spring is a time of new beginnings, new growth, planting seeds, purification, and for clearing out the old. Following the rhythms of nature and developing harmony with the ways in which nature cares for itself, we can also create balance within our own lives. Trees, plants, grasses, and seeds that have laid still throughout the winter slowly emerge from their dormancy. Buds develop and grow into new leaves and flowers, plants, and grasses emerge through the ground from their resting roots as seed sprouts; all from the extended sunlight, warmth, rains, and Spring's nourishment.

Jasmine: (Jasminum gradiflora) is a bold, sweet scent. Jasmine is the greatest aphrodisiac of all. These night blooming flowers are picked during a full moon, at their height of potential, to become one of the sexiest scents. Associated throughout history with the compassionate Goddess of the Moon, Jasmine, grown along the Nile in ancient Egypt, represents the Goddess, Isis, the Egyptian Mother Goddess who held the secrets of fertility, magic, and healing.

Patchouli: (Pogostemon cablin) is a sweet, earthy scent. Its smell is intense and spicy. From an energetic point of view, patchouli, like jasmine, is warm and yet anti-inflammatory in action. It combines a calmative property with a gentle stimulating effect that uplifts the spirit. Patchouli is a sweet and grounding harmonizing fragrance.

Neroli: (Citrus aurantium) is distilled from bitter orange trees. It has a refreshing, spicy aroma and is known for its sensual, exotic effect. Neroli oil is emotionally unifying and soothes with harmonizing effort. This sensual yet uplifting oil, helps to bring both mind and body into sync. Neroli opens our heart and mind to accept more happiness within us.

Rose: (Rosa damascena) The mother of all flowers, the Rose has amazing powers of love, trust, and self-acceptance. Roses are representative of faith, hope, and love and have the qualities to restore the very center of one's being. A gentle tonic of the heart, rose oil's psychological properties lie mainly in its effect on the mind, the center of our emotional being. Rose oil calms and supports the heart and helps to nourish the soul.

Peppermint: (Mentha piperita) is the most extensively used of all the volatile oils, both medicinally and commercially. The characteristic antispasmodic action of this essential oil is most often used and greatly adds to its power of relieving pain. From its stimulating, stomachic and carminative properties, it is valuable in certain forms of dyspepsia, being mostly used for flatulence and colic. It may also be used for other sudden pains and for cramps in the abdomen.

Lemon: (Citrus limonum) is a fresh, sunny scent that is cold pressed from the rind itself. Lemon has antiseptic-like properties and contains compounds that have been studied for their effects on immune function. It may serve as an insect repellent and may be beneficial for the skin. Diffuse it in your home for a fresh alternative to air spray. This oil can make the skin photo-sensitive to sunlight. Be cautious if wearing it outside.

Eucalyptus: (Eucalyptus globulus) was first employed by Australian aborigines, who not only chewed the roots for water in the dry outback but used the leaves to treat fever, cough, and asthma. European settlers quickly adopted it as medicine. You can use a few drops of eucalyptus oil in boiling water as an inhalant or in a bath. Eucalyptus is often used for sore muscles, insect repellant, tension headache, cold, cough, sinusitis, rheumatoid arthritis and strains/sprains.

Orange: (Citrus sinensis) is obtained from the rind of the fruit and used principally as a flavoring agent. Orange oil is an anti-depressant, antiseptic, antispasmodic, carminative and digestive tonic. Orange oil helps spreads sunshine when gloomy thoughts or depression set in. It has a very comforting and warming effect and dispels tension and stress. It has a beneficial effect on colds, bronchitis and fever when rubbed into the head and chest. Helps with anxiety and insomnia. Orange oil helps dry skin conditions, softening wrinkles, and dermatitis. An excellent skin tonic. Orange oil can make the skin photo-sensitive to sunlight.

Cycle Celebrations

The celebration of the seasons and the passing of time have been celebrated since its beginnings. Before there was a monotheistic religion or the worshipping of one God in our culture, there was polytheistic or the worshipping of nature and many gods.

The process of claiming and adopting styles, religious beliefs, and rituals have been repeated over and over again throughout history. Like the cultures before them and every culture after, our celebrations for life and the seasons have evolved over centuries with a history and folklore rich in myth, mystery, and magic!

Greeks and Romans celebrated the turn of each season to please different Gods. As they conquered the Celts, they took over their temples, traditions, and ideas and made them their own.

What we know about the Celts is often taken from the literature recorded by the Greeks and Romans, early Christians, and archaeological evidence. We know that the Celts, like other cultures before them, found methods of healing primarily through the bounty of nature, the sacred honoring of places and objects, and respect for their Gods and Goddesses.

When Constantine, Emperor of Rome from AD 306 to 337, legalized Christianity, he made Sunday, "keeping the Law Day". Constantine was a pagan sun-worshipper, who greatly loved and revered the sun.

His new sabbat would be on Sun-day in order to please the Christians by giving them a new day, different from the Jews. This kept his love for the sun, intact. Therefore, the sun god day, turned into the Sun of God day. His infamous Sunday enforcement law of March 7, A.D. 321, reads as follows:

"On the venerable Day of the Sun, let the magistrates and people residing in cities - rest, and let all workshops be closed." (Codex Justinianus 3.12.3, trans. Philip Schaff, History of the Christian Church, 5th ed. (New York, 1902), 3:380, note 1.)

Later, on his death bed, Constantine professed conversion to Christianity, but at heart, remained devoted to the sun.

I have attempted to honor the original seasonal celebrations, in which most of our current holidays are now based upon.

The Coligny-Calendar, found in France, at the end of the 19th century, is a compilation of pre-Christian Celtic systems of timekeeping, including the Gaulish Coligny calendar, used by Celtic countries to define the beginning and length of the day, the week, the month, the seasons, quarter days, and festivals.

The Gaulish Coligny calendar is possibly the oldest Celtic solar/lunar ritual calendar. The year was divided into a light half and a dark half. As the day was seen as beginning after sunset, so the year was seen as beginning with the arrival of the darkness, at Samhain. The arrival of the light half of the year started at Beltane. This observance of festivals, started on the evening before the festival day and is still seen in the celebrations and folkloric practices among the Gaels, the Irish and the Scots.

The Wheel of The Year or four seasons are known as Solar Festivals. The cross-quarter days are marked by Fire Festivals. Together they form The Wheel of the Year. These holidays are celebrated from sundown on the day before the holiday through sundown the next day.

Imbolc

Imbolc (February 1st or 2nd) is also known as St. Brigid's Feast Day and in the Catholic holidays as Candlemas. It celebrates three occasions according to Christian belief: the presentation of the child Jesus, Jesus first entry into the temple, and celebration of the Virgin Mary's purification. Imbolc is a Gaelic festival marking the beginning of Spring.

An Irish Gaelic word, Imbolc pronounced im-molk, literally means "**in milk**" or "**in the belly.**" It is a time for honoring creativity, fertility, and receptive, feminine energy. It occurs when daylight begins to lengthen as we approach the **Spring Equinox**. It is where ancient connections mix Irish spirituality with Celtic pagan traditions and Christianity.

Celebrated all over the world in different cultures including Imbolgc Brigantia (Caledonni), Imbolic (Celtic), Disting (Teutonic, Feb 14th), Lupercus (Strega), St. Bridget's Day (Christian), Candlemas, Candlelaria (Mexican), the Snowdrop Festival, The Festival of Lights or the Feast of the Virgin.

When: February 1st or 2nd
Season: Cross Quarter: (Mid-way point between Winter and Spring)
Represents: Festival of the Maiden, St. Brigid's Day, Candlemas, Groundhog's Day, and divination by weather
Virtues: Fertility, Patience
Symbols: Candles, Ewe Lamb, Crocus Flowers, Corn Doll, St. Brigid's Cross, Priapic (acorn-tipped) Wands, Bride's (baskets) Beds, Seeds
Gemstone: Amethyst, Aventurine, Fire Agate, Bloodstone, Carnelian, Citrine, Rose Quartz, Snow White Quartz
Color: Red, Green, White, Yellow, Brown
Essential Oils: Basil, Cedar, Geranium, Myrrh, Pine, Rose, Rosemary
Remedies: Angelica, Basil, Dandelion Root, Dill Weed, Rosemary, White Willow Bark, Yellow Dock
Flowers: Ancyrensis, Chrysanthus, Crocus, Sieberi, Tommasinianus
Element: Water
Direction: Northeast
Life Event: Quickening
Lunar: Ice Moon or Full Snow Moon
Body Healing: Strength
Mind Healing: Intuition
Spirit Healing: Sacred Spirit

Mid-Winter Ritual Bath

~Mix together in a blender 3 cups of whole milk, 2 teaspoons of honey and 1 sprig of dried sage.
~ Light 5 white candles to represent the power of fire and light. The candles embody the winter white snow.
~ If you would like to encircle your bath tub with crystals, consider placing 4 crystals in 4 corners (rose quartz, chiastolite, moonstone, and aventurine.) Add milky white quartz stone into the bath water.

Run the bath water into the tub and add your blended mixture of milk, honey, and sage into the running water. You can repeat a prayer or positive affirmation as you sit in the water.

Relax in your bath for 15 – 20 minutes. Think positive, creative, and fertile thoughts as you enjoy this ritual to cleanse, purify, and love yourself for the turn of a new Spring to come.

Gemstone:
Sacred Spirit: Imbolc Blessing

"O Brigid our most patron saint,
of craft and poem and home so
quaint.
From cross you wove with field rush,
to dollies made with care and such.
You bless our home, our brides, our
land,
with mother Nature close at hand.
We honor up these charms so dear,
to bring good joy, when Spring is
near."

~ Andrew Pacholyk MS L.Ac

Ostara

Eostre or Ostara of Spring is a goddess in Germanic and Celtic tradition who is the namesake of the festival of Easter.

In her various forms, she is a spring-like fertility goddess associated with dawn. She is also associated with Eostre or the **Norse Goddess, Freyja.** Her focus is on balance and the equilibrium between night and day at the Spring Equinox.

Ostara has transformed into Easter, the Christian holiday celebrating the resurrection of Christ. It is the transforming of life to spirit and the raising or transition into a new beginning.

In both the **Celtic and Russian** traditions, placing eggs on burial sites or burying their dead with eggs, reinforced the fact that the egg was a powerful symbol of immortality, resurrection, and rebirth.

The coloring of eggs has also been a long-standing tradition representing the promise of joy, happiness, and rebirth. The Christian concept of Easter connects the holiday of Easter with the renewal of life through the egg. It is a representative of the renewal, resurrection, and rebirth of Christ.

The "World Egg" is an ancient story about how the Universe "hatched" and the Hindu's believe the yolk became heaven and the white became earth. The Shinto believed the entire Universe was contained in a huge egg, standing upright.

Celebrated all over the world and in different cultures including Easter, Feast of the Annunciation (Christian), Lady Day, Celebration of the Goddesses, Venus (Roman) and Aphrodite (Greek), Eostre or Ostara (Old English), Hewsos or Austro (Proto-Indo-European goddess of the Dawn), Easter, Eastre (Old High German).

When: March 20 or 21
Season: Spring or the Vernal Equinox
Represents: Spring Equinox, Easter, balance of day and night
Virtues: Growth, Union, Renewal
Symbols: Eggs, Egg Coloring, Rabbits, Flowers,
Gemstone: Amethyst, Blue Lace Agate, Aventurine, Bloodstone, Chiastolite, Citrine, Rose Quartz
Color: Green, Pink, Violet, Yellow
Essential Oils: Eucalyptus, Lavender, Rose, Sandalwood
Remedies: Bee Pollen, Bilberry, Blessed Thistle, Burdock Root, Calendula Flower, Catnip, Chamomile, Chaste Tree Berry, Cramp Bark, Dandelion, Eye Bright, Hydrangea Root, Milk Thistle Seed, Mullein Leaf, Nettle Leaf, Passion Flower, Wild Cherry Bark
Flowers: Daffodil, Gorse, Iris, Narcissus, Peony, Violet, Woodruff
Element: Air
Direction: East
Life Event: Renewal, Rebirth
Lunar: Growing Moon or Full Pink Moon
Body Healing: Cleansing
Mind Healing: Sun Walk
Spirit Healing: Sacred Spirit

Spring Rituals

~ Light a colorful candle or Easter candle – to celebrate rebirth and new beginnings. "Renew your spirit" as a source of promise. Say a prayer, state an intention or make a positive affirmation.

~ Blend essential oils of rose absolut, lavender, and jasmine to use as a perfume. You can anoint candles, eggs, or jewelry, to "embrace the goddess" or to "honor the renewal of life."

~ Gather some of your favorite crystals together to use as powerful tools representing love and fertility (rose quartz), heart's desires and Spring (aventurine), the sun and renewal (citrine), the veil of the goddess/virgin (blue lace agate), courage and the martyr stone (bloodstone) or the cross stone (chiastolite).

~ Light some incense and burn them as a cleansing ritual, or rite of Spring, to clear away negative thoughts or bad energy.

Gemstone:
Sacred Spirit: Ostara Blessing

"Balance of light and dark are here,
Take this time to find what's dear,
creative spark and fertile life,
release me from this winter's strife.
With promise of renewal strong
Those days of winter nights are gone,
So bless me with rebirth of light,
And start this season off, alright."

~ Andrew Pacholyk MS L.Ac

Season of the Sun: Sunrise

The sun is symbolically found in all cultures and religions throughout history. The sun represents the rising of Spring, the start of a new day, or the beginning of life.

It represents the cardinal direction of East. The East represents our capacity in honoring our source of new beginnings, broader awareness, and spiritual wisdom. This is done through vision, a sense of touch, a glimpse of listening, and our own vocal expression. It is the rising of the warming sun, which allows us to look at the developments within us. We feel surer about embracing our creative wisdom, our own growth spurts, or our need to expand outward in life.

Gemstone:
East

*"Great sun does rise above
your head,
With grace and silent thunder,
red,
with power, strength, and
gracious prayer,
you represent a wisp of air"*

~Andrew Pacholyk MS L.Ac

The Sun represents the conscious ego, the self, and its expression of personal power, pride, and authority. The sun exemplifies leadership qualities and the principles of creativity, spontaneity, health, and vitality. The sum of which is named "life force."

The ruler of Sunday, the Sun (in Greek: Helios, in Latin: Sol) is the star at the center of our Solar System and is by far the most important source of energy for life on Earth. It is a nearly perfect spherical ball of hot plasma, with internal convective that generates a magnetic field via a dynamo process.

According to the tenets of paganistic Roman, "Sunday" was the day for the God of the Sun. It was adopted on Saturday by the Jewish faith, called "Shabbat" (the original Hebrew word) and then by the Christians on Sunday, as the sabbath. The symbol of light was a pagan ideal that was adopted by Christians and other religions using the symbol of the sun as guiding light.

The Sun is viewed as a goddess in Germanic paganism, Sól/Sunna. Scholars theorize that the Sun, as a Germanic goddess, may represent an extension of an earlier Proto-Indo-European Sun deity because of Indo-European linguistic connections between Old Norse Sól, Sanskrit Surya, Gaulish Sulis, Lithuanian Saulė, and Slavic Solntse.

In ancient religions, the sun was a source of life-giving warmth and illumination to mankind. It was the center of a popular cult among Mayan, Greeks, and Romans, who would stand at dawn to catch the first rays of sunshine as they prayed. The sun symbolizes our conscious mind. The sun symbolizes our determination to live and the creative force of our life energy.

The celebration of the winter solstice (which influenced Christmas) was part of the Roman cult of the sun. It was standard practice for the Christian church to construct each house of worship so that the congregation faced toward the sunrise in the East.
In the Vedic text, "Surya", The Sun God is Son of Aditi and Kashyap. Surya means "the supreme light." The "sun cross" or "solar wheel" is often considered to represent the four seasons and the tropical year, and therefore the Sun. In *The Review of Religions*, Fazal Ahmad wrote:

"As man observed eclipses, comets, meteorites and other phenomena, he sometimes related to these larger, more powerful elements as substitute deities... In Ancient Egypt, the sun took on a huge significance in the religion of the Egyptians and the status of Pharaoh.

As a central focus in early spirituality, the sun was worshipped and adorn. It was the first of the monotheism religions and gave birth to a new understanding. Monotheism has been defined as the belief in the existence of only one God that created the world. It is believed that He is all powerful and intervenes in the world. This brief change over occurred during the Egyptian time of the pharaoh, Akhenaten. Akhenaten tried to shift his culture from Egypt's traditional religion (polytheism ~ or the belief in many gods), to the belief in the sun God, Amun-Ra.

Gemstone:
The Sun God Worship

*"In Ancient dust of desert sand, stand testaments of time and
space,
to those who searched beyond the realm for answers to embrace.*

*From temples pointing starward bound and circles made of
stone,
to look moreover, heaven bound for answers they have known...*

*within their minds and hearts, they find a way to just explain,
the constant change and ever moving world that they have
gained.*

*For all at once they came to learn the fast and shifting world,
was due to rise and setting sun, as mysteries unfurled.*

*It taught them lessons, far unseen, as masters of this game,
It ruled day and brought on night, and weather, it would tame.*

*The sun it warmed the crops in day and left for shorter nights,
or came around and stayed less time and took life to new
heights.*

*So if the year grew long each day there had to be a peak,
of time when it no longer shared and gave us days more bleak.*

*These days of wrath were overcome by giving Sun more reign,
attention seemed to be the way to wrangle bout their way."*

~ Andrew Pacholyk MS L.Ac

The Morning: Sun Salutation Music

You can certainly call me a sun worshiper. Being born on the Summer Solstice, I have always been attracted to the warmth, power, and glow of the sun! Sun worshiping or sun salutation as we referred to it in yoga, is the greeting of the day as you embrace the power of all things rising before you. Sun salutation is a series of poses or asanas done to not only wake up the body but to encourage the soul. This music is inspired by my love for any morning, the Summer solstice, and the beauty of the sunrise. I hope you add these songs to the playlist of your life. I call this list,

The Sun Salutation Playlist!

1. Morning Mood, "Peer Gynt" Suite No.1, Op.46, Grieg
2. Aquarius/Let the Sunshine In, Hair
3. Sun Salutation, David Moore
4. Seasons In The Sun, Studio 99
5. The Warmth of The Sun, The Beach Boys
6. House of The Rising Sun, The Animals
7. Walking on Sunshine, Katrina and the Waves
8. Sunshine, Jonathon Edwards
9. Sunshine on My Shoulders, John Denver
10. Halo / Walking on Sunshine, Glee Cast
11. You Brought the Sunshine, The Clark Sisters
12. You Are the Sunshine of My Life, Stevie Wonder
13. Morning Has Broken, Cat Stevens
14. A Beautiful Morning, The Rascals
15. Sunrise Serenade, Glenn Miller
16. Blissful Soothing Soundscapes (Sun Salutation) Spiritual Journeys
17. Indian Sunrise, Classical Indian Music
18. Moon Salutation – Chandra Namaskara, Winter Hill Records
19. The Red Pony Suite I: Morning on the Ranch, Aaron Copland
20. 98.6, Keith
21. Haydn: String Quartet in B flat, Op.76 No.4 – "Sunrise" , Haydn
22. Certain of the Dawn: Hymn to the Eternal Flame, Barry Abelson
23. Seasons in The Sun, Studio 99
24. Appalachian Spring: Doppio movimento, Aaron Copland
25. Symphony No. 6 (Pastoral), Beethoven
~ Honorable Mention: (great for sun salutation): Sabrina's Theme, John Williams

Solar Meditation with Crystals

The sun has been prayed to, worshiped and adored for thousands of years. It is the center of our lives on earth and we would not exist without it! What better way to start your day by offering your intention outward to the Universe or with the last rays of the setting sun in the evening to give thanks.

Using a crystal as a meditation tool is a practice, I have done for over 30 years. Introduced to me by my yoga teacher, Deva Inglesia Germana and reinforced over the years by several other dear mentors, including Jean-Claude Van Itallie and Zachary Selig, it is a wonderful way to empower your intentions. Consider using one or all of these stones:

Sunstone: This stone is a kiss of sunshine, crystallized. It honors the God within, brings good luck, and fortune. It energizes and empowers one's self. Used to warm the heart and lifts/rejuvenates the spirit. Sunstone is used for protection, life force, and grounding. Sunstone is a great stone to use with "energy vampires," or those who drain your energy from you. This includes parents, children, lovers, patients, bosses, or anyone who is possessive, aggressive, or overbearing. Sunstone breaks these bonds and allows light, separation, and clarity from these energies. This stone clears and brightens both the entire Chakra and clears the Aura. Sunstone does great justice when placed on our power center or Solar Plexus Chakra. Sunstone is a wonderful stone to relieve stress and overcome fear.

Citrine: Citrine energizes every level of the aura, cleansing, and balancing the subtle bodies as it aligns it with the physical body. Citrine crystals are invigorating and positive and help steer us in a positive direction. They are used for mental and emotional clarity. Considered the "merchant stone", citrine is very versatile and is used for mental and emotional clarity, problem solving, memory issues, will power, optimism, confidence, and self-discipline. It reduces anxiety, fear, and depression. An energizing crystal, citrine absorbs, transmutes, grounds, and dissolves negative energy, which makes it a very protective stone. Citrine crystals are invigorating and positive.

Yellow Calcite: Also called Golden Calcite, is a stone that boosts overall energy levels in a peaceful, gentle manner. Yellow calcite increases strength and health. It stimulates the intellect. It can help organize intellectual thoughts and information and is used by people who meditate because the color is linked to the Solar Plexus Chakra, sun and light. It is also an important stone for astral projection. It has been used for centuries as folk remedies as a detoxifier. In the bath, Egyptians used it for decalcifying joints. Use this stone to boost life energy and to encourage will power.

Tiger's Eye: The stone for bringing more luck into your life, Tiger's Eye is the most recognized for attracting money, psychic protection, courage, confidence, and willpower. Used for clear thinking and speaking, it shows us the personal power in life that we have. Very versatile for the Solar Plexus Chakra, Third Eye Chakra, and Crown Chakra.

Working with These Stones

These unique stones are full of sun and a bright spot in anyone's day. You can lay on the floor with one stone at your solar plexus or two inches below. These power centers embrace your own radiance and light. They are encouraging and empowering centers and help bring a sense of awareness through knowing ourselves and sparking our intuition.

You can sit in a comfortable position on the floor, ground, or in a chair. Face the sun, in order to feel the warmth (and promise) on your face. Hold one or more of these stones in your dominant hand with the other hand underneath it. If you are using two stones, hold one in each hand. If you are using 3-4, place them in a circle around you.

Create a meditation circle on the floor, in your meditation space or on your yoga mat. Anoint each crystal with a "sunny essential oil" such as orange, lemon, neroli, or sunflower oil. Invoke each direction by creating a circle with the 4 stones. Invoke the 4 elements by placing crystals in a circle in each direction, starting from the east, south, west and moving in a clockwise direction ending with the north.

> *"Stones in circle round, give peace,*
> *Quiet, calming, great release.*
> *To bring about a welcome change,*
> *To meditate and then exchange,*
> *The flow of love and light and such,*
> *To find what serves me very much."*
>
> ~ Andrew Pacholyk MS L.Ac.

119

Close your eyes and breathe in deep, exhaling as if you were breathing life into your stone(s). This sense of regeneration, stimulates yourself and your crystal. The exchange of energy you take from the stone, engages your core. It is like a battery jolting back and forth between your body's energy and the living presence of the crystal. Take as much time as you need to recharge.

Whether it is the morning sun, full of promise or the setting sun, with grace and thanks… give your attention to it. Feel its power and energy. It is the second most powerful force we can sense in the Universe.

With each deep breath, bring the power of your intention to your Solar Plexus Chakra. This power center is our greatest force of movement and motivation. It is from here that we energize our will power. Breathe into this energy center. Sense your connection between the crystals around you and the center just below your heart.

Expand and contract as you inhale and exhale. Take in the sun's rays and exhale out the unpleasant thoughts. Release, as the sun releases. Expand as the sun expands. Take as much time as you need to recharge.

When you are ready to finish your meditation, simply (and slowly) bring your focus back to behind your eyelids. Sense your surroundings as they come back to you and slowly open your eyes.

I always recommend journaling about your experience. Include any references that may have come up so you can look at them later.

Sun Walk

My dear friend, Jean Claude has a farm and theatre company called Shantigar, in the rolling hills of Massachusetts. He often takes morning constitutions over the sprawling landscape on a "sun walk." This morning ritual allows you to take the sun on your skin and face. It enables the sun's rays to trigger the synthesis of Vitamin D and can be a very spiritual process, as you commune with nature.

His ritual includes one or several chosen stones in his hand, as he slowly walks, taking in all that is before him. He slowly turns the stone(s) in his hand or rubs their smooth surface with his thumb and forefinger, while either reciting a mantra, saying a prayer, or just focusing on his daily intention.

This meditation can be done anywhere outside your front door. It should be done for at least 20 minutes. Consider leaving your cell phone behind. It is your chance to connect with the environment around you. It does not have to be in nature, but it should be on a sunny morning!

The goal is for you to connect with your thoughts, take in your surroundings, and appreciate where you are right NOW. It is a chance for you to drink in the morning sun, which is imperative to our body's function. Enjoy a little sun today. It will make you feel better.

Please note: our bodies need sun. Without sun, we would wither and die. It is recommended to take in morning sun, without sun screen, for a period of 15-20 minutes, during early morning hours. As we all know by now, the sun is strongest from 12 – 3 pm and sun screen should be worn to protect your skin. But, over the past decade, vitamin D deficiency, lack of calcium absorption and osteoporosis have doubled due to the lack of sun we are getting. This case is even more so in women and especially women in the Northeastern part of the United States, in particular. The sun is an element to be respected and revered. Allow the sun to help your body in its natural processes. Protect yourself from its ominous power.

Chapter 6

Summer

Summer is the peak of the yang cycle when the daylight is at its longest. The "summer" time, represents the **shaping of our lives**. It is our second quadrant of development from our 30's throughout our 40's. It is our greatest introduction and realization of our "selves." We usually find our passions, use our power, and find strength in laughter, joy, and humor. We have the confidence to follow our dreams and make them a reality. The summer is more right-brain activities such as focusing on synthesizing or putting together different elements to understand the whole. This too is the time of our lives when we are more able to manage temporal and spatial relationships and are more prone to analyze non-verbal cues we get from others. By this time in our lives, we are better able to communicate our emotions.

Summer is ruled by the Fire element and is expressed in nature, as well as in the body. Growth, joy, and spiritual awareness between the heart and mind are the focus during this season and time of life.

Late Summer is also considered a separate season in Ayurveda and Chinese Medicine, as hotter days bring about damper conditions. This time is associated with more pensive and worried emotions, connecting to the Earth element. This too can be seen as our transition from the Summer of our lives to the Fall of our lives.

Gemstone:
Ode to Summer

~ *"O longest day of summer's light,*
I come to honor the sun, so bright
With light of new beginnings grow,
With daylight during summer's glow
To rise as sunlight does each day,
And offer joy on journey's way"

~ Andrew Pacholyk MS. L.Ac.

The Priorities of Life

Our "summer" priorities are focused more on the **material things in life** and how we can get them. It is part endeavor, part luck. It is wishful thinking and the struggling with love, money, and happiness to obtain strength and success.

Confidence

Although finding confidence in our teens and 20's is possible, (and very commendable) in the "Spring of our years," we tend to feel like we are at the mercy of other people, as well as situations that are beyond our control. Because of this, we tend to lack confidence or the foundation to feel more confident.

In the "summer of our years," or our 30's and 40's we are more aware of who we are, take control of situations around us that we can command, and have the power to know when we need to be more self-aware and courageous.

Gemstone:
Confidence

"With focus and assurance strong,
I'll go the distance, ever long.
I'll step out on the precipice,
I'll know that I can master this.
Assertive in my nature be
I'll walk with pride for all to see."

~ Andrew Pacholyk MS, L.Ac

My goal is always to promote self-worth and promote body awareness. Identity works to raise consciousness. Building self-confidence makes us more approving of ourselves. Improving our ego, boosting our self-esteem, and finding emotional balance helps strengthen our positive personality traits. When we are self-assured, we will allow ourselves to see all the beauty our eyes touch.

Self-esteem issues are different in different people. Although you may feel great about yourself in one area of your life, you may be extremely down on yourself in another. Welcome to the world. We can all seek to improve ourselves. It is time you became committed to truly loving and appreciating yourself and who you are.

1. Walk with your head up – do not look down. Keep your eyes even with the horizon. Tell everyone who you are with your eyes.

Affirmation: I keep my head up high. I choose to be a very loving, humble, and secure me.

2. Stay positive, patient and keep your temper in check – Breathe. Think of positive thoughts and choose the sunny side of each situation. Avoid getting extremely angry or having fits of anger.

Affirmation: I am calm, cool, collected. Nothing, absolutely nothing bothers me today.

3. Stop taking things personally – guess what, it is not all about you. Everyone is not against you and they are not ganging up on you either.

Affirmation: It is not about me. I rise above all that is in my way. I soar free and independent of that, which is around me.

4. Stop playing it safe – It is time to be a risk taker. The worse thing that could happen is that you fall on your face. If you do not go out on a limb sometimes, you will continually be ruled by your fear.

Affirmation: I honor all that I am. I deserve the best. I am the best.

5. No more hiding – Your lack of belief in yourself may want to keep you hidden away behind closed doors and from reality. Get out there. Meet and greet. You never know who you will encounter. Make it a challenge. You just might meet your next employer, love of your life, or bridge partner.

Affirmation: I am powerful and brave. I know we are all in the same situations. We share the same consciousness. I will be the better person and take my place in the world.

6. Change your vocabulary – NOW. Words and phrases like: "I can't", "It figures", "Just my luck", "I'm only human", "I should have", "Life sucks" or "it's impossible" … should never cross your lips…again.

Affirmation: Yes, I can, ~ I'm so lucky, ~ I'm so fortunate, ~ I will, ~ I'm deserving, ~ It's possible, ~ I love my life.

7. Limit the apologizing and drop the guilt – Enough already. You have nothing to be guilty of. Nothing. Continuous apologizing is not only annoying to hear, it shows that you are not grounded and cannot find comfort in your own skin.

Affirmation: I am guilt free. I have nothing to be guilty about. No more excuses or apologies.

8. Make direct eye contact – Do this every time you meet someone… and keep it. Looking down or looking away only shows how insecure you are. You have nothing to be insecure about and everything to be sure of.

Affirmation: There is nothing more beautiful, than a confident person.

9. Accept a compliment – with praise and graciousness. They are not often given out. Take them with pride and honor. Be happy that someone else has found their own security - enough to give a compliment to you. Show them how secure you are, by thanking them.

Affirmation: I appreciate a compliment. I deserve a compliment. I am grateful.

10. Less taking and more giving – shows you are confident that what you have to give is worth something. The more we take, the more we think we deserve, and the more we feed into our poor sense of self.

Affirmation: I am happy to give my time, my love and my charity to all who need it.

Good Luck

Luck. What exactly is luck? Is luck being at the right place at the right time? Finding that lucky penny? Always landing on your feet? Finding a four-leaf clover? Discovering bird droppings on your shoulder?

Gemstone:
Good Luck

*"I create my own good luck,
with bright ideas,
where lightning struck.
I maximize the gift of chance,
expect good fortune to enhance,
the best I wish to bring to me,
and always keep me on the sea
of luck and lady fortune shine
upon me as I make it mine."*

~ Andrew Pacholyk MS L.Ac

Whatever your idea of luck, research has found that people are divided. Thanks to the research of Dr. Richard Wiseman in collaboration with Dr. Matthew Smith and Dr. Peter Harris, *The Luck Project* discovered some incredible results. "The results of this work reveals that **people are not born lucky**.

Instead, lucky people are, without realizing it, using four basic principles to create good fortune in their lives."

The Four Principles to Manifest Luck

Principle One: Maximize Chance Opportunities
"Lucky people are skilled at creating, noticing, and acting upon chance opportunities. They do this in various ways, including networking, adopting a relaxed attitude to life, and by being open to new experiences."

Principle Two: Listening to Lucky Hunches
"Lucky people make effective decisions by listening to their intuition and gut feelings. In addition, they take steps to actively boost their intuitive abilities by, meditating and clearing their mind of other thoughts."

Principle Three: Expect Good Fortune
"Lucky people are certain that the future is going to be full of good fortune. These expectations become self-fulfilling prophecies by helping lucky people persist in the face of failure and shape their interactions with others in a positive way."

Principle Four: Turn Bad Luck to Good
"Lucky people employ various psychological techniques to cope with, and often even thrive upon, the ill fortune that comes their way. For example, they spontaneously imagine how things could have been worse, do not dwell on the ill fortune, and take control of the situation." The authors' most recent research has shown that these four principles can be used to enhance the amount of good fortune that people experience in their lives.

Seven Tips for Good Luck

Why do you think people around you are so lucky and you never seem to be? Part of the problem could be how you choose to look at your "lack of luck." This is usually where the problem lies. The old adage "energy follows thought" plays a big role in how you choose to see what is lucky and what is not. Discover the 7 tips for turning your luck around:

1. The expression of confidence is a definite component of luck. Confidence can best be classified as a subset of optimism. Gaining confidence is easy when you put your mind to it. It is the most attractive and powerful trait we can have. We are drawn to those who are confident and sure of themselves. This often plays a hand in how lucky we can be.

2. Networking in one form or another, is like planting seeds. Seeds of good intention are seeds of good luck. You never know when the seeds will sprout, grow, and express themselves as a good lead. A client that shows up at your door, or a referral from someone else, who was in your networking circle are examples of the seeds that you plant.

3. Preparation, practice, and study. The motto of the Boy Scouts is "be prepared." This idea, when actually executed prior to a crisis, can literally mean the difference between life and death. In less extreme circumstances, it can mean the difference between a comfortable and interesting life, or a mediocre, painful, and boring one. Preparation in life is like creating a safety net. It gives you a head start or allows you to be aware of a current or future situation.

4. Putting fear aside is often essential for good fortune. Our bodies have a fight or flight response. A certain amount of fear/stress is normal and allows us to avoid dangerous situations. It also helps improve our performance and gets us motivated to act. Fear holds you back and locks you in a cage, if you allow it. What are your really afraid of?

5. Risk-taking can be either voluntary or not, but just as you must usually pass through a doorway to gain access to a new environment, you must usually take a risk to find or exploit new opportunities. Risk accompanies virtually every breath and step we take in this world. It's a part of living.

6. Timing is the metaphysical correlation to the modern affirmation that "location, location, and location" are the three most important aspects to real estate values. If a person could fully exploit the timing of events, even just in the daily circumstances of our own lives, we could, in many cases, accomplish amazing things. "Be here, be aware, be in the now". This means pay attention to the actions, circumstances, and present moment.

7. Self-discipline. Mastering your own life through discipline is essential for bringing luck into your life. Self-discipline is committing to a task one day at a time. Self-discipline brings awareness. Awareness brings change. Change helps us to understand fluidity. When you are more fluid with your thinking, you are more able to see the great luck you are given… daily.

Happiness

"Greater personal fulfillment." This should really be the "full name" for happiness.

Research by the *Journal of Positive Psychology* found that meaningful experiences, even if they were due to hard work or some stress, added up to happiness. Stronger, personal relationships, making a positive difference, and better self-expression for one's own personal satisfaction, are the building blocks of happiness.

The opposite would be those fleeting, less connected moments of joy or short-term gratification. Another words, real happiness comes from the long-term goals of self-awareness, making a difference in other's lives. and those things, which give us a sense of purpose!

Gemstone:
Happiness

"O. Bright light, open up my heart,
allow a smile to be apart,
of my day, today, always be,
a little more a part of me.
Like rising sun, upon each morn',
the graces in my life, adorn."

~ Andrew Pacholyk MS L.Ac

Whatever your idea of happiness, research has found that a great deal of unhappiness stems from negative thoughts. Not acknowledging what you already have, not seeing what is important in your life, or mentally blocking yourself from gratitude. This undermines your foundation of joy. Humility, self-love, and appreciation really show us where happiness comes from. Having positive images of yourself and others, diffuses negative thought.

Consider this:

1. The Power of Positive Thinking: Negativity is the root, which undermines our happiness. The negative ideas we think of, manifest in the words we speak. The minute the words leave your lips, is the minute they manifest. Change your thoughts to positive, uplifting ones. Think hope, not hopelessness. Think goodness, not evil. Think joy, not despair. When you program thought to be positive, your energy will reflect it.

2. Get Social: Do this with those who have a good outlook on life. Do not be around others who are negative, self-serving, or do not know how to express genuine kindness. Staying in the circle of positive light and the bright energy of others, feeds your soul and keeps your spirit light bright.

3. Affirmations: are a positive word, expression or term to guide us and give us reassurance. "I am happy," "nothing will deter my happy thoughts, today," "I am full of joy." These are all great affirmations to live by.

4. Focused, Happy Thoughts: bring a long lasting, enduring enjoyment of life. It is being in love with living. Happiness is what we receive by achieving life markers along our journey. These include valued friends, a loving romance, a career in a field we love, and enjoyable hobbies. All of which stimulate our mind and body on some appreciative level. Achieving these values requires rationality and takes effort and skill. Put yourself to work. Start by focusing on the area(s) you value most. Where ever you put your intention, is where you will be most successful. So instead of focusing on "being happy," start by focusing on being happy with...

5. Learn Your Happiness Skills: with two types of skills that you can use. These are thinking skills and valuing skills. Learn to have confidence in your own mind and discover the virtues that make it possible for you to achieve your values. This makes your life worth living. Do this and you will experience the result.

6. The Metaphysics of Happiness: has everything to do with our belief system. Belief is one of our most powerful assets. With the ability to believe, you can accomplish nearly anything! The more you believe in yourself, the more you will definitely accomplish. Happiness comes to those who BELIEVE THEY ARE HAPPY! It's just as simple as that. When we face situations that are near physical or mental impossibilities, then it is our belief system, or belief in ourselves, that determines IF it is possible.

7. Our Belief System: is one of the major factors that can get us through situations or can cause our life to crumble around us. How we "program" ourselves to see our real happiness, shows us just how happy we are.

8. Our self-confidence and self-love: are often the key to opening and strengthening this portion of our thoughts which, in turn, emanates from ourselves. This "allows" happiness to find us.

9. Really appreciating what we DO have: as opposed to what we would like to have, makes a significant difference. Crying over what you don't have, feeds into the negative thought cycle that makes it more difficult to let go. This is always an important element in a happy person that is often neglected.

10. Find happiness in simplicity: and you will find the greatest joys yet revealed to you. Smile when you talk on the phone. Greet everyone you pass by or meet today, with a smile. Appreciate the smell of the air, the warmth of the sun and the laughter of children. Make that your happiness. These are the seeds that grow into the wealth that is joy.

The Happiness Checklist

√ I will think positively: If negative or unhappy thoughts comes into my mind, I will think positively, instead.

√ I will show love and kindness today. I will compliment someone, show love with words or actions, instead of shutting down.

√ I will concern myself with the present moment. I will not get caught up in the minutia that weighs my spirit down.

√ I will find any way to fulfill one of my passions today. By doing something I love, I will lead myself to a place of joy.

√ I will be open to endless possibilities. When I expect something, I limit my options, chances, and goals. I am open to the path that comes before me.

Love

Love is the most relevant, moving, painful, joyous experience we can practice. It transcends all barriers, moves mountains, springs eternal, and manifests the hardest of stone into the most liquid of emotions.

Love and all its divine power can be manifested from within us. We can accept no more love than we are willing to give ourselves. The way we love others, STARTS with the way we love ourselves. Learning how to love ourselves begins with a relationship with the self.

Research has shown, that there are three components to love and creating a happy relationship with another. This theory, developed by *Robert Sternberg*, is called the *Triangular Theory of Love*. These components are the fundamental building blocks on creating, nurturing, and developing a long-lasting relationship.

Gemstone:
Love

"Circle round these thoughts of love,
encourage peace like hand in glove.
To honor, praise and love myself,
So I may give more to the rest,
of those who truly seek my light,
of Universal grace and rite."

~ Andrew Pacholyk MS L.Ac

Self-Love Is Not Selfish Love

Self-love is probably the most important love we can do for ourselves AND others. It is very important that we love ourselves, first. When this truly occurs, the Universe allows all things to fall in to place very nicely.

Self-examination is the only way to know.

1. To live feeling fully alive is our own choice and responsibility. There are many examples of people living their passions from many different walks of life. These choices re-affirm the love and respect for ourselves.

2. Self-Love is NOT Selfishness. Selfishness is always voluntary, showing regard to our own interests, and gratification, which is sought after and indulged at the expense, and sometimes, to the injury, of others.

3. Have the courage and determination to feel good. This is our personal business.

4. Deciding to feel good, to whatever degree we can manage, is the most important decision that we can make.

5. Spending even a few moments each day doing something that simply delights us, will increase our feeling of wellness. This makes it easier to do even more of our soul's passion, allowing us to find the confidence to love, and respect ourselves that much more.

6. The renewal and invigoration received from doing the activities we find absolute passion in, are vital to the quality and performance of our lives. Without this "fire" for our creative soul's desire, our lives seem less fulfilled.

7. When something is so wonderfully important to our overall well-being, it is essential that we pursue it.

8. Self-love can often be found by doing something that brings out the passion in our lives. Doing exactly what it is that makes us happy, is up to us. When we follow the path that we long to follow, we can always find this love in ourselves.

9. It is this passion, which gives us reason in our lives. It allows us to "see" the reasoning behind why we are here in the first place.

10. Bring your love and light to others by truly loving and respecting yourself, first. Lead by example.

"You yourself, as much as anybody in the entire Universe, deserve your love and affection" ~ Buddha

---

<u>Gemstone:</u>
A Wake-Up Call

*"You tug at my heart and make my life sing,
I found a new person through journeys you bring,
me here at the crossroads where I have been found,
just waiting and waiting for you to come 'round.
I'm grateful and humbled to come to this place,
Of self-realization, no matter the take...
I've found my soul's bounty, more greater and dearer...
I then realized, that it's me in the mirror."*

~ Andrew Pacholyk MS L.Ac

The Triangle Theory of Love

The Triangular Theory of Love is a theory developed by Robert Sternberg, a member of the *Psychology Department at Yale University*. During his time as a professor, Sternberg emphasized his research in the fields of intelligence, creativity, wisdom, leadership, thinking styles, ethical reasoning, love, and hate. In the context of interpersonal relationships, "the three components of love," according to the triangular theory, are an intimacy component, a passion component, and a decision/commitment component.

The three components of the Triangular Theory of Love are:

Passion:

Feeling physically aroused and attracted to someone. Passion is what makes you feel "in love" and is the emotion most associated with love. It also rises quickly and strongly influences your judgment. Passionate love involves continuously thinking about the loved one and also involves warm sexual feelings and powerful emotional reactions.

Intimacy:

Feeling close and connected to someone (developed through sharing and very good communications - over time). Intimacy is what makes you want to share and offer emotional and material support to each other.

Commitment:

This is pledging to yourself and each other to strengthen the feelings of love and actively maintain the relationship. Commitment is what makes you want to be serious, have a serious relationship, and promise to be there for the other person if things get tough. Compassionate love is trusting and having tender feelings for someone who is close to you.

Why We Need to Love

√ Life is not a fulfilled journey without the attachment, connection, and ultimate letting go of great love.

√ It is the key to the greatest opening of your heart and consciousness with another.

√ Giving love, selflessly, unconditionally, and without limits, is our soul's true recognition of its counterpoint in another.

√ We need love, to find within ourselves, our ability to express compassion, humility, and care.

√ Offering our heart, is the letting down of our guard, the unveiling of our vulnerability, and the trust and security it takes to go there.

√ Love is the greatest expression of our spirit.

√ Love conquers all. No matter what we experience in life, our condition is held higher, more secure, and much easier with love in our lives.

√ When we pain from love, it is the complete giving of ourselves, that reminds us how truly lucky we have been to have embraced it in the first place.

√ Manage to nurture yourself and others with an unconditional heart. We all love in different ways. Accept those ways. They may not be yours, but the expression of someone else's love, is their way of reaching out to find your favor. Your lessons are to gain the experiences from them.

√ Eternal love will always stay with you. It is the accumulation of moments, where the good outweighs the bad. Eternal love comes together in a potpourri of self-expression, honesty, and attention. It is the will to understand - that at the root of it all, you will maintain a golden place in your heart for them, forever.

Money

Money is one part of your abundance in life. Money is your reward for hard work. Abundance is a long lasting, enduring enjoyment of life. It is being in love with living. Abundance is not merely money, but a life lived by accumulating moments, both materialistic and spiritual.

Abundance is your reward for achieving good character, and rational, personal values in life. Whereas, money teaches us values about receiving, giving, sharing, accepting compliments, and recognizing new beginnings. Discover how your money beliefs can change your life.

In the *Spring of our lives*, we are figuring out who we are, how we will follow a career or job, and how we can use this to support ourselves. But, in the *Summer of our lives,* we should be familiar with money's value and what it can do for us. We may be saving money by now, using money to invest in a home, or going back to school. We need to realize how money should be only one part of our "**abundance plan**" and how we can utilize this *currency* to our advantage.

<u>Gemstone:</u>
Money

*"Oh will of power, money come
To draw the most, a total sum
To keep me happy and fulfilled
But not too greedy to rebuild,
the confidence and focus lost
to bring abundance at no cost."*

~Andrew Pacholyk MS L.Ac

Positive Belief About Money

The Metaphysics of Money can be explained as "emotional currency!" Our belief system about money comes from our own emotional, psychological, and symbolic ideas about it. Belief is one of our most powerful assets or one of our most destructive foes. With the ability to believe good things about money, you can accomplish nearly anything. Almost every decision we make, and so much of our personalities are formed in some way, shape or form by our beliefs around money. Abundance comes to those who MAKE ROOM FOR IT and for those WHO HAVE POSITIVE BELIEFS ABOUT MONEY. It's just as simple as that.

1. What You Believe about Money

Positive beliefs about money come from how we choose to use it. If we see it as a means of exchange, we most likely allow it to flow. If we see it as an end to itself, we most likely never seem to have enough.

2. Visualize a Sea of Abundance

If you are able to truly conceive of more money, more will come into your life. This gives you the opportunity to "see" how you can make this happen. Visualization is a brilliant tool. The Universe can only distribute to you what you have in your consciousness. You can ALWAYS create more in your consciousness by visualizing abundance. The practice of meditation helps us temporarily let the physical world go so that we can begin to see ourselves as we truly are – spiritually enlightened beings in a sea of abundance. The ability to visualize what we want, sets us up to believe that we can have what we manifest. If we choose to think we never have enough money then, clearly, we never do.

3. Gaining Abundance through Giving

Like everything else in life, money ebbs and flows. Giving, is the natural process that leads to the flow of receiving. Allowing yourself to "let go" and to give freely, creates more abundance than you can imagine. When we gather and hoard, hold on to and amass, we simply restrict the free flow of this energetic currency from moving, and in turn, the flowing of prosperity.

4. Allow Yourself Pleasure

Give yourself pleasure with your money. You truly deserve it and if you don't think so, you need to go back and re-evaluate as to why you don't think you deserve it. Enjoy the spending of money. What old belief is stopping you? Change it!

5. Pay Your Bills with Great Thanks

If you feel resentment every time you have to pay a bill, the money will come back to you even slower. If you pay with love and joyfulness, you open the free-flowing channel of abundance. Remember, a bill is an acknowledgment of your ability to pay. Someone gives you the product or the service first, entrusting you for good reason; that you are able, capable, and a dependable person. So, pay each bill with thanks and appreciation.

6. Make Room for Money

Cluttered space means a cluttered mind. Remove everything in your life that you do not absolutely LOVE. Making order out of chaos is the natural way of the Universe. Clutter means confusion and the fact that you do not have a handle on things. Money is one of those things. It is a hard concept to accept, but you will see, that once you clear the clutter, you open yourself and your environment up for new change.

7. Enough, Not More

"Insatiability is the glutinous act of never having enough." When we are never content with what we are given, then it is simply greed. There is a fine line between what we want and want we need. Finding this balance, is enough (not more). The constant desire for more is not only damaging to us personally, but feeds into a greater belief that there is never enough to go around.

Create A Money Jar

Known as the "**Mason Jar Money Method**" because it's not only fun to do, but it's easy to start, even if you're broke. All you need is a mason jar or similar jar and a few bucks.

The basic plan starts with just $1 on the first week and you can ease your way into saving big bucks. For each week of the plan, you save an extra dollar.

You can label your jar, tie ribbon around it, spruce it up with stickers, or symbols, but give it an intention. For example "my intention for this jar is to save money for the... "holidays," "school," "mom"....whatever the intention, make sure you have a purpose.

Week 1=$1. Week 2=$2. Week 3=$3.and so on. Of course, by the end of the plan you'll be putting away $52 in one week, but you'll have weeks of time to lead up to the biggest saves, which takes the sting out of saving those extra bucks each week.

The good thing about this plan is that you know in advance, how much you need to put away for the week. This mentally prepares you to plan each week and motivates you to prepare the money for your jar.

Best of all, when you're finished, you'll have well over $1,300 in the jar to spend on something special - a vacation, holiday travel, or that emergency fund you know you should have but haven't started.

If you've missed starting your Mason Jar of Money on January 1, no problem. You can either play catchup (do you have an extra $1 or 2 lying around?) or find another holiday or milestone to save towards. Start today!

"Capital as such is not evil; it is its wrong use that is evil. Capital in some form or other will always be needed." ~ Gandhi

Strength

Strength has many definitions. When we think of strength or being strong, it could refer to your own physicality or muscle strength. Are you emotionally strong? How strong are you spiritually/mentally?

Here, you can discover the secrets to having physical strength. Understand the power behind your emotional strength and lastly, you can use these tips to build and maintain your mental strength. I have learned that these **three strengths are interlinked** and by becoming more mentally strong, our emotional, and physical strength follows. It will also lend itself to our spiritual path and beliefs.

<u>Gemstone:</u>
Strength

"O four directions ~ I do call,
To assist and build foundation strong
I am the one with strength and power,
Built upon this mental tower.
So bring about my inner sense,
Of self-awareness, this point hence."

~ Andrew Pachoyk, MS, L.Ac

Tips for Building Strength

What makes us strong? You need to find the right balance that works for you. Strength is about relinquishing weakness, gaining courage, and releasing limitations. We will find strength when we truly believe in ourselves. The more strength you find in yourself, the more you will believe is possible. When our mental capacity feels we can do something, it is our body and spirit that easily follows.

1. Courage: is extending yourself beyond your own limitations. Courage is defined as the risk of losing something for the benefit of something else. Courage is the idea of standing up for what you believe in. Courage comes when we start to reassure ourselves. Courage manifests from a desire to want to do better, take care of ourselves, and honor who we are. This is strength.

2. The Belief in Yourself: We will find strength when we truly understand ourselves. The more you understand who you are, the stronger your foundation becomes. When our foundation is built, we are more able to stand up for our beliefs. We trust our judgments and believe we can surmount the challenges.

3. Let Things Go: Learn to let things go once in a while. Learn to recognize the things that do not have great impact on your life and release them. Let go of the thing you cannot control.

4. Confidence Empowers Strength: Allow confidence in your life and you will let in strength. Be sure of yourself, without doubting or second guessing your decisions. This is the road to confidence. Confidence gives you power. The benefit to this, is that it makes you a more assured person. Have the guts to not care what others think and you will become empowered with confidence. This lends itself to great strength.

5. Celebrate All Your Success: This is the one place that is often the most out of balance. Our lives are filled with endless checks, balances, and to-do lists. It is important to stop and take stock in the goals you have accomplished. Don't forget to celebrate your successes. They are important to recognize and celebrating them will build strength.

6. Explore Your Options: We can all feel overwhelmed with our work or family responsibilities. These emotions can undermine our strengths. Take control. Consider re-organizing your day. Delegate work. Focus on one task in front of you. Set priorities. Be satisfied with doing a few good things in a day instead of too many.

7. Trust: The more knowledgeable we become, the more we believe in ourselves. When we believe in ourselves, we are more likely to trust the outcomes that occur. This is strength. You find it when trying to achieve a physical task, a mental challenge, and even more so with your spiritual beliefs. Trust is the foundation of faith.

8. Simplify: When we pile too many bricks on a foundation, we weaken the ground it stands on. Simplifying is not weakness. Simplifying is strength. It is learning to take on just the right number of tasks to gain the same outcome. We often overdo something, due to our own insecurity with it. When we simplify, we are clearing out the clutter, gaining confidence.

9. Strength Gained by Appreciating the Little Things: Really appreciate when something in your life comes into balance. Acknowledge it. Be grateful. This empowers and builds inner strength. Inner strength reflects in your actions. Your actions relay a sense of knowledge. This shows the world your obedience to the task and therefore, the strength in your convictions. Strength comes from appreciating something small.

10. You Are In Control Of Your Life: With every decision you make, you shape your own reality. Strength is simply a matter of knowing what you want and making good decisions. By deciding what you want, making a plan, and actively going for it, you can create the life of your dreams. When you come up against something you have no control over, you are then able to accept this with faith and trust that there is a "greater plan behind it."

Create A "Building Strength" Journal

An empowerment or strength building journal is a book or record you create to chart progress. You can take steps to follow and create a path to building strength. It can be used for writing down experiences, words that empower you, or help you to work toward your success. This journal is a good place to record information so that you can use it as a re-enforcement tool.

Tips for Power Journaling

1. Strength building is about creating balance. Upon waking, pick up your journal and write down a goal for the day. Commit yourself to doing one thing that will empower you today.

2. It is a good idea to focus on one specific thing that will bring about a change, no matter how awkward it may feel. Be focused. Start with your identity. Make a list of traits/strengths that people identify with you. Then make a list of traits/strengths that you identify as yourself.

3. Determination is the key element you must apply to see your goal through. Be diligent. Be strong. Be direct. How do you act according to your decisions? What will you do to make yourself stronger today?

4. Jot down an affirmation that you will repeat throughout the day. "I am a brilliant, strong life force today." "I am proud of myself and I will extend my pride even further today." "I will achieve a strong new goal today." "I feel empowered to…"

5. Standing up for what you believe in is the sign of a confident person. You can achieve this by having faith in what you choose to set as your goal. Make a short list of what you believe in today.

6. Have faith in your abilities by trusting your heart's desire. No one can deny your heart's desire. You are able to do anything you put your mind to.

7. Take a look at the people or situations that TAKE AWAY your strength. Write them down. Now, is the time to realize what, when, and who disempowers you. These are the people or areas of your life you need to detach from.

8. Take a look at your positive attributes. These are your strengths you will use as tools to detach from your disempowering situations and take you further, creating the powerful person you choose to be.

9. Reflect on your past empowering times. Use these as stepping stones in order to reach your goal. You have done it before and you will do it again.

10. As you inspire yourself and build your self-esteem, you inspire confidence in others. This natural progression is one of the most rewarding gifts you can receive. Write down 7 items, people, places… which inspires, empowers, or gives your life strength. How do these inspirations figure into your life? How will you use these as tools to boost your potential and encourage your goals?

"Strength does not come from physical capacity. It comes from an indomitable will." ~ Mahatma Gandhi

Success

What does success mean to you?

Some people equate success with fame or amassing huge sums of money. Others measure success by achieving simple goals they have set for themselves each day or week. So, what goals have you set for your life? Have you achieved these goals? Do you have a time frame defined in which you intend to reach them?

Short term, immediate goals are the best way to achieve long-term success. Setting simple, achievable goals are similar to building a stairway to your life's ultimate dream. Each time you reach a new goal, you reach a new plateau on your way to fulfilling your life's success. Each new goal you reach gives you an incentive to set a new one.

> ## Gemstone:
> ### Success
>
> *"O. Universal truth, be told,*
> *success is found be seeking, bold.*
> *Enjoy each morning as you rise,*
> *eager to keep on late, anigh,*
> *for this is truly passion found,*
> *and where success will follow,*
> *round."*
>
> ~ Andrew Pacholyk MS L.Ac

The Path to Success

The greatest successes come from the ideas we are most passionate about! When we are passionate about something, we devote our time, money, resources, and most of all, our love to this new idea.

When you follow your dream and see it through, the greatest reward is your success. This is done in two ways: passion and persistence.

Passion is the root of what you love to do most. It is a blinding force of energy that you desire to do, every waking day. If all you could do is your passion every day, then that is what you MUST do. It will drive you to success.

Your passion will assist you in finding the right audience, attracting those who are drawn to your passion, and make you successful.

Why will your passion do this? Because you will find the answers through what you love doing most... or these answers will find you. This passion can turn into a profession. A profession from your passion is one of the greatest rewards.

There is also the fact that when someone genuinely enjoys their profession and are motivated by their passion, they tend to be more satisfied with their work and more psychologically healthy. When these same people begin to get positive feedback and see results from their passion, they are motivated to work harder to ensure that this passion continues. It is a profession they will always have in their lives.

Persistence is the other part of this equation.

When you are passionate, you do not give up. It is not an option. No matter how long something can take to become a realized dream, this persistence is guided by your passion.

So many times, in my life, I have seen patients, friends, and colleagues give themselves a "time limit" for their passion. They would tell me"

"if I don't make it by next year..."

"if I don't publish my work by next Spring..."

"if I don't get this promotion next week.... I'm done."

More often than not, they give up. They let go of their dream or relinquish their passion. It is a tragic end and it hurts to see someone give up on a dream. They block their progress by giving it an "expiration date."

I think this also shows that perhaps, they just were not *passionate enough* to truly pursue what they desire.

Success are steps up a ladder. Reaching for the top rung of that ladder is great. But do you even know what that top rung is? Success is often a definition we have in our heads, which we do not seem to stray from. But in reality, success often comes in ways you do not even imagine. At the top rung of that ladder, are other, endless possibilities, that we have never thought of.

Many people who have experienced successes, tend to not see them or recognize them as such. They may pass over the fact that...

~ "They finally got a meeting with the top brass", unfortunately they do not recognize that they have been waiting a year for this meeting.

~ "They just sold products to their first big box store concept" but now they are more concerned about getting 10 more contracts with other big stores and fail to realize, that this was the best success they have had in 6 years.

In achieving a success, it is important to remember how far you've come. Even though there's a part of you that wants to grow and yearns for more, acknowledging each achievement, no matter how small, is necessary.

Success is notoriously elusive for many people because their definition of success sets them up to never quite have it. We may have minor achievements, but yet do not feel they are successes, because it's not the end goal. Success is an achievement in any form, on any level.

If your definition of success has the room to include who you are and what you have right NOW, you'll continue growing and refining, even when you make mistakes. You will realize you are defining success.

It is important to recognize, honor, and appreciate the little "rungs on the ladder" as these are the real successes. This is the real definition of success.

Success is money and power to most people. What also must be included is:

1. Peace of mind, which is the result of self-satisfaction in knowing you did your best to become the best you are capable of becoming.

2. Well-being, which is the long-lasting end result of your success and how it makes you feel.

3. Wonder, is your own amazement of where you came from and what it took for you to succeed.

4. Wisdom, from the long journey it took for you to get here and the brain power you discovered to make it all happen.

5. Giving, is the gift you offer back for your success. It is probably the most rewarding of all.

6. Success is a mirror of yourself. It is how you like yourself, how you accept yourself, and how you like how you do it.

7. Success is the expansion of your happiness through worthy goals.

"Put your heart, mind, and soul into even your smallest acts. This is the secret of success." ~ Swami Sivananda

Personal Growth

Within each *season of our lives*, we are faced with new challenges, often because of our age or our mindset. Personal growth tools are those which help us to stretch and learn. They are situations that present themselves in some form or fashion that can either be a natural progression or issues that force us to pay attention.

Hopefully, throughout your life, you will work to improve and benefit from these situations. We should never stop growing mentally and spiritually. Our personal growth defines our lives, guides our path, and offers new opportunities.

In the *"summer" of our lives*, we tend to search out more movement or exercise, if we have not done so already in our 20's. Our bodies are hitting their peak of physicality and we may already be feeling the effects of aging as it slowly makes an appearance in very subtle ways. Your doctor may have recommended that you start adding exercise into your life.

Exercise/Movement

Exercise is what the body craves. Movement is essential to our bodies. A sedentary lifestyle not only stifles our mind but wreaks havoc on our physical body.

Exercise is what your body instinctively wants to do, especially when stressed or under mental distress. It burns off some of the stress chemicals which tension produces. Therefore, a tired muscle is a relaxed muscle. Regular exercise builds stamina that can help anyone battle stress. But even something as casual as a walk around the block can help you burn off some of the tension that you carrying with you.

Exercise gives you energy. Study after study supports those words, including one by the National Aeronautics and Space Administration. More than 200 federal employees were placed on a moderate, regular exercise program. The results: 90 percent said they had never felt better. Almost half said they felt less stressed, and almost one-third reported they slept better.

What motivates you? What is it that moves you or makes you want to get up? Use what motivates you! Find purpose. No more excuses! You'd be surprised what you could do if you put one foot in front of the other.

The summer is the best time to do exercise. The muscles are easily warmed up during this time of year. They do not have to work against the cold and are more attuned to the weather conditions.

Summer gives us the opportunity to workout outside. We can enjoy nature and the great outdoors, natural air and light, and a feeling of oneness with the earth. Summer offers a great variety of exercise and movement choices.

The Power of Yoga

As a yoga student and teacher for over 20 years, I have dedicated much of my life to the healing and rejuvenating effects of yoga. Over the years, the fitness craze has become very interested in the ancient "art of yoga." There have been many different types of yoga "workouts" that have been created. But many times, in our quest for fitness and a hard body, it becomes just a workout and not yoga.

There is a spiritual side to yoga that has been synthesized out of these practices. If you come to this path with fitness in mind that is important, but yoga is extremely powerful on a mind/body/spirit level. If you try to rush it, you will only slow yourself down. If you disregard the mental challenge, you will only sweat. If you do not recognize the spiritual lessons associated with why you do each pose or asana, your practice is no more than aerobics.

Yoga is harmony between mind and body. In yoga, the mind is used to perceive (understand) and guide (heal) the body, not "control" it or force it.

Yoga takes time. Time for muscles to coordinate. Time for tissues to become more aware. Time for breath, spirit, and energy to flow. The time you invest in yoga comes back with life lessons full of consciousness, more vitality, a peaceful mind, reduced stress, and a life richer in spirit.

Yoga should be a conscious action, not "repetitive routine." It is skill, grace, and poise developed through regular practice. The awakening of the body and mind develop awareness.

Gemstone:
Life on the Mat

"I roll it out and step inside a world of self-discovery, mine.
Here is where I challenge myself, to learn just how to be myself...
to grow and reach and stretch and sweat,
I push my boundaries, no regrets.

For this is where I seem to be, a stronger, better newer me.
And when my body's fully spent, my spirit takes a forward step,

I contemplate the wisdom's known,
relinquished now, in Child's pose."

~ Andrew Pacholyk MS L.Ac

Reasons to Incorporate Yoga as a Lifestyle

Incorporating yoga into your life can be one of the most rewarding and fulfilling experiences you can take on your journey. A nurtured yoga practice can transcend you by creating a disciplined mind, a strong, and physically fit body. No matter what religion you practice, yoga can be a bridge to enhancing your spirituality.

Practicing yoga is associated with establishing harmony, balance, and conscious awareness. It has been well-publicized in mainstream media, recommended to patients by their doctors, and praised by practitioners.

1. Creates Discipline: Discipline is a necessity in life. Discipline is essential for achieving any kind of success in life. It is the secret to the most effective, efficient, and well strategic plan you can give yourself. Being successful, losing weight, maintaining relationships are not tasks that come easy for most people. They are all things we must work hard at creating, keeping, and maintaining. Yoga assists in understanding this process.

2. Improves Circulation: Poor circulation is the cause of over 1000 diseases. From a healthy heart to a good sex life, the proper flow and circulation of blood in our arteries is one of the most important things we can do to maintain good health and push back the aging process. There is a common denominator between good arterial health and disorders such as heart attack, obesity, diabetes, and high glucose levels, as well as sexual health. That common denominator is blood circulation.

3. Increases Flexibility: Yoga is the way to a more pliable, flexible body. It creates a supple and more resilient muscular structure, suited to react quicker to falls, accidents or any kind of sports. As we age, the flexibility improved by doing yoga has shown to be a deterrent in injury related accidents.

4. Quiets the Mind: A disciplined mind is a free mind. Gain control over your thoughts and you maintain control over your life. Retrain your mind and you regain your freedom. Calming the mind is a behavioral technique used to interrupt, minimize and eliminate "psychological noise." Obsessive, repetitive thoughts and fears are all apart of negative, self-destructive patterns that benefit from the power of yoga and mind quieting.

5. Improves Breathing: Breath is life! Exchange of electrons. Flow of energy. Your breathing is the voice of your spirit. It's depth, smoothness, sound, and rate reflect your mood. If you become aware of your breath and breathe the way you do when you are calm you will become calm. Yoga helps us to practice regular, mindful breathing, and can be calming and energizing. With the addition of music and its rhythm, the "musical breath" can even help stress-related health problems ranging from panic attacks to digestive disorders. Fall into the rhythm of the music and breathe. Focus on your breathing as you move through your yoga poses.

6. Brings Awareness: Through your yoga practice, you can gain a broader perspective in self-awareness. Being able to open up your mind, allowing a free flow of thoughts and ideas can be liberating. Welcoming a new opinion or way of doing something can bring new meaning to your life. If you give up your closed thoughts and make way for a different opinion, you may be surprised at the outcome. Through your yoga practice, you learn to strive to meet difficult goals as you are pushed to stretch the horizons of what you think is impossible. This is conscious living.

7. Improves Nutrition: The source of fuel you find to nourish you on a daily basis changes as you become a yogi. The demands for a healthier diet make your journey more important. The Ayurvedic science of food is based on incorporating the 6 flavors (salty, bitter, sweet, pungent, sour, and astringent) into each meal. The Three Humours or Tri-dosha are the Ayurvedic body types that classify a diet and lifestyle routines that are best suited for you.

8. Betters Your Sex Life: As mentioned earlier, a healthy heart and the proper flow and circulation of blood in our arteries is one of the most important things we can do to maintain good health and a satisfying sex life. Not only that, just think how much more limber you will be. Not to mention, stamina.

9. Improves Your Quality of Life: With yoga in your life, you are now breathing better, are more flexible, have found a new sense of purpose, drive, and direction in your life. Welcome, change. Through this gateway, your idea of nourishment has changed. Not just what you put in your body, but what you allow or don't allow in your life anymore. Yoga is like the lotus flower. It teaches us to unfold one petal at a time in order to reveal the raw beauty underneath.

10. Brings You Closer to Nature/Spirit: Finding spirit and a higher sense of purpose comes to you as you evolve in your yoga practice. Yoga can show us what is truly important in life. It allows all those "things", that monopolize our time, to have less value or stress-inducing effects on us. Especially, as we grow as a yogi practitioner.

Gemstone:
A Hindu Dance

"All I ask is that you choose to find a path to lead you down,
where travels are, fulfilling, true, for many paths exist to reach ~ your liberation, bound...

to find just what you're looking for, a unity with God, you see. It's how you break the cycle here, of birth and death no more.

The Divine resides within us all, regardless of your choice. We all have the ability to achieve this liberation. Let go the pain and suffering and release your passive voice.

No one person is condemned, to suffer due to class or place, but rather earns the fruit of their own actions, words, and grace.

To advance your spirituality by acting on these facts, in accordance with their righteousness, and that, which we attract."

~ Andrew Pacholyk MS. L.Ac

Summer's Element: Fire

Throughout the centuries, the elements have come to be associated with each season. The elements are the forces of nature that express their energies on earth, in the Universe, and within us. They are the fundamental building blocks of many paradigms from every culture.

Fire is one of the four classic elements from ancient Greek philosophy, science, and astrology. In astrology, there are four classical elements.

In the *Summer of our lives*, our personalities tend to match that of the element, fire.

The element, Fire is associated with the Summer season and with heat.

In the Chinese Medicine paradigm, the element is associated with the heart, pericardium, small intestines, and is related to the tongue.

The heart is the "seat" of the mind and therefore, its highest expression is love. Enthusiasm, warmth in relationships, and conscious awareness are "fire traits." Fire represents physical strength, force, courage, desire, initiative, fertility, passion, purification, and rejuvenation. It represents both light and heat.

Emotionally, this element is associated with the mind and its stability. When the fire element is balanced, sensitivity and expression, true fulfillment, and the equilibrium between heart and mind are our greatest rewards. When the fire element is balanced, the heart properly governs and circulates the blood and ensures proper assimilation of the beginning breakdown of food in the small intestines.

When imbalanced, we may either lack joy (depression) or have an excess of joy (maniac condition). Fire is symbolic of maximum activity or greatest Yang energy. It is nature at its peak of growth and fire's "motion" is upward. Agitation, nervous exhaustion, heartburn, and insomnia are other physical indicators of imbalance in this area.

The Fire Signs of the zodiac are Aries, Leo, and Sagittarius. They are passionate in their desires, leaders in their fields, and are honored and looked up to. They are broadly intuitive, use their gut instincts, and have an emotional sensitivity. On the other end of the spectrum, they can have high and low bursts of energy, experience "burn out" much faster than other signs and have a pigeon hole passion, which can be destructive. A positive fire person is strong, courageous and bold, dramatic and passionate in all areas within themselves.

Within the Celtic, Mayan, and Indian cultures, fire has been used for its powerful healing, purging, and cleansing properties. Offered as a tool of celebration in many of the major holidays and seasonal transitions, fire, smoke, and ashes were deemed to have protective properties.

Cows were driven between two pillars of fire as a cleansing ritual, while tribes would jump over bonfires to achieve fertility, prosperity, and protection. Fires were lit to represent stages of the sun and its light was shared between communities. All good examples as to how fire plays a major role in ritualistic themes.

Within the Hebrew Bible and culture, fire was an element of theophany represented in the burning bush, pillar of fire, and the flame of the Menorah. The highest form of sacrifice was the Korban Olah, performed twice daily, which was an animal sacrifice consumed by fire.

In Hinduism, fire is a central element in the Yajna ceremony, with Agni, "fire", playing the role as mediator between the worshipper and the other gods. In Hinduism, Agni or Fire is thought of as the tongue of Superior Lord Narayana.

Fire worship in Roman tradition had two separate forms: fire of the hearth and fire of the forge. In Rome, it was the infamous Vestal Virgins, who cared for Vesta, the goddess known as "protector of home and hearth." This sacred flame was known as the symbol of Vesta's presence within Rome.

The Greek equivalent of the goddess was Hestia. The fire, which represented the forge, was associated with the Roman God, Vulcan and the Greek equivalent, Hephaestus. They seemed to serve their reign as protectors against accidental fires in cities and as forging craft patrons. Prometheus, the Titan God, was also associated with fire and was known to have stolen fire for man, from the gods.

Fire

June 21 to September 22

(Summer solstice to the eve of autumn equinox)

Abilites: Warmth, sexuality, activity, excitement, entertainment, insight, liveliness, swiftness, renewal, purifying, transformation, change, transmutation, destruction, creation, passion, energy, intuition, inspiration, will, desire, heat, communication, strength, courage.

Stones: Amber, obsidian, rhodochrosite, ruby, lava rock, garnet, jasper, pipestone, citrine, beryl, hematite.

Plants: Basil, carnation, cedar, chrysanthemum, dill, ginger, heliotrope, holly, juniper, marigold, peppermint, ash, betony, cinnamon, tobacco, witch hazel, cactus.

Direction: South (North in the Northern Hemisphere)

Colors: Red, gold, yellow, orange.

Season: Summer

Cycle Celebrations: Litha (Summer solstice)

Number 1

Time: Noon

Zodiac: Aries, Leo, Sagittarius.

Planets: Sun, Mars.

Angel: Ariel

Sense: Sight

Time of life: Young Adult

Gemstone:
Fire

"For passion burns with fire's fury, its central to our heart and mind. Desire blazes forward reaching, even when our love is blind.

We surge ahead and go with gusto, taking all we want and need, consuming everything around us, retaining every bit, through greed.

But there's a lesson here to take with, even when we cannot see, that fire may be less aggressive, when its simply smoldering.

Obtain the things you want in life, with ambition, strong, don't force your hand and you will have them greater and lifelong."

~Andrew Pacholyk MS L.Ac

Musical Landscape

Music is the soundtrack to our life. Whether we know it or not, our lives are mapped out by the important moments we encounter. And most often, there is a song associated with it. Quite often, when we hear a familiar tune, it can take us back to the exact time and place, along with the experience that went with it. This "musical landscape" is the map of our lives.

From celebrations and ceremonies to proclamations and processions, music marks the empirical reference we associated with time and place. Music is a magical medium that has always been a metaphor for our spirit!

Musical Playlists for Life's Journeys

Gemstone:
Melodies of Love

"Oh song so sweet, I hear your call,
when music brings the memories all
~ from heartache, flirting, precious
love,
to certain times I rose above
~ so here's a list of songs most true,
to offer up a special few ...."

~ Andrew Pacholyk MS. L.Ac

Love in Song

This list of love songs is the tip of the iceberg. You could only make a list of songs related to your loves if they are meaningful to you.

This list was a daunting task. There are so many hundreds of magical songs about love, that it would be impossible to list everyone's favorite.

Regardless of this challenge, you could ideally say, that any song could remind you of love if it has a connection to you and something or someone you love.

If one or more love songs you find on this list are ones you can relate to, I am grateful to have introduced it to you or brought back a memory you may have forgotten.

No matter what song is or isn't here, you must always have love around you, even if it is just in song. I thought it would be a wonderful gift to share the love songs that have made a life-long impression on me.

Love expressed through song, is a centuries' old tradition that has changed the course of history, brought together the most unlikely duos, and touched our hearts when we least expected it.

Many of these songs have a personal meaning to me and are songs I treasure and hold dear to my heart. These melodies cross several eras, yet they ring true for me as the indelible mind set and the amazing way love can be expressed in song. I call this list:

Andrew's Greatest Love Songs

1. Right Here Waiting, Richard Marx
2. When I Fall In Love, Nat King Cole
3. Reward, Basia
4. My All, Mariah Carey
5. Every Road Leads Back To You, Bette Midler
6. Baby, Baby, Amy Grant
7. Time After Time, Cyndi Lauper
8. I Will Always Love You, Whitney Houston
9. Forever And For Always, Shania Twain
10. Loving You, Robert Preston, (The Music Man)
11. Always And Forever, Heatwave
12. My Heart Will Go On (Love Theme From "Titanic"), Celine Dion
13. Whole New World (Aladdin's Theme), Peabo Bryson/Regina Belle
14. Longer, Dan Fogelberg
15. When I Think Of You, Janet Jackson
16. Endless Love, Diana Ross/Lionel Richie
17. Lost In Your Eyes, Debbie Gibson
18. How Deep Is Your Love, Bee Gees
19. Somewhere, My Love, Doctor Zhivago
20. Without Love, Hairspray
21. Somewhere, West Side Story
22. Flying Sequence/Can You Read My Mind, Superman, John Williams
23. Songbird, Fleetwood Mac
24. At The Beginning, Donna Lewis, Richard Marx
25. All I Ask of You, Phantom of the Opera

Gemstone:
Songs of Luck
"Of Irish brogue or positive lilt,
the songs of luck bring a world that tilts,
in our direction, filled with light,
for good intentions, make it bright,
with songs of fortune, good will bring,
by way of wind or bird that sings...."
~ Andrew Pacholyk MS. L.Ac

Feeling Lucky: Music to Motivate

Music is a great catalyst for empowering dreams, boosting motivation, and invigorating life itself. Here to inspire you are special songs that encourage, empower, and entrain you to feel lucky. I call this list:

The "Feeling Lucky" Playlist

1. Luck Be A Lady, Frank Sinatra
2. With A Little Luck, Paul McCartney
3. Some Guys Have All the Luck, Rod Stewart
4. Good Luck Charm, Elvis Presley
5. Good Luck & True Love, Start Station
6. Lucky One, Amy Grant
7. With a Little Bit of Luck, My Fair Lady
8. Lucky, Britney Spears
9. Lucky, Jason Mraz
10. Lucky Now, Ryan Adams
11. Lucky Strike, Maroon 5
12. Lucky That Way, Joe Walsh
13. Lucky Man, Emerson, Lake & Palmer
14. I Feel Lucky, Mary Chapin Carpenter
15. How Lucky I Am, Brian White
16. Lucky Star, Madonna
17. God Luck and Good Speed, Season of Mist
18. Third Time Lucky, Basia
19. Fortuosity, Tommy Steele
20. The Luck of the Irish, Blarney Music

160

Gemstone:
Binding Magic
"A union of two is sacred time,
when we are shown the great divine,
the best we wish to be as one,
we strive to keep this spell we've spun.
So honor, love and cherish thee,
for all and all, eternity..."
~ Andrew Pacholyk MS L.Ac

Fairy Tale Weddings

June is one of the most popular months for weddings. Music is one of the most important elements within this celebration. I have attended many weddings and the magic of the music is truly what makes it such a memorable ceremony. I have gathered some of the most beautiful and infamous music for the union of two people.

1. Bridal Chorus, Wagner (Processional)
2. The Wedding March, Felix Mendelssohn (Recessional)
3. Lullaby for String Orchestra, Gershwin (Prelude)
4. Make Our Garden Grow from Candide, John Williams
5. Gloria: I. Allegro vivace,St Albans Cathedral Choirs
6. Rustic Wedding Symphony / In the Spring, Goldmark
7. Ave Maria, Op. 52 No. 6, Leopold Stokowski
8. Homage March – 'Sigurd Jorsalfar, Edvard Grieg (Processional)
9. L'Arlesienne Suite No. 2Hungarian Orchestra (Offertory)
10. Fantasie und Fuge Ãuber den Chorale, Joseph Nolan (Processional)
11. Waltz in A-Flat Major, Op 39, No. 15, Johannes Brahms
12. Gloria, Antonio Vivaldi (Recessional)
13. Canon In D, Pachelbel
14. Air on a G String, Johann Sebastian Bach
15. Butterfly Waltz – Piano and Cello, Brian Crain
16. Wedding Processional, "The Sound of Music"
17. Finale (from Water Music Suite), George Frederick Handel
18. Minuet in G Major (The Lovers Concerto), Johann Sebastian Bach
19. Ode to Joy – Symphony No. 9 In D Minor, Beethoven (Recessional)
20. Wedding Song (There Is Love), Captain and Tennille

Gemstone:
Summer Shakes
"From bop and shake, to rattle and roll.
summer music lends us soul,
to be just who we need to be,
today~ in almost every way.
It brings us joy, light-heartiness,
and "rules", by motivating us!
~ Andrew Pacholyk MS L.Ac

Summer Song

Music and summer go hand in hand. What better feeling than the sounds of music bursting in your ears as you sun bathe, surf or hit the pool. So, on my walk back from the beach today, I thought of the songs of summer that make up my consciousness. These melodies are an amazing way summer can be expressed in song. I call this list:

Andrew's Summer Consciousness Play List

1. Summer Breeze, The Isley Brothers
2. On the Beach, Chris Rea
3. The Second Summer of Love, Danny Wilson
4. Beach Baby, First Class
5. Someone Somewhere (In Summertime), Simple Minds
6. Staying Out for The Summer, Dodgy
7. Wake Up Boo! The Boo Radleys
8. Walking on Sunshine, Katrina & The Waves
9. This Summer, Squeeze
10. Here Comes the Summer, The Undertones
11. Sunny Afternoon, The Kinks
12. In the Summertime, Mungo Jerry
13. Up, Up and Away, The Fifth Dimension
14. Green Grass, Gary Lewis & The Playboys
15. Turn Down Day, The Cyrkle
16. 98.6, Keith
17. Daydream, The Lovin Spoonful
18. Stoned Soul Picnic, The Fifth Dimension
19. Feelin' Groovy: Best of Featuring 59th St Bridge So, The Hit Crew
20. Lazy Day, Spanky & Our Gang

Seasonal Landscape: Sea

The mysterious and amazing healing power of water has been utilized for centuries. Water cleanses, refreshes, and restores all life. We are always drawn to water. Be it a soothing fountain, majestic waterfall, or the churning sea.

Water is a carrier. It flows. It moves along the lines of least resistance to find its way to the sea where it comes and goes in the ebb and flow of tides and waves. The appeal is inexplicable. We crave water. Perhaps because our bodies are made up of a large percent of it. Maybe we instinctively know how it can heal us.

Healing Power of the Sea

Every summer I take a long-needed vacation to the sea. This powerful source of nature yields some of the most essential healing tools and additional benefits that are hard to compare with anything else. We already know the necessary and soothing abilities water offers. Here are some of the best tools and tips the sea can give:

1. Sun – is the best source of Vitamin D synthesis. The sun is the source of all life and feels good, especially after a long, cold winter. Prevention and precautions are the most important methods when you go out in the sun. More than 15-20 minutes can be harmful when you are not protected. Applying sunscreen (SPF 15, at least), wear UV-protective sunglasses, and clothing. Limiting your time in the sun from I pm. to 3 pm, if possible.

2. Sand – is a natural exfoliator. These finely ground shells, coral, and carbon matter become an amazing tool for cleansing your skin. Wet your skin in the sea and rub the sand gently over your face and body. Use some in a bowl to create a Zen garden or "sea garden" display.

3. Salt Water – the healing abilities of salt water are profound and well documented. Salt water is an astringent and speeds wound healing. A cup or handful of water in your hand or neti pot is a wonderful cleansing therapy for sinusitis or blocked nasal passages. Slowly inhale the salt water into your nose to cleanse your sinus and open up the air passages. Floating in seawater is an extreme release of tension and stress from the day. Allow yourself to float weightlessly in the water. You deserve it.

4. Sponge – a natural cleanser and exfoliator, a sponge can be dried in the sun and placed in a decorative bowl or on the bathtub. Rewet your sponge and use it in the bath or shower.

5. Coral – comes in many forms. When this beautiful "art of the sea" washes up on the beach and bleached by the sun, it's beauty can be awe-inspiring. Coral is rich in calcium. This "stone" can be used as pumice to exfoliate dead skin cells, bring blood and circulation back to the feet when used as a massage stone, and can make a wonderful decorative piece.

6. Sea Air – deep breathing of ocean air helps us to relax and let go. The faint smell of salt in the air can take us to a place of pure joy. Sea air has a certain aliveness found nowhere else. This deep breathing can help release tension and the problems associated with it.

7. Exercise – yoga, body toning, running on the beach, or breathing exercises are all great ways to stay fit and take advantage of the outdoor activities offered us in summer. Make exercise enjoyable. In the summer months, it is a good idea to exercise early in the morning or late afternoon. Make sure you drink plenty of water before, during, and after activities to ensure hydration.

8. Seaweed – rich in iodine and other minerals, seaweed and other sea vegetables are fat-free, low calorie, and one of the richest sources in the vegetable kingdom. Seaweed has access to the abundance of minerals in the sea. Seaweed can also be ground into a wonderful exfoliant and used in mineral and mud treatments.

9. Seashells – these magnificent works of Universal creation are wonders to behold. Finding and searching them out is a great past time that can last for hours, taking us away from ourselves and giving us a carefree adventure that is rewarding on many levels. Your favorites can be taken home and cleansed. Shells can make beautiful decorative pieces. Seashells are natural vessels that can be used for cleansing and make a great carrier for sage or incense. They can be placed on your personal altar as a reminder of good times or as a tribute to nature and all her powers.

10. Stress relief – the best combination to relieve stress is combining the above elements of light, air, and surf to create the best prescription for good health and relaxation. They will melt away stress and bring you back to yourself. Leave your laptop and cell phone behind.

Gemstone:
A Mermaid's Tale

(for mom)

*"Life's a beach and then you
sigh,
a sigh of relief, for days gone
by.
With time, it gently, slowly
drifts,
on clouds of light and sand that
sifts,
between your toes and with
each day,
invite a little sun your way.*

*And though you may not be with
me,
where sand comes up to meet
the sea,
remember you can always take,
a long deep breath to let
escape,
the tension as you let it out…
all fear and anger, restless
doubt"*

~ Andrew Pacholyk MS L.Ac

Meditation: Inspiration as Deep as The Sea

Take a minute. Find your center. Close your eyes. Allow a deep breath. Now… listen to your subconscious mind as you reach back to find that which gives you pleasure, makes your heart sing, and moves you to do what really brings you happiness.

Sense the sea air gently blowing over your body. Let it tussle your hair as the warming sun, slowly kisses your face. Feel the warmth.

Smell the rich floral scented flowers and the ripe smell of sunbaked fruit as the salty air fills your lungs with each breath.

Give your whole body up to the support of the sand you are sitting in, beneath you. Let the sand take all your weight. The deeper you breathe the sea air, the more your body releases and let's go of its tension.

Feel the gentle air wisp up from your bare toes as it glides over your body, massaging each center of energy. Slowly air flows up and over you. Time and time again.

You now feel the gentle lapping water of the warm Caribbean Sea at your feet. You see in your mind's eye, the beautiful blue green color of the water. Allow your mind to clear and feel as vast and wide as the sea before you.

Sense your toes at the water's edge by gently wiggling them. Let the sand fall slowly through your fingers as you move them.

Your subconscious mind is the key to dreams. It holds, locked away, the desires and inspirations that you seek to find. What do you see? With each exhale, what is brought to the surface? Like the deep sea, we hold on to our treasures, only to be brought up by a gentle stirring…**Expand the breath** in your lungs as you press deeper into the supporting sand. Exhale and realize. Exhale and discover what is rising to the surface.

Now, relax and breathe. Relax and let go.

The Mineral Kingdom

Crystals are profound gifts and a great integrative therapy that can be used in conjunction with any other form of health care for personal pleasure, meditation, stress relief, and healing. Crystals are not always thought of as being associated with the sea, yet the sea has many gems that it gives up, like treasures from a treasure chest! Crystals, stones, and organic matter (such as shells, pearls and coral) bring together the blend of earth and sea, sun and fun.

Crystals Associated with the Sea

These stones, crystals, and shells are associated with water and relaxation, mermaids and sea goddesses, sailors and journeys. Rich in history, metaphysical energy and mystery, this crystal menagerie incorporates some of the best jewels of the sea.

Abalone Shell: Shimmer of the Sea

Although not a crystal, abalone shell has been used for centuries in jewelry and carvings. Nicknamed the "sea ears", the Abalone's flattened, oval shape with the iridescent interior was used by the Native Northwest American Indians as a natural vessel for cleansing, offerings, and prayers. Embracing the colors of the ocean, the shell displays iridescent colors in blues, greens, purples, and yellows. This unique shell embodies all the aspects of the water element including love, beauty, gentleness, caring, comfort, peacefulness, delight, and solace. It is soft to the touch from repeated tumbling in the sand and water.

Abalone is useful for handling and calming emotional situations and is very soothing to the mind/body. When working through any emotional situation, have abalone nearby, as it is believed to be beneficial and promotes cooperation. Abalone is associated with all the Chakra energies. In particular, it seems to work the best on the Solar Plexus Chakra, stimulating that gut feeling. Abalone is especially good for the Heart Chakra, as it gently clears the heart of fear, sorrow, and negative emotions. Abalone allows your intuitive resources to stimulate psychic development and intuition through the Third Eye Chakra.

Amazonite: Unique Adventures in Self-Discovery

This stone represents prosperity. It is great over a door to bring in new business. It is wonderful for entrepreneurs and those in sales. This "hope stone" is important to have when starting a new business or financial venture. Amazonite's energy works very well when combined with other feldspar stones such as topaz and aqua aura. It is a gentle, friendly, calming, stone, which opens Throat Chakra, Heart Chakra, and Solar Plexus Chakra. Used for self-expression, artistic creativity, and healing. This is a great stone for communication, confidence, and leadership.

It is said to reduce self-damaging behavior, impart self-respect, and grace. It is a stone for trust, feeling self-assured, and improves communication. This green stone is instrumental in distilling the raw information used for personal expression. It helps filter information and combines it with natural intuition. Use to enhance masculine qualities. Good for anyone involved in the arts. Utilize Amazonite in order to encourage the pursuit of your unique path in life. Amazonite is used to disperse negative energy.

Aquamarine: The Soothing Energy of the Sea

This stone has the calming, soothing energy of the sea. This is the stone of courage. Known for being tranquilizing, bringing innocence, lightheartedness, stimulating creativity, communication, and self-awareness. It is a stone for confidence and purpose. Throat Chakra, Sacral Spleen Chakra, and Heart Chakra all benefit from this stone. Used for protection on journeys, especially those who travel on water. Affects etheric and mental levels. Helps stabilize and harmonize unsettled surroundings. Helps reduce fears.

Excellent stone for meditation. Helps one attune to nature. Quiets the mind and reduces stress. Aquamarine brings about a tolerance toward others. It clears blocked communication and assist the user in verbal expression. Throughout history, this stone has been used to find our individuality and to help us be ourselves. It's been used to increase clairvoyance, intuition, and psychic awareness. It will also provide a good focus for meditation and visualization. It is the stone of distance healers, ecologists, and long-distance travelers.

Beach Stones: Gifts of Gratitude

Piled high or rolling up to your wet, sandy feet, beach stones can be any class of stone that has been embraced by the water, moved and nurtured, tumbled and tossed through a long journey from its beginnings until it finds you. We tend to be drawn towards symmetrical, smooth, and energetic things, and beach stones offer us a vision of gratitude and kindness, gentle energy, and a subtle approach. These stones will take on the metaphysical properties that they are created from when combined with nature's folly.

Beach stones teach us humility. They have undergone great stress, wear and tear, as they find their way to the seashore. Yet, when discovered, they bring new light to our thoughts and can offer deep recognition in our hearts. These stone are believed to bring luck and peace.

Chrysocolla: The Sage of the Sea

This solid light blue to blue green stone has a very gentle, soothing, and friendly energy. It is considered the "wise stone" or "sage stone ", as it offers up its wisdom and sagely advice to those who pay attention. Excellent for the Heart Chakra, this stone is used to flush and heal "heart blocks" such as loss, hurt, guilt, fear… This stone helps us to find "peace in our hearts." Use this stone for allowing what you need into your life. It helps us to be flexible, self-forgiving, and patient. It keeps us in light, love, and healing on a daily basis. Utilized at the Throat Chakra, it assists in expressing our feelings through verbal and artistic creativity. Helps one feel more comfortable speaking the truth. This stone helps develop personal confidence. Because of its blue green minerals, it has been used for helping with dreams and dream work.

Known as an Earth healing stone, its elements help enrich the planet. It is therefore, one of my favorite "garden stones" and reminds you of a natural forest, a distant mountain top, or the stillness of the sea. Calming and tranquil, this stone allows us a feeling of unconditional love. It has been used traditionally to bring about quiet peace, where there is upset and can be used to purify a place or restore balance to a person. Chrysocolla symbolizes prosperity, luck, and fortitude. It is forged into jewelry to bring about these traits to those who wear this very special stone. Chrysocolla has the ability to bring harmony, increase wisdom, and remind you about discretion.

Coral: Living, Breathing Stone

Coral is not a crystal but has been used for centuries for its healing properties such as shells, pearls, and resins. Coral is a blend of calcium and calcite. In various languages, the word for coral often translates as "small stone." Since the time of the Hebrews, coral has been used as a divination tool for casting lots. In the Bible these "small stones" determined an uncertain fate as it was considered a "truth teller." This stone was said to tap into your intuitive nature and help with psychic energy work.

Coral brings diplomacy and concurrence, quiets emotions, and brings peace to the inner self. Used for centuries to facilitate intuition, imagination, visualization, and accelerate the transfer of knowledge. Coral was known as a protective stone against negativity while also preventing loss of energy. White coral soothes, clears, and heals the Chinese meridians. It helps one manage stress, especially when stress affects the back.

Larimar: When Sky Meets Sea

A gentle, soft, sky-blue Caribbean healer, Larimar brings the tranquility of sea and air to heart and mind. Soothes and uplifts hurt, fear, depression, the pain of life, and changes with love. Beneficial for self-expression, patience, acceptance, simplicity, and creativity. When this stone has red spots, it helps gentle people to be assertive. Larimar is an extremely rare gemstone that has been found in only one location: in a mountainous, relatively inaccessible region of the Dominican Republic overlooking the Caribbean Sea. This gemstone first surfaced in 1974, although the inhabitants of the region and their ancestors have long been aware of the stone.

The name Larimar was given to the stone by a Dominican, Miguel Mendez, who combined his daughter's name LARIssa, with MAR, the Latin word for sea. The stone is also called the "Atlantis Stone", since claims surfaced that the Dominican Republic was part of the lost continent of Atlantis. An association that has been affirmed by various spiritual and metaphysical authorities.

Ocean Jasper: Gifts of the Sea

This stone helps one to accept responsibilities, develop patience and helps with circular breathing during meditation. Ocean Jasper allows for mental stabilization and assists in emotional detoxification and elimination. Ocean Jasper is found in only one mine near Marovato, Madagascar. The deposit, is located at the edge of the ocean and can only be seen and collected at low tide.

Technically considered "Orbicular Jasper" in reference to its colorful orbs, some have adopted the name "Moon Jewel Jasper." But "Ocean Jasper" seems most fitting, as it was found right along the shore. Orbicular jasper's distinctive patterns are made up of round or spherical inclusions of contrasting colors floating in solid jasper. The orbs can range in diameter from a millimeter to a centimeter and frequently show a particularly dramatic concentric banding. How orbicular jasper forms is still a scientific mystery.

Opal: The Rainbow of the Sea

Opals are mysterious stones. This silicate stone contains water, metaphysically, correlating with our emotions. Opals help by clarifying, amplifying and mirroring our feelings. They can bring up buried emotions, or desires (including love and passion). With opals in your life, you can find less inhibition, more spontaneity. These stones have often been associated with the higher or Crown and Third Eye Chakra. They assist in visualization, imagination, dreams, and the power of healing. They are efficient as they can easily absorb and store our emotions and thoughts.

Opal is a "stone of inspiration", which enhances the imagination and creativity. It helps one release inhibitions and enhances the memory. Opal is also said to be a very spiritual stone. The Renaissance period perpetuated the story that opals helped one be "invisible" in situations where they didn't want to be noticed. It has been known to bring happy dreams, and also to ease the process of change. With that said, opals are extremely sensitive and must be treated with great care. They may change color with high energy/intensity people. They easily diversify and scatter energy.

Pearl: The Sea's Gift of Beauty

In tune with emotions, water, and women, especially pregnant women, pearls are a symbol of pure heart and mind; innocence and faith. Because it is from the sea, it has watery and lunar connections, therefore it is used for balancing emotions, especially for water signs. Absorbing by nature, this mineral takes in thoughts and feelings. Remember, pearl is the result of layer upon layer of substance produced to combat irritation. Pearls can cool and soothe anger. They are very nurturing.

If using pearls in conjunction with other gemstones, consider diamonds (to amplify and purify), or emeralds (to bring negative energy out) to amplify its energy. It has been recommended for occupations as varied as artists, chiropractors, and farmers. Pearl is a cold and independent mineral, which is used, ironically at the Heart, Solar Plexus, and Sacral Spleen Chakra, to stimulate the heart and emotional issues. Pearl powder is used for stabilizing and generating beautiful skin aqs well as, clearing toxins. Ancient divers wore pearls for shark protection. Pearl attunes to the astrology sign of Cancer and is one of the 9 sacred Vedic stones associated with the moon.

"The sea, once it casts its spell, holds one in its net of wonder forever." ~
Jacques Yves Cousteau

Top 10 Crystals for Summer

This season is full of action and activity. Summer is a joyful time of sun, surf, and sand. It brings out in us adventure and desire to be the most engaged with life. Summer keeps us on the go. Crystals echo the colors and energy of the season. You will find some of the best gems for passion, relating, and honoring who you are. Heartfelt and connecting, these gems offer the insight and playfulness that is appropriate for this time of year.

Summer is my favorite season! Born on the solstice, the Gemini in me is attracted to everything and anything that I find curious, communicative, and intriguing. Crystals draw me in and introduce an entire world of mystery and joy. My favorite crystals for summer have several connections. The element associated with summer is fire and the associated color, red. These crystal's energies are fiery, passionate, and spark the Kundalini energy into motion. The other theme, synergistic to these crystals, are pink and green stones relating to the Heart Chakra. This Heart is most associated with summer in the Chinese medicine paradigm. Lastly, some of my favorite stones of the sea are sprinkled in to honor my love for the beach and ocean.

Fire Agate: Most often found in North America, this stone comes in shades of orange, brown, blue, or green. It has a strong connection to the energies of earth and fire. Excellent stone to use when meditating. Induces a feeling of relaxation. Helps you examine and deal with problems in a calm and safe manner. They help take the edge off difficult experiences. Recommended for dentists, optometrists, and those in the healing profession.

Aquamarine: This stone has the calming, soothing energy of the sea. This is the stone of courage. It is tranquilizing, uplifting, encourages innocence, lightheartedness, and creativity. Use it for communication, self-awareness, confidence, and purpose. The Throat Chakra, Sacral Spleen Chakra, and Heart Chakra are where this stone is most helpful. History has used it for protection on journeys, especially those who travel on water. Helps stabilize and harmonize unsettled surroundings. Helps reduce fears. Excellent stone for meditation. Helps one attune to nature. Quiets the mind and reduces stress. Helps bring about a tolerance toward others. Clears blocked communication and assist the user in verbal expression. This stone allows us to find our individuality and be ourselves.

Chrysoprase: This stone allows greater flexibility, wisdom, generosity, and self-confidence. Place over the heart, neck, or brow for meditation. This stone uplifts the Heart Chakra. It soothes the energy of the heart when you are heart heavy. It, therefore, brings internal peace, harmony, and contentment. This stone symbolizes clarity of thought. It soothes the central nervous system and creates calm. It is a stone that leads its user to new and intellectual approaches. Helps one achieve greater personal insight and lessens our egotistical behavior. Stimulates creativity and draws out unknown talents.

Garnet: This stone symbolizes faith, love, devotion and trust. Garnet is most famous for balancing our emotional states. Therefore, garnet is one of the best stones for soothing emotional stress and balancing out anger that is held in and not expressed. Garnet is good for those who have anger issues directed to themselves, NOT for those who expel anger outwardly! Garnet is a stone of passion. It is given as a gift of love's attraction, a gift of estranged love, or a gift for a loved one's quick return. The birthstone of January, it represents love and helps the user to strive for improvement in moral conduct.

Ocean Jasper: Ocean Jasper is produced from only one mine near Marovato, Madagascar. The deposit, is located at the edge of the ocean, can only be seen and collected at low tide. Technically considered "Orbicular Jasper" in reference to its colorful orbs, some have adopted the name "Moon Jewel Jasper." But "Ocean Jasper" seems most fitting, as it was found right along the shore. This stone helps one to accept responsibilities, develop patience and help with circular breathing during meditation.

Peridot: This stone is traditionally used for health, wealth, and protection. Helps understand relationships and other realities. Alleviates anger, fear, jealousy, and anxiety. A "visionary stone", it helps connect us to our destinies and to an understanding of the purpose of existence. It can help us visualize not only the ultimate peak of physicality but of spiritual continuation, as well. The greener the stone, the more useful it is at the Heart Chakra, to clear a pathway, strengthening the breath of life, and the ideals of prosperity, growth, and openness.

Rhodochrosite: Gentle and yet probably the most vibrant loving stone to heal the Heart Chakra. It is especially for giving/receiving love. Rhodochrosite is the "stone of love and balance". Also, for loneliness, loss, heartache, fear, insecurities, and inner-child issues. Helps self-forgiveness, trust issues, spirituality and self-love. It is used in times of transition by providing comfort and support. It will enhance the dream state.

Rhodonite: This stone symbolizes "self-realization." Rhodonite works with the Heart Chakra by soothing the heart center, as well as, the Root Chakra for grounding and balancing, due to the presence of black oxides in this stone. This balance of colors allows for a powerful vibration of caring for one's self. Helps us express confidence and love on a physical plane in day-to-day ways. Calms and feeds the soul through the heart; with love and service. It helps us with confusion and allows us to focus. This stone helps to strengthen mantras, chanting, affirmations, singing and toning.

Rose Quartz: This stone represents love, beauty, peacefulness, forgiveness, love, self-love, and emotional balance. Rose Quartz works with the Heart Chakra. It is a soft, gentle, soothing stone that warms the heart center. Its value as a nurturing friend cannot be overstated and neither can its soothing influence. Helps diffuse negative stimuli and uncomfortable memories. Helps us discover the ability to love ourselves and makes us more open to other people. It is of particular value in helping us to forgive ourselves, hastening self-acceptance.

Ruby: Famous stone worn for wealth, joy, love, sexual energy, and power. This July birthstone warms and energizes. Strengthens physical and emotional Heart Chakra issues pertaining to love, courage, confidence, vitality, stamina, strength, leadership, and success over challenges. Intensifies all emotions (passion, jealousy, impatience, love...)   A wonderful stone whose stimulating energy can bring startling things to light.

Food for Thought: Eating for Summer

When eating along with the seasons, there are two elements that should be taken into account. The "nature" of the food and the "flavor" of the food. The nature of the food refers to the food's innate temperature ie: cold, hot, warm, cool or neutral. According to Chinese Medicine, eating a moderate amount of all flavors including sweet, salty, pungent, bitter and sour, can help to keep your body balanced and regulated.

Summer is actually divided into two categories. The first category is the early part of the summer, which is the transition from Spring to the Summer Solstice. The second category is classified as Late Summer. This is when summer wanes into the real "dog days" or the hottest days of the season.

In general, eating light and easily digestible foods are most important. Fruits and vegetables are at their greatest peak, giving us an abundance of choices for eating the right way.

It is particularly important to avoid overeating, especially as the summer moves on. Therefore, heavy, greasy fried foods should be avoided as they tax the heart, small intestines, stomach, and spleen. Foods that are cooling in nature are what the body craves.

Although the temptation for ice cold drinks, ice cream, and other frozen treats seem to be appropriate, moderation is very important. Eating too much cold or raw foods can injure the spleen and stomach, cause headaches, upsetting digestion. and slow metabolism.

In Chinese Medicine, a bitter taste is attributed to the heart and small intestine while sweet taste attunes to the spleen and stomach. Therefore, adding some bitter foods in your diet during early summer and more sweet tasting foods in late summer, can improve the body's function.

Consider watermelons, honeydew, and cantaloupe. These fruits, in particular, have a tendency to clear summer heat, cool inflammation, and benefit the stomach.

Juice therapy is a great way to take advantage of seasonal fruits and vegetables and helps your daily nutrition. You might also consider drinking mint, chamomile, and chrysanthemum teas.

Food as Medicine

Written in 203 AD, the *Taisho Tripitaka* contains a Buddhist sutra called *"The Sutra Containing Pronouncements of Buddha on Buddhist Medicine"* (adapted from Paul Unschuld's "Medicine in China: A History of Ideas")

Buddha says: *"There are nine causes for the premature, unexpected end to human life."* The first five of these are related to how we choose to eat and are listed here. The others are related to proper conduct:

1. It is not recommended eating foods which are out of season or improper for you as an individual.

2. It is not necessary to eat beyond your comfort zone or more than you should.

3. You should avoid eating at inappropriate times (other than breakfast, lunch, dinner) and eating a large number of foods your body is not yet used to consuming.

4. It is not advised to eat again before you have finished digesting your previous meal, as well as eating when you are not hungry.

5. It is not advised to suppress elimination and defecation.

Consider eating these foods for Summer:

1. Foods for summer are cool or cold in temperature and should be eaten in moderate amounts. Foods that are more cooling in nature are bamboo shoot, banana, bitter gourd, clams, crab, grapefruit, lettuce, persimmon, salt, seaweed, star fruit, sugar cane, water chestnut, watermelon, lotus root, cucumber, barley, bean curd, chicken egg whites, marjoram, oysters, pear, peppermint, radish, strawberry, tangerine, yogurt, broccoli, cauliflower, zucchini, corn, tomatoes, pineapple, turmeric.

2. Grilling is a big part of summer eating yet, grilling often dries out the natural juices in food. If you grilled or fry meats in summer, serve them with cooling, moisturizing fruits and vegetables such as cucumber, kiwi, mango, papaya, pineapple, squash, and tomatoes. These fruits and vegetables can be lightly grilled or marinated in a side salad or side dish as they complement the drying effects of grilled meats.

3. Keep food out of the sun. Direct sunlight causes the immediate loss of vital essences or vitamins and can spoil food. Consider keeping foods refrigerated until they are ready to be served, especially foods containing mayonnaise, oils, vinegar, or sauces.

4. Enjoy vegetables such as bamboo, sprouts, bok choy, broccoli, Chinese cabbage, corn, cucumbers, mushrooms, snow peas, spinach, summer squash, water crest, seaweeds, potatoes, and mung beans.

5. Eat spices, condiments, olive oil and herbs such as cilantro, mint and dill.

Essential Oils for Summer

Summer is a time of full growth. Life is at its greatest potential in the summer. Trees, plants, grasses, and seeds are now at their full peak, offering up the "fruits of their labor." Take a minute to enjoy this most "Yang time of energy" and production. These essential oils are great for your first aid kit, as insect repellent, for soothing sunburn, along with re-freshening and cleansing. Enjoy these soothing scents for relaxing and letting go.

Bergamot: (Citrus bergamia) bergamot orange is a hybrid of lemon and bitter orange. This sunny and beautiful oil captures a sun-drenched orchard on a southern Italian coast. This oil lifts your spirits and helps us communicate better, by nature of its color and fragrance. Do not apply to the skin before going out into the sun for it can increase the susceptibility of the skin to severe burning (photo toxic/sensitivity)

Chamomile: (Chamaemelum nobile) is the common name for several daisy-like plants of the family Asteraceae. Two of the species are commonly used to make herb infusions thought to have medicinal uses. The word "chamomile" derives, from French and Latin, meaning "earth apple", or from "on the ground". This oil is often applied to the pulse points of the wrist, neck, and tops of feet to help with anxiety, stress, and insomnia. Best for external inflammation, teething, nervousness, irritability, depression, burns, sunburn, asthma, hay fever, sprains, strains, nausea, and fever. Avoid during the first trimester of pregnancy.

Citronella: (Cymbopogon) Citronella oil is an essential oil obtained from the leaves and stems of different species of lemongrass. The oil is used extensively as a source of perfumery in soap, candles and incense, cosmetics and flavoring. Citronella is also a plant-based insect repellent and has been registered for this use in the United States since 1948. "The United States Environmental Protection Agency considers oil of citronella as a bio-pesticide with a non-toxic mode of action." Citronella oil has strong antifungal properties and is effective in calming barking dogs. Works as a germ killer

Eucalyptus: (Eucalyptus globulus) is the principal source of eucalyptus oil. Eucalyptus oil is steam distilled from the leaves and can be used as an antiseptic, for deodorizing, and in small quantities for food supplements, especially sweets, cough drops, toothpaste and decongestants. It has insect repellent properties and is an active ingredient in some commercial mosquito repellents. Eucalyptus is also used to help with muscle aches and pains. Avoid if you have high blood pressure or epilepsy.

Grapefruit: (Citrus paradisi) is a subtropical citrus tree known for its sour to semi-sweet, somewhat bitter fruit. Grapefruit is a hybrid between sweet orange (C. sinensis) and pomelo or shaddock (C. maxima). When found, it was named the "forbidden fruit"; and frequently, it has been misidentified with the pomelo. The grapefruit's name alludes to clusters of the fruit on the tree, which often appear similar to that of grapes. This invigorating oil is known for its uplifting and stimulating, crisp citrus scent. A great oil for treating anxiety and depression, easing stress. Do not apply to the skin before going out into the sun for it can increase the susceptibility of the skin to severe burning (photo toxic/sensitivity)

Lavender: (Lavender cassia) is one of the most accepted and most notable essential oils in the Materia Aromatica. This flower oil is used as an antiseptic, antibiotic, anti-depressant, and immune stimulant. It helps with issues of sleep or anxiety due to its sedative properties. Best known for treating burns and blisters, wounds (cell regenerator, minimizes swelling and scarring) insect bites. Stings, and heat exhaustion. Avoid during the first trimester of pregnancy.

Lemon: (Citrus limon) is a refreshing, stimulating, uplifting essential oil. Lemon essential oil enhances the immune system by boosting white blood cells. It is best for fighting infection, cools fever, stops bleeding, tightens and tones tissue, while softening and soothing skin It has been used for centuries to lower both blood sugar and blood pressure. Do not apply to the skin before going out into the sun for it can increase the susceptibility of the skin to severe burning (photo-sensitivity).

Orange: (Citrus sinensis) is a warm, fresh, citrusy, sweet essential oil. It has been used to stimulate lymphatic circulation and improve immunity, helps fight infection, reduces inflammation, relieves muscle spasm, and eases digestive disorders. This bright and sunny oil helps lift depression. Do not apply to the skin before going out into the sun for it can increase the susceptibility of the skin to severe burning (photo-sensitivity).

Peppermint: (Mentha piperita) is a crisp, cooling, and soothing essential oil. It can be used to massage over the stomach and chest to soothe indigestion, flatulence, flu, colds, coughs and cool fever. Massage on the

179

head and neck for headaches and migraines. Massage over the gums with clove oil to soothe toothache (do not swallow), Inhale to open congested sinuses. May irritate sensitive skin and mucous membranes of the nose. Avoid during pregnancy and while nursing. Do not combine with homeopathic remedies as mint will de-sensitize the remedy as an antidote.

Rosemary: (Rosmarinus officinalis) is a pungent, woody evergreen essential oil. Its name means "dew of the sea". Rosemary was considered sacred to ancient Egyptians, Romans, and Greeks. A bride would wear a rosemary headpiece and the groom would wear a sprig. Known also as an "herb of remembrance" during funerals. Mourners would wear rosemary as a lapel sprig and throw it into graves as a symbol of remembrance for the dead. Ancient myth also tells the story of the Virgin Mary, who was said to have spread her blue cloak over a white-blossomed rosemary bush when she was resting, and the flowers turned blue. Best for muscular aches and pains sprains, fatigue (mental and physical) relieving headaches, migraines, coughs, flu-like symptoms. This oil should not be used during pregnancy or with those with a history of epilepsy.

Tea Tree: (Melaleuca alternifolia) is a camphorous, pungent, woodsy scented essential oil and is considered a "first aid kit in a bottle." Its properties are antiseptic, antiviral, antibacterial, antibiotic, antifungal, insecticide and is one of the best wound healing oils. Has been used historically to fight infections, ringworm, athlete's foot, sunburn, irritation from shaving, bruises and cuts, warts, and acne. May irritate sensitive skin.

The Power of a Summer Garden

Gardens have been associated with our spirituality throughout history. From the Gardens of Eden and Gethsemani to the Gardens of Haifa and Earthly Delights, these sanctuaries have great healing and curative powers. I love being able to meditate in a summer garden. The air is clean, the scent of flowers drift by throughout the day, and offer up a visually breath-taking combination of colors. It is a wonderful way to connect with God.

For as long as I could remember, my mom and dad created beautiful gardens around our home each summer. I will never forget the unbridled pageantry and natural allure the gardens would offer. From every color in the rainbow to the creatures they would attract, it seems everyone is attracted to flowers and herbs growing in a garden.

From "secret gardens" and Japanese style gardens to floral, vegetable, and English gardens, the opportunity for creating a bed of flowers is endless. A garden is a sacred place. It is a place to contemplate, entertain, meditate, or simply to wander and enjoy its beauty.

Creating a garden is as easy as marking out the area for the plantings and bringing to it, all the items that make it your own.

Planting a garden for summer flowers should start around mid-April and no later than early May. Till and turn up the soil. To keep away such pests as snails and slugs, create a border with crushed egg shells or coarse sand around the perimeter of the soil.

Have a clear intention for your garden. Will your garden have a theme? Which plants and flowers will you add to it? What colors are you hoping to see? Will you add additional elements such as a bird house, crystals, garden objects? How will you place these elements in your garden?

You can grid your garden out, either in your head or on paper. Sketch out what you would like to see. Create borders, high and low points, areas with space around them so that larger flowers will have room to grow and spread out. Learn which two flowers look good together, which flowers will attract butterflies and where you will place a garden bench, fountain, or bird bath.

A tribute to the elements may be added to enhance the "flow of energy" by placing the appropriate color of plant, object or shape into your garden. In

Feng Shui, we balance the five elements of wood, fire, earth, metal, and water. Therefore, the water element may be assisted by adding a fountain in the north. Red flowers in the south would enhance the fire element, bringing more sun energy. A wind chime in the west and white flowers in the northwest would enhance the metal element. Tall, thin trees in the east and a wooden arbor in the southeast can be used to strengthen the wood element or growth. A stone sculpture as the centerpiece of the garden with yellow flowers in the northeast and decorative rocks in the southwest would add a balancing touch.

Like any spiritual practice, once your garden is planted, you must nurture it every day. As the flowers grow tall, you can stake them so that they won't fall over. Pull the weeds and water the soil. The more you nurture something, the better the possibilities of it rendering you all the love and joy right back. Your spiritual practice will benefit in the same way.

Your garden will grow and offer you a beautiful respite from your day. It will give you bouquets of flowers or handfuls of vegetables. It will bring you to a place of love and tranquility. Your garden will offer you sensory experiences from the birds, colors, and smells it brings to you. It will give you a place to meditate.

Bring yourself to your garden with the intention of finding peace and solitude.

Sit in front of your garden. Cross your legs in a comfortable position and close your eyes. Take several deep breaths in and slowly out through your nose. Take your time and simply visualize your perfect surroundings. What feels "right" to you? At some point, listen to the sounds around you. Breathe in the aroma about you.

Allow your intuition to guide you. Give yourself time without distraction or urgency.

Open your eyes when ready and admire the garden before you!

Gemstone:
The Morning Glories (for mom)

"When the morning dew is nipped by the sunshine,
as it rises over hill and dale...
You will hear the lovely buzz of the garden,
as the nuances prevail.

There are lovely blooming roses and the scent of sweet
perfume, you can feel begonias smiling, as the birds all chirp
in tune.

You will sense the peonies as they burst forth,
in each color, as they tell their tale.
You will know the wind is gently blowing,
as the daisies they regale.

They have stories they must tell you, as the bees ring in their
ear, and the pansies they must wake up, as the butterflies
come near.

The entire garden stirs as the sun roams,
past the turning point of now, high noon,
While the caterpillars crawl and the weeds grow,
all the crickets are in tune.

So the flowers they look up toward the noon sky,
as they hope for just a kiss of rain.
But it looks like they will have to wait, still,
for another passing day.

Now the twilight grows and makes long shadows,
as it passes by the flower beds...
And the occupants are all a-yawning,
so it's time to bow their heads.

They will fall asleep and dream of a new day,
when it comes to bring them all great news...
Of the stirring of the dew and sunlight,
as once again day passes through".

~ Andrew Pacholyk MS L.Ac

Cycle Celebrations

The celebration of the seasons and the passing of time have been honored since the beginning of time. Before there was a monotheistic religion or the worshipping of one God in our culture, there was polytheistic or the worshipping of nature and many gods.

The process of claiming and adopting styles, religious beliefs, and rituals have been repeated over and over again throughout time. Like the cultures before them and every culture after, our celebrations of life and the seasons have evolved over centuries with a history and folklore rich in myth, mystery, and magic!

Beltane

Celebrated all over the world and in different cultures including Roodmas (Old English) May Day (British, Welsh, Celtic, German, Irish), Beltain, (Gaelic), Feast of the Cross (Christian), Rite of the Catholic Church (Gallican) commemorating the finding by Saint Helena of the True Cross in Jerusalem in 355. First day of summer (Ireland), Festival of Flora, the Roman Goddess of Flowers (Rome), the Walpurgis Night Celebrations (Germanic).

The Celtic beginnings of Summer, May Day is the celebration of life, procreation, and the start of the "light days" of the year. Half way between the Spring Equinox and the Summer Solstice, this time of fun, frolicking, and dancing are done to honor the blessing of nature including the gift of love and fertility, cleansing and purity, and the return of the Earth's abundance.

Throughout history, the "mating" of Mother Earth and Father Sun or the god and goddess of fertility is an important time to impregnate the earth with life by planting seeds and nourishing the beginning of this fertile season.

The Beltane Fire is symbolic of light returning and days lengthening. The lighting of bonfires is a ritual done in order to sanctify, purify, and cleanse the body and soul of old habits and negativity.

The phallic Maypole, was an ancient tradition of dancing clockwise (sunwise or disoleil) around a large tree or brightly decorated pole with ribbons and flowers. On Beltane eve, the Celts believed it was the fairies who were returning from their winter respite in time for summer.

When: The eve of May 1st
Season: Cross Quarter: (Mid-way point between Spring and Midsummer)
Represents: Fire Festival, Bonfires, Maypole Dancing, Union
Virtues: Sex, Union
Symbols: Maypole, Fire, Flowers, Mirrors, Priapic Wand
Gemstone: Abalone Shell, Angel Aura, Chalcopyrite, Fluorite, Labradorite, Rainbow Moonstone, Rainbow Obsidian, Peacock Ore. Titanium Quartz, Tourmaline
Color: Green, Pink, Violet, Yellow
Essential Oils: Eucalyptus, Lavender, Rose, Sandalwood
Remedies: Bee Pollen, Bilberry, Blessed Thistle, Burdock Root, Calendula Flower, Catnip, Chamomile, Chaste Tree Berry, Cramp Bark, Dandelion, Eye Bright, Hydrangea Root, Milk Thistle Seed, Mullein Leaf, Nettle Leaf, Passion Flower, Wild Cherry Bark
Flowers: Lilac, Lily of the Valley, Peony, Agapanthus, Amaryllis, Anemone, Calla lily, Cherry Blossom, Corn Flower, Dahlia and Hyacinth.
Element: Fire
Direction: Southeast
Life Event: Creativity, Consummation
Lunar: Moon of Winds or Full Worm Moon
Body Healing: Sacred Sexual Secrets
Mind Healing: The Power of Love
Spirit Healing: Sacred Spirit

<u>Gemstone:</u>
Sacred Spirit: Beltane Blessing

"O fire clear this way to hope,
and purify my spirit whole,
to bring me to a place I see
a deeper, loving part of me.
So I can share myself with you
and not get lost in tales untrue
that I become that better half
for you to sing and dance and
laugh."

~ Andrew Pacholyk MS L.Ac

Beltane Oil Perfume Recipe

In a two-ounce, dark bottle, combine essential oils of romantic rose absolut, pungent patchouli, and sexy sandalwood. Add small pieces of red garnet and rainbow moonstone crystals. Add pieces of passion flower, wild cherry bark, lily flower, or rose petals.

Allow this combination to ruminate for 2 evenings.

Use this sexy oil for enticing and "that come hither" feeling. It is great for bathing, anointing candles, crystals or other metaphysical tools. Blend with other oils to encourage their properties. Bless your body or sacred space by massaging a few drops where needed. Freshen up potpourri or seasonal decor by adding a few drops to a spray bottle full of water and spritzing anywhere to invite tantric energy, romantic arousal, or the bonding of emotions.

Litha

This is the Summer Solstice or Midsummer, celebrated on June 20th or 21st. It is the summer solstice at its peak. Symbolically, this day represents solar power and strength and is celebrated when the sun reaches its zenith. The summer solstice is celebrated all over the world.

Historically, it is the time to celebrate the Greek and Roman Sun God at his highest point. This is the longest day of the year when light and life are most abundant. In *Shakespeare's Mid Summer's Night Dream*, on this night's eve, it was believed the "faery folk" were most active and visible by their actions.

As the solstice sun rises on its day of greatest power, it kisses the landscape, drawing up with it, the power of nature and its most fruitful benefits. In his book, *The White Goddess*, the author Robert Graves proposed that the mythological figure of the Holly King, represents one half of the year, while the other half is personified by his counterpart and adversary the Oak King:

The two battled endlessly as the season turns. At Midsummer, the Oak King is at the height of his strength, while the Holly King is at his weakest. The Oak King continues the reign of his power and at the Autumn Equinox, the tables finally turn in the Holly King's favor, as his strength peaks at Midwinter.

The author, Graves identified a number of paired hero-figures which he believes are variants of this myth, including Lleu Llaw Gyffes and Gronw Pebr, Gwyn and Gwythr, Lugh and Balor, Balan and Balin, Gawain and the Green Knight, the robin and the wren, and even Jesus and John the Baptist.

When: June 20th or June 21st
Season: Summer Solstice
Represents: Peak of Power, Fire, Full Potential, Culmination
Virtues: Self Power
Symbols: Flowers, Fairies, Fire, Sun, Wheel
Gemstone: Fairy (Crackle Quartz) Carnelian Chalcopyrite, Fluorite Labradorite, Moonstone, Rainbow Obsidian, Sunstone
Color: Green, Orange, Yellow
Essential Oils: Chamomile, Clary Sage, Cypress, Geranium, Grapefruit, Lemon, Orange, Peppermint, Rosemary, Tea Tree, Thyme

Remedies: Bee Pollen, Bilberry, Calendula Flower, Burdock Root, Calendula Flower, Catnip, Chamomile, Chamomile Flower, Eye Bright, Echinacea Purpurea, Elder Flower, False Unicorn Root, Fennel Seed, Fenugreek Seed, Goldenseal, Lemon Balm. Oatstraw, Red Raspberry Leaf, White Willow Bark

Flowers: Black-Eyed Susan, Butterfly Bush, Coneflower, Garden Phlox, Lavender, Moonbeam Coreopsis, Russian Sage, Salvia, Shasta Daisy, Speedwell, Stella de Oro, Yarrow

Element: Fire

Direction: South

Life Event: Self-Empowerment, Strength

Lunar: Moon of Horses or Strawberry Moon

Body Healing: Physical Activity

Mind Healing: The Power of Happiness

Spirit Healing: Sacred Spirit

Solstice Rituals

* Bathe in the light of the sun ~ Visit a beach, pool, or park and bathe in the light of the sun for 15-20 minutes. The perfect amount of time to get your vitamin D and enjoy the power of the warmth and joy the sun offers.

* Get crafty ~ Making a flower crown on the summer solstice is a traditional way to celebrate. Wined the stems of flowers around a crown of wire. Intertwine the stems and line the flower heads up along the outside of the wire crown. Try using flowers with a variety of colors and textures.

* Make a solstice lantern. With a mason jar, glue or tape a variety of color strips of tissue paper, (or just use yellow) around the outside of the jar. Place a candle inside and light it when you are ready.

Gemstone:
Sacred Spirit: Litha Blessing

"O brightest day of Litha's light,
I come to honor in circle, bright
With light of new beginnings grow,
and sunlight during summer's glow
With midday-summer passing by
Till fall and winter time, anigh
I honor light by candle's flame,
To praise each day in summer's name
To rise as sunlight does each day,
And offer joy on journey's way"

~ Andrew Pacholyk MS L.Ac

Season of the Sun: Sunset

The sun is symbolically found in all cultures and religions throughout history.

The sun represents the high noon of Summer, the end of the sun's reign over the light half of the year.

It represents the cardinal direction of South. The South represents our greatest expansion yet. It is an alignment with love, a connection to our "emotional wisdom," a greater ability to trust, a stronger yearning for faith, and a time of much more empathy towards others.

This is a peaking of ourselves. The grand awakening with an ability to look back in wonder and look forward to more possibilities, yet with boundaries more defined.

*"High noon ablaze with
powerful sun,
You show us full fruition done,
With elements of fire a top,
You show us how you never
stop."*

~Andrew Pacholyk MS L.Ac

Soul Satisfying Journey: Sensational Sunsets

You can certainly call me a sun worshiper. Being born on the Summer Solstice, I have always been attracted to the warmth, power and glow of the sun! I have listed a few of my favorite experiences with the "setting sun."

In my travels, I tend to be an observer. These particular instances occurred on my first trip to the Tucson Gem and Mineral show in Arizona, my visit to the island of Santorini, and my subsequent return to Los Angeles for a visit, after living and working there as a dancer and choreographer.

This was a sacred journey, which focused on sunsets. Before my first twilight in Arizona, I had spent the day gathering crystals at the Tucson Gem and Mineral Show. My friends and I wanted to create a large circle for a desert meditation at sunset. My mentor and friend, Zachary Selig invited several of his friends he knew from years past, to participate in this meditation circle. We traveled West to a wonderful energy vortex about 15 minutes outside of town. We set up a healing mandala of quartz points in a large healing circle. We laid out four selenite wands, one for each direction.

In between the four directions of south, east, west, and north, we laid tumbled stones out to represent each element. Angelite for air, carnelian for fire, black tourmaline for earth, and aqua aura for water. An inner circle was then created with spheres of septarian, rose quartz, and golden calcite, topped with Atlantean pyramids we gathered from the crystal show.

The eight of us then sat within the inner circle holding rare pieces of Tibetan Quartz. This type of quartz is considered a "teacher of humanity." Based on Tibetan beliefs, these stones have been used to promote contact with the ancient cultures of the East, bringing knowledge concerning healing and spirituality to its user.

This was a silent, sunset meditation done within the crystal mandala circle as the Arizona sunset painted a picture across the desert floor. This sunset was a staggering burst of fire that flared up over the mountains. As the sun set, the play of light and shadow stretched across the desert floor, kissing the cactus as it began its introduction to the night. From the desert floor, the darker hues of the Chakra rainbow offered its cooling colors such as deep blue, intriguing indigo, and vibrant violet washing over us as we ended the meditation.

The next sunset was probably the most beautiful exhibition of light and color I have ever seen in my life. We were leaving Tucson, flying at about 17,000 feet. We were eye level with the mountains as the sun seemed to make a commanding, silent gesture that got everyone's attention. I was sitting on the side of the plane that was facing west. The sky looked as if it was ablaze with fire, seeming to come from the mountains. As the sun gave its last peek over the ridge, the real show started. Large swatches of red-orange color splashed over green blue skies as yellow then merged with a deeper blue indigo over the mountain tops. As the sun was completely out of sight now, the violet flame washed over the other rainbow colors creating a color palette I have never seen in the skies before! I could hear someone on the plane say, "the Arizona sunset… the most amazing spectacle in the world!" I had to agree.

Santorini is famous for its sunsets. I was inspired by this beautiful island in the southern Aegean Sea. I have created breathtaking memories from my precious moments spent in the azure waters and multi-colored beaches. Famous for its white buildings and churches and some of the most eye-popping sunsets in the world, Santorini is a shining jewel in the Crown of the Greek Islands.

Santorini is essentially what remains after an enormous volcanic eruption destroyed the earliest single island and created the current geological caldera. Due to even more recent evidence, the island's pre-eruption shape and landscape frescoes located under the ash, both strongly resemble Plato's description of the lost city of Atlantis.

A giant central, rectangular lagoon is surrounded by high, steep cliffs on three sides. It was from here, that I witnessed the sun relinquishing its reign, as it spilled into the cooling sea. As if it were exploding as it passed beyond the horizon, bright red and orange streaks pined upward as cooling indigo and violet rays washed across the apparent waterline. It was a spectacular site and lived up to its infamous reputation. No matter what the appeal, this island embraces the magic and color of an endless summer.

Back in Los Angeles, my final sunset of the trip came at the top of Sunset Blvd. I was in a yoga class and the large windows of the studio faced west. The sun began setting over the Hollywood Hills as we did our final namaste and meditation. I was flooded with memories of my previous life and career as a choreographer here.

The setting sun brought back the good experiences Los Angeles offered me in the early 90's and as the sunlight diminished over the hills and the city lights started popping on like popcorn from the flickering flames, I just remembered feeling forever grateful for all that had been offered me.

"Each day is born with a sunrise and ends in a sunset, the same way we open our eyes to see the light and close them to hear the dark. You have no control over how your story begins or ends. But by now, you should know that all things have an ending. Every spark returns to darkness. Every sound returns to silence. And every flower returns to sleep with the earth. The journey of the sun and moon is predictable. But yours, is your ultimate ART."

~ Suzy Kassem

Chapter 7

Fall

By the season of Fall, our lives have "turned a corner." It is our third quadrant of development from our 50's through our 60's. This period in our lives represents an awareness of how life is perceived. The "new" ideas that come around now, tend to be seen through jaded eyes, as by now, we feel as if we have seen and done it all. Our caution comes as we seem to question more and take other things for granted much less.

Fall also represents a new-found knowledge of prosperity. It is often the time in our lives when we actually understand the basis of prosperity, not just being money or fame, but flourishing and thriving in our productive years. This suggests that "sensing" actually means the use of our perception in a much keener approach. We tend to be more observant and are more conscious of our intuition or 6th sense.

Fall is the raw, unprocessed information we take in and discern more directly and with immediate consciousness. We no longer take things for granted as we look for much deeper connections. We are more discerning in our relationships and have a better grasp at the art of sensuality.

In this season of our lives, we tend to switch to more left brain thinking or perform tasks that have to do with logic, such as making better informed decisions, comprehending our surroundings faster, and seeing further ahead into our thoughts. These are steps out of the peak of our enthusiasm and into our waking consciousness. This is now the exact opposite of our "Spring."

Fantastical Fall is the approach of our Autumn shadows. Shadows we start to see and feel, yet we simply push away or choose to ignore. These are shadows of darkness, aging, loss, and death.

Fall represents a time of gathering. As an expression in nature, this is the time when crops are harvested. Leaves are changing to brilliant colors as they mimic the change in us. Gathering and elimination are the traits of this season and can be seen in nature, as well as human health.

This is a good time of year to be more conscious about and take care of the lungs, large intestine, and our skin, by nurturing them well. The change in weather affects our respiratory and immune system, so it is a good time to build up our defenses. Sometimes, we feel "stuck" in Fall, both emotionally and physically. Eating a diet with more fiber can help the large intestine to better move things along, while our mind must be clear and focused in order to process the emotional changes of the season. Our skin is our first line of defense, so keeping it moisturized and supple will both protect it and allow for a smoother transition during a time of colder more harsh weather ahead.

Gemstone:
Approach to Fall

~ O harvest mother, bring us near,
a place of love when Fall is here.
To bless and honor hearth and home,
when chill comes round and changes
so...

~ Andrew Pacholyk MS. L.Ac.

The Priorities of Life

In each aspect of our lives, there are certain "priorities" we find important and tend to focus more on. This is often based on our age or need to fit in, our self-discovery or need to be recognized. Our priorities of life are the cornerstones we use to define ourselves, better understand who we are, or are sometimes forced to recognize out of circumstance.

Our "Fall" priorities are focused more on the spiritual approach to life and how we can understand it. It is part intuition, part conscious thought. It is believing more in the metaphysical than the physical. It is taking in the better understanding of divination and intuition, the strength of forgiveness and the gathering of knowledge through journeys and therefore, enhancing our prosperity.

Divination

Traditionally, metaphysics refers to the branch of philosophy that attempts to understand the fundamental nature of all reality, whether visible or invisible. It seeks a description so basic, so essentially simple, so all-inclusive that it applies to everything, whether divine or human. It attempts to interpret what something must be like, in order to BE at all.

As far back as biblical times, divination was considered the art or practice that would seek to foresee or foretell future events. Discoveries of hidden knowledge, usually by the interpretation of omens, dreams, or by the assistance of supernatural powers, was how the divine intervention was perceived. Today, the idea is not so different.

Gemstone:
A Divine-nation

"O rhythm come, let nature flow,
of sacred balance ~ to and fro
I seek to know the truth, betold,
by sensing all to which unfolds,
before me ~ watching, hearing too,
the telltale signs that give us clues."

~ Andrew Pacholyk MS L.Ac

Divination is considered unusual insight or intuitive perception. As intuitive beings, we often tend to let go of or lose sight of this ability as we age. Children are extremely intuitive and utilize this ability daily. As we grow older, it seems that we tend not to trust these feelings, images, or concepts from our mind's eye. They almost seem odd, irrational or just something that is hard to believe. So, now is the time to "reconnect" with your child-like wonder and start re-examining your trust in that "gut feeling" or intuition. It is time to pay attention to the synchronicity that shows itself to you.

Divination is the attempt to gain insight into a question or situation by way of inner knowledge or insight.

Divination itself can take various forms, including:

1. The direct observation of events, which may or may not have occurred yet.

2. The interpretation of patterns formed by objects or on surfaces or symbols that come our way.

3. The selection of objects with meanings assigned to them by some form of random process.

While divination is often a structured and methodical procedure it is never a purely rational one, for it depends on the awakening of (latent) psychic abilities or your simple insight.

Game Playing or Role Playing

Game playing or role playing is a great way to get back into discovering your divinity and trust in your intuition. I remember studying acting with Uta Hagen, at HB Studios in Greenwich Village, in the early 1980's. Ms. Hagen was famous for her "object exercises." As an actor, it was our job to explore all aspects of who we are.

Each week, based on a particular reading or character study, we would have to decide on a moment in our daily lives when we could apply these principles discussed in a particular reading. Specifically, we would need to think of something where we were able to answer the following questions:

1. Who am I?

2. What time is it?

3. Where am I?

4. What surrounds me?

5. What are the given circumstances?

6. What is my relationship?

7. What do I want?

8. What's in my way?

9. What do I do to get what I want?

Although, it is not the throwing of dice or reading of cards, it is the raw unveiling of the "leaves of the lotus" to reach our inner core. As actors, we tend to seek the person within our central core. We lure that person out by role playing, word associations, or exercises which cause us to dig deeper into our untamed spirit.

When you get to know more about yourself, you also get to look at different archetypes of people around you. Learning more about the categories we fall into, paints a better picture of understanding of who we are and how we think.

Most people are afraid of divination. I think because they equate it with the occult or searching into information that seems random but yet is tied to who we are and where we are headed.

This brings me back to the rituals of game playing and role playing. Even the word, "ritual", some people shy away from, because they tend to think it is Satanic or conjures up images of evil, like we see in the movies. This cannot be further from the truth. Of course, there are all kinds of ritualistic aspects from soup to nuts, but some of the greatest rituals we do every day, are done to improve our lives. In history, there are many examples of game playing rituals and here are a few:

The Medicine Wheel is a representation of all of creation and how it works within the seasons. This Native Indian tradition, shows the sun, moon, and earth in a circle called a medicine wheel. Each stone or color in the circle tells us a part of the story. The circle represents all of the cycles of nature, day and night, seasons, moons, life cycles, and the archetypes of mother, father, animal spirits, and more. This circle is just one example of how early man used this tool for divine right.

The Tarot are cards which, are filled with archetypal references. They are seemingly chosen at random to explain life's events and prophecies. What is more interesting about the Tarot, I found, is the knowledge that can be gained by the "characters" within each card. From Mother/Queen and Father/King personalities - to the young Fool or the Lovers, these cards are filled with people just like us, in different stages of our lives. They are based on archetypes. They really show us more about who we are and how we are

197

reflected within each personality - depending on the day, situation, age or circumstance. Since the beginning of time, archetypes have appeared in myths and stories all over the world. They are defined as symbolizing basic human drives, desires, motivations, and goals. These archetypes resonate with us, as they represent a group of personalities, including, the innocent, orphan, hero, caregiver, explorer, rebel, lover, male, female, creator, magician, healer, and death.

Dreams have been interpreted, identified, and debated for centuries. They are the quintessential (divine) tool, we all share. They are a window into our own subconscious mind. One of the great dream interpreters of our age, was Carl Jung, a Swiss psychologist. In the 1920s he made a connection through "synchronicity."

"Synchronicity is the simultaneous occurrence of events that appear significantly related but have no discernible, causal connection. Jung believed synchronicity to be a glimpse into the underlying order of the Universe." He coined the term "synchronicity" to describe what he called the "a-causal connecting principle" that links ritual, mind, and matter. He said this underlying connectedness manifests itself through dreams, flashbacks, and meaningful coincidences that cannot be explained by cause and effect. Such synchronicities occur, he theorized, when a strong need arises in the psyche of an individual.

He described these three "needs" that he had observed:

1. The coinciding of a thought or feeling with an outside event

2. A dream, vision, or premonition of something that then happens in the future.

3. A dream or vision that coincides with an event occurring at a distance.

No one has come up with a definition that has superseded his.

Divination, therefore, is a look at these signs, symbols, and coincidences that are all around us. It is simply up to us to pay attention.

Rituals: Taking Away the Taboo – The Empowerment of Everyday Magic

A ritual is a set of actions, performed for their symbolic value or to reach an outcome. Brushing your teeth or eating breakfast is a ritual. We do them every day. Some rituals are done monthly, like paying our bills or paying the rent. We do seasonal rituals like planting the garden, harvesting the fields, or once a year ritual like celebrating a birthday or a holiday.

Rituals give us the opportunity to start anew, refresh, and reboot our lives, our intentions, or goals. Rituals can be done with simple words (like a prayer or affirmation) while other rituals use tools such as incense, water, candles, or oils.

Since the start of the New Year, I have participated in several rituals that many people experience… the countdown to a New Year, the cleaning and sweeping of our home after the holidays, and the family ritual of lighting a candle on New Year's Day.

In year's past, I have always had the privilege of working with and studying herbs from Ecuadorian Shamans in the upcountry outside of Quito and valley of Vilcabamba. This past year I had the great honor of working with a spiritualist/psychic, Sylvia Mendez, who privileged me with a sacred "spiritual" cleansing, called "Levantamiento" (to wake or rise up). It is basically done with prayers, candles, meditation, and a cleansing bath with a special castile soap and a dowsing of a prepared herbal bath used for cleansing, clearing, and refreshing the mind/body/spirit. A baptism is another perfect example of a cleansing bath.

There are not necessarily any religious or denominational beliefs one needs to have to do a cleansing. I do feel that a belief in a higher or Universal power is important. To realize that we are not always in control of our lives, is a humbling and moving experience. I think your own belief system can make your rituals that more powerful.

The components of a ritual can be anything. For instance, the ritual of brushing your teeth, need only be the toothbrush, toothpaste, and some water. The process of that ritual, everyone knows. You set your intention: "I'm going to brush my teeth in order to have a clean mouth and avoid cavities." Maybe you wet the brush and add the paste. Brush up and down and all around. Maybe you brush your tongue. Rinse and finish. You may repeat this twice or three times a day. It is the same sequence of events for any ritual.

You gather your tools, prepare your intention, act upon the intention, and then you finish, allowing for your actions to take effect. Here are some examples of healing rituals you can do:

A ritual meditation or affirmation are several words or images that you can use to create a base for your ritual. A meditation or affirmation can be done once or several times a day. It implies a connection between your inner life and your mind's eye. Your inner life (or spiritual center) becomes in tune with your mind's eye (or focus and intention.)

A wonderful and powerful tool for creating self-love and confidence is to stand, facing yourself in the mirror. Repeat a positive affirmation "I will be filled with pride and confidence today." "I will remain at peace and calm all day." "I look handsome and confident." Whatever your words, the power of repeating your affirmations to yourself in the mirror (and throughout the day) is a ritual of self-empowerment.

A great meditation you can do at the beginning of the day and at the end of the day, can simply be sitting (grounded) on the floor and closing your eyes. Taking some very deep breaths in, so that each breath reaches all the way down to your pelvic bone and then exhale s-l-o-w-l-y each time. Choose an image, person, or scenario that empowers you. Always go back to it when you find your mind drifting. Take your focus to the back of your eyelids. Let whatever comes into your mind pass through, then let it go. When you are ready, move your focus to between your eyebrow, to your Third Eye. Sense it opening and filling your mind with your chosen image. Allow it to expand outside your head and fill the room. Your image is now, all around you. When you are ready, slowly bring the image back and contain it with your Third Eye again. Move your focus back to behind your eyelids. Then, when you are ready, slowly open your eyes.

A ritual bath is a "magical" ceremony involving the use of water to immerse or anoint a subject's body and/or feet. It prepares one to be more aware, conscious, and open for new opportunities. It can be used to cleanse the mind, the body, as well as embrace the spirit. Ritual baths can clear negative energies and prepare yourself for accomplishments. First, clean your bath tub. Run the warm/hot water. As you do this, add a cup of sea salt, perhaps a tablespoon of lavender, clary sage, or rose essential oils and as a final touch, a handful of flower petals. Swirl these ingredients around in the bath water and immerse yourself for 15-20 minutes. You can add some nice stress reducers, such as incense, low lighting, or candles and soothing music. Make this magic ritual "your time", as you deserve it!

A ritual tea or tea ceremony has been done for centuries to honor ancestors, embrace the change of seasons, or as a "time out" from the day. I always like using fresh or dried herbs sans the tea bag. One or two teaspoons of herbs per serving. Use clear spring water. Warm the steeping pot. Pour the measured, fresh water into a saucepan and place over medium heat. Heat the water until it just comes to a rolling boil. Add the tea leaves to the warmed steeping pot (one teaspoon per cup, plus one "for the pot.") Immediately pour the boiled water over the loose leaves; cover the pot. Steep three to five minutes for most teas. Longer, to taste. Also, be sure and steep the herbs longer for the teas made from sticks, twigs, roots, or berries.

A ritual with crystals is another way to relax and find stillness after your day. You can use 7 or 9 crystals and place them on the floor in a circle. Choosing the crystals that call to you that day are often the ones you need the most. You can choose crystals to use for your circle based on their colors, names, mineral make-up, or the power they give to your life. Lay down within the circle and close your eyes. Sense the ground beneath you accepting your weight. Feel your body relax with each breath as you allow yourself to melt into the floor. Sense the energy of the crystals as they have something to lend you which is their subtle energies for healing. After your session, you can carry one or a few of these crystals with you throughout the day or place them in a room where you need some energy. Your instincts will never fail you.

These are just a few rituals we can do in our lives in order to bring about, peace, confidence, and empowerment. I encourage you to get back in touch with your intuitive self, through games of self-awareness and divination.

Forgiveness

"Forgiveness is the healing of wounds caused by another." It is our choice to learn to let go of a past wrong and it is our choice to no longer allow ourselves to be hurt by it. Remove your ego from the equation. Now look at the situation. Does it appear differently? As it was so eloquently stated by *Henry Ward Beecher*, when someone says "I can forgive, but I cannot forget," it is only another way of saying, "I will not forgive."

Understanding how to forgive is a well learned lesson, which will only make you stronger. So why should we forgive?

"We must develop and maintain the capacity to forgive. He who is devoid of the power to forgive is devoid of the power to love. There is some good in the worst of us and some evil in the best of us. When we discover this, we are less prone to hate our enemies." ~ Martin Luther King, Jr.

Gemstone:
Forgiveness

*"I ask for clarity to see,
and bless those persecuting me.
Allow me to forgive myself,
for holding on, release the past,
So I can move on forward to
that which keeps me strong and
true."*

~ Andrew Pacholyk MS L.Ac

The need to understand the power and place of forgiveness is important in the healing process. It is urgent that we examine the steps that lead to justice and strengthen society. We need to understand how forgiveness improves the human condition. How do we choose to forgive? What are the effects of holding grudges and seeking revenge? We can find a way to balance our need for security with the potential for granting forgiveness.

Forgiveness offers the possibility of two types of peace: *peace of mind* -- the potential healing of old emotional wounds, and *peace with others* -- the possibility of new, more gratifying relationships in the future.

"The weak can never forgive. Forgiveness is the attribute of the strong." ~
Mahatma Gandhi

In his article, *"Forgiveness, What Its For?",* adapted from **Larry James's** books, he writes"

"Forgiveness works! It is often difficult, AND it works!

"We often think of forgiveness as something that someone who has done us wrong must ask of US. There is always another way of looking at something. My thoughts on forgiveness suggest that you focus on offering forgiveness TO the person who has wronged you. To not forgive them is like taking the poison (continuing to suffer for what they did or didn't do to you) and expecting THEM to die."

"Forgiveness is a gift you give to yourself. It is not something you do FOR someone else. It is not complicated. It is simple. Simply identify the situation to be forgiven and ask yourself: "Am I willing to waste my energy further on this matter?" If the answer is "No," then that's it. All is forgiven."

"Forgiveness is an act of the imagination. It dares you to imagine a better future, one that is based on the blessed possibility that your hurt will not be the final word on the matter. It challenges you to give up your destructive thoughts about the situation and to believe in the possibility of a better future. It builds confidence that you can survive the pain and grow from it."

"Telling someone is a bonus. It is not necessary for forgiveness to begin the process that heals the hurt. Forgiveness has little or nothing to do with another person because forgiveness is an internal matter."

"Choice is always present in forgiveness. You do not have to forgive AND there are consequences. Refusing to forgive by holding on to the anger, resentment, and a sense of betrayal can make your own life miserable. A vindictive mind-set creates bitterness and lets the betrayer claim one more victim."

"If we really want to love, we must learn how to forgive." ~ Mother Theresa

A Checklist for Forgiveness

√ Forgiveness is for YOUR peace of mind.

√ Forgiveness helps to heal our emotional wound.

√ We are not perfect.

√ By holding on to this, we continue to be the victim of this circumstance.

√ Those who are weak, can never forgive.

√ When you forgive, you change your future.

√ Forgiveness offers you another chance for a new start.

√ If perfection was possible, there would be no need for love or forgiveness.

√ The final acceptance in your life, is forgiveness.

√ Why are you losing sleep over transgressions, that another may not even know they committed?

√ Forgiveness is making peace with yourself, as much as it is releasing the offense against you.

Create A Forgiveness Workbook

This Forgiveness Worksheet or Life Workbook, is a great way to bring the power of your thoughts, good energy, and a generous way to express your true feelings on paper.

This journal can be used for writing down situations and how you have experienced them.

These journals are good places to record your positive outlook, your goals for achieving a path to your truths, and your daily affirmation.

It can allow you to look at that information later for understanding inspiration and guidance.

Tips for Understanding Forgiveness

1. Upon waking, write down the name of the person you are forgiving. Write down what it is you are forgiving them for.

2. It is a good idea to write words such as I am, I can, I will.

3. Write down your perception of the misunderstanding.

4. Jot down significant words/phrases, that signify your mindfulness, today. "My partner", "my great career", "my respect for myself".

5. List what negative feelings you are still holding on to. Explain in your journal.

6. Now learn about the power of letting go of these feelings. Write down each day, something new that you find forgiveness in doing, seeing, saying, hearing...

7. Understand, it is now time to let go, which you do by_____... (write them down). Look at it periodically. What impact does it have on your thoughts?

8. Do you see failure as a stumbling block or a stepping stone to forgiveness? Find three things in forgiving that make it a stepping stone to the next level. List them now.

9. Be sure and write the time and day on the top of the page.

10. Make this journal your own. Buy or make a book that you are eager to go to each day. Use stickers, color, doodles that all express your journey to forgiving yourself and others.

11. Our ability to forgive is in direct proportion to our ability to receive forgiveness.

12. When we are able to forgive all parts of ourselves, this allows us to be that much more perfect and whole. This in turn helps us to forgive others for any past mistakes.

13. Remember: mistakes come from good people who, from time to time, made some bad choices.

14. Judgments, resentments, and grudges are destructive emotions. When left unchecked, unresolved, or not under control, they can wash away the foundation of any relationship.

15. A wake-up call is in order. Talk it out. Resolve issues, disputes, and misunderstanding by expressing your feelings in a calm, well thought out, civil conversation. Preferably in person.

16. When we hurt ourselves, we hurt each other. Learn to forgive yourself by releasing your guilt. Learn to forgive others by letting go of your ego.

17. Remind yourself that we live in each other's hearts and when we look at ourselves, we see each other. When we love each other, we love ourselves m ore.

18. Learn to understand the relief you gain from forgiveness.

19. Step up to the plate and speak your peace.

20. Forgiving is the ultimate in acceptance of yourself and others. It reveals a path to our true selves.

Questions to think about:

Who am I going to forgive today?

Why am I going to forgive them today?

I am going to benefit greatly from doing this. Why?

Does it matter what the issue was about?

I am forgiving this person for who's sake?

What lesson will they gain from this?

Intuition

What is often called the sixth sense, intuition can be defined as "the ability to sense or know immediately without reasoning." We all have hunches, gut feelings, or intuitive insight. The feeling one gets when first hearing about something or someone, or the first impression when we meet someone new…these are all simply our intuition.

Intuition is often considered the ability to synthesize and deduce from all of our accumulated unconscious experiences. Therefore, we "know" much more than we realize. It is also through the perception of our (other) five senses, which, allows us to "tune in" to our intuition. Those who pay attention can find intuition a useful tool in their lives.

Gemstone:
Intuition

"I seek to see what's deep inside,
O' clear mind, open up Third Eye.
To grant me vision, set the tone,
I seek to find the answers, known.
So come, reveal all that I ask,
And take the challenge of this
task."

~ Andrew Pacholyk MS L.Ac

The Intuitive Learning Process

There are three stages our mind goes through in learning to comprehend a situation or idea:

1. Sensory perception is the process of discerning and deciphering information we receive in the cerebral cortex from the lower sensory or motor neurons. It is the understanding and interpreting of information from what we sense, touch, smell, hear, or see. From this information we deduce what the mind interprets based on our knowledge of signs, symbols, and what our mind recalls. **Then**, you should ask yourself, "is it the perceived notion of what feels good? Is it the intuitive act of what you know in your heart?" I had a teacher who answered that question by asking, "is there a presence or absence of harmony around the situation?"

2. Surrender is the action of yielding one's person or giving up the possession of something or into the power of another. By letting go, it leaves us exposed, opened, vulnerable, and defenseless. Only by surrendering, are we completely and fully able to allow the Universe to take over and truly lead us to the most natural and simple path. By allowing this path of least resistance into your life, you receive what is intended. Use your tools of love, gratitude, and assurance to trust your perception. When the choice seems effortless, inspiring, associated with synchronicity, clarity, or a profound sense of peace, surrendering to it is the only and best choice available.

3. Illumination is receiving power. There is nothing more enlightening than looking at something you do not understand or quit comprehend until that moment when suddenly, it becomes so very clear to you, that you just cannot believe you did not see it in the first place! This self-discovery or illumination we experience is one of the greatest gifts we can receive. There is no personal agenda or hidden reasoning behind the illumination, as it is a product of pure clarity, harmony, and profound peace. This is due, in many ways, to our sensory perceptions, which takes place in this discovery process and the ability to allow ourselves to surrender.

This Intuitive Learning Process is something we can apply to ANY situation in our lives. Whether learning a craft, understanding a lesson, or accepting any given situation, this process will help you to "open your mind" and allow new ideas, new creativity, and new insight to flow freely. Try it.

Your Intuition Exercise

Based on the sensory perception/surrender/illumination model, it often becomes clearer, when you dig deeper. This can be done by asking certain questions and then answering them truthfully:

Write out your situation

1. On a piece of paper, write out your specific concern:

a. Are you having an issue with family? ___

b. Is there a relationship problem? ___

c. Are you having a problem at work?___

2. Are you at a crossroads with this situation?___

a. Explain it out by writing down where the conflict occurs.___

"What I really want this outcome to be is:"

3.My natural response to this would be:___

a. Finish the sentence.___ .

Now keep asking the question and answering 3 more times, each with a different response:___

What I really want this outcome to be is:

What I really want this outcome to be is:

What I really want this outcome to be is:

What this situation really needs is?

4. Write out an answer to this question.___

a. Finish the sentence.___

b. Do not add the phrase "from me" to this answer.

c. Now keep asking the question and answering 3 more times, each with a different response:___

What this situation really needs is?

What this situation really needs is?

What this situation really needs is?

If you have reached/revealed your illumination (true intuitive answer)

5. Write out the solution below.___

6. Explain why this worked for you!

"Cease trying to work everything out with your minds. It will get you nowhere. Live by intuition and inspiration and let your whole life be a Revelation." ~ Eileen Caddy, Spiritual leader, Scottish Writer

Journeys

Many people, who have now gone through many of their life markers or milestones, realize that it may be time to leave their empty nests and see the world. In the Fall of our lives, more people have the financial means and available time to travel.

Trip the light fantastic! Whether you are traveling for business, taking a family vacation, going on retreat or taking a trip through your mind's eye... here is a guide to keep you safe, healthy and aware.

Gemstone:
Journeys in a Balloon

"As I fly upon the air
let breezes blow, without a care.
To reach new heights and journey
through,
adventures far and wide and new.
To float as if without directions,
minding all of earth's perfections,
streams and mountains, valleys too,
they show their better self to you.
Let gentle winds blow through your
hair,
Oh, travel swift, upon the air!"

~ Andrew Pacholyk, MS L.Ac

"The journey is not finding satisfaction in the end but savoring each moment on the road there." ~WC Fields

Soul Satisfying Journeys

Our journeys are about making choices. Whether it is a choice about where to go, how to go, or when to go, the choice determines our outcome. Soul satisfying journeys are mindful trips that include self-awareness and a look within ourselves. This pertains to any journey, be it from place to place, action to action, or decision to decision.

The sum of our choices constitutes our life. The journey we take from start to finish. We may not always make the proper choices, but we are always allowed the ability to make another. No matter how far down the "wrong" road we may be, this road we chose, we chose for a reason.

Herein lies life's lessons. Learn the lesson, then make your next choice. This is how we discover the daily journeys in a span of time that is ours and ours alone. Your journey in life always begins with a single step.

This accumulation of steps over time is what brings you to your life's path. So, make the decision to live YOUR life and follow the path you desire. You have the ability and right to change that path, whenever you are ready.

"Life is designed by our soul and spirit as our moment-by-moment opportunity to expand our consciousness." ~ unknown

Tips for a Soul Satisfying Journey

Our personal journey is a path we seek to find happiness. The journeys we take represent our attempts to find more about who we are. Whatever your idea of a journey is, here you can learn how to take a soul satisfying trip:

1. The Power of Positive Thinking: Negativity is the root that undermines our free flow of thought. The negative ideas we think can manifest in the words we speak. The minute the words leave your lips, is the minute they manifest. Change your thoughts to positive, uplifting ones. Allow the process to flow without judgement. Stay in the moment. Energy follows thought. Program thought to be positive and your energy will reflect it.

2. Networking: When traveling on any journey, take the time to meet those who cross your path. If you believe in Universal attraction, then your purpose for those you meet will unfold.

3. Find Quiet Time: Turn off the cell phone, power down the laptop, cut yourself off from the constant world of communication. Try doing it for 15 minutes. Then add another 15 minutes. Build your time up to an hour.

4. Find Time to Meditate: Become aware of your breath. Learn to close your eyes, sit comfortably, and smell the air around you. Enjoy the sounds of nature, your new surroundings, or your favorite music.

5. Enjoy the Company of Those Around You: If you are on vacation with your significant other, your family, or children, give them your full and undivided attention. Not only will you understand your willpower but you will truly show your loved ones how important your time is with them.

6. Pamper Yourself: Take this time to enjoy a massage. Take a yoga class, or give yourself a soothing bath or spa treatment. Do something for yourself that you would not normally do.

7. Be Flexible: You have a rigid, set schedule at work, with the kids, or in your daily routine. Learn a lesson from the willow tree and its ability to bend in the great wind. When we are rigid like the old oak tree, we can easily break apart under the stress of change. Learn to relax and follow the path unfolding on the journey before you.

8. Become More Mindful: Mindfulness is the act of being fully aware of what happens in each moment. Try living in the NOW. Be present. Honor each moment you are given. Acknowledge each task you take.

9. Really Appreciating: what we DO have as opposed to what we would like to have, makes a significant difference. This is always an important element in any journey that is often neglected.

10. Find Happiness in Simplicity: and you will find the greatest joys yet revealed to you. Have patience on your travels. Greet everyone you pass by or meet, with a smile. Appreciate the smell of the air, the warmth of the sun and the laughter in children. Make that the stepping stones of your travels.

The Path Less Taken

What is the path less taken? This is often referred to as the path to our dreams. There are more paths not taken than there are those who stumble down it. The sheer number of people who dare not to venture down the road of their desires is much more than those who do. But why? Is it fear, insecurity, poor self-esteem?

In my practice, I have heard it over and over again. I wanted to be this, or I wanted to do this…, BUT I, (fill in excuse here) …

The number of reasons for NOT perusing your dreams is staggering. But when I ask someone in my practice to list 3 reasons why they SHOULD follow their dreams, not too many people can come up with them.

The real key to success is **persistence and perseverance**. I have seen so many people give up, fall by the wayside, or just stop trying. The excuses I hear are often about their lack of persistence. If you already have a perceived timeline as to how and when you will achieve your goal, you have already lost. As you can see, your expectations are already in the way and keeping you from your goal. This is the number one means of failure. Instead of taking your dreams a day at a time or allowing things to naturally transpire on their own timeline, you have given them an expiration date with your expectation.

What do you really want to do with your life? What do you want to be? Where do you want to go? Here are my top tips for "following your path…"

1. Make a list of fears: This could be a short list or a long list. The idea is, to create a list of fears you recognize. Once you know what each one of these fears is, you can then look each one of them in the eye and find the "opposite" reasoning behind it. It is going to be your way of debunking these reasons.

2. Do not use money as an excuse: Money comes and goes. You will sometimes have it and sometimes you may not. But I bet you that whenever you really need it, it somehow comes to you. It is often your fear of not having any that stops you from doing anything.

3. Let go of "what if": You will never have the answer to this question. So, let it go. The anticipation of anything is a fool's game. Your goal is to look at the moment. The past is behind you and the future has not happened yet. You must learn how your attention in the present moment will help you focus on the task at hand.

4. Choose ways to reach your goal: Perhaps you have to go back to school or travel far to pursue your desires. Maybe you need to find a teacher or climb the corporate ladder. Make a list from point A to point B. Map out ways to get you on that path to your goal. Come up with a plan A, B or even C. Look at how these possibilities can work for you.

5. Take the first step: Without this, you can go nowhere. You can pave that path with good intentions, but if you do not take that first step, you are no further along than sitting and dreaming about it. It is important not to get bogged down in the negative feedback from others. The family members that don't want you to leave your day job or those who think you can't do it, are deterrents. Focus on your path. Use your energy to follow your positive thought process and take one step forward.

6. Do something every day that brings you closer to your dream. If you wish to keep one foot in your current job, do so, BUT, the other foot should be reaching with each toe, inching forward on that path. Send a resume, take your class, go to an interview. Each day make a journal or just write down what you did to achieve your day's goal.

7. Make Room for Change: Make it a nourishing, self-respecting place for change to take place in your mind. In the same way, create a life affirming, positive path to reach your goal. Make no excuses. Procrastination is the bi-product of feeling unworthy. Self-worth leads us in the right direction.

What you will realize by taking these steps, is that before you know it, you are actually looking back over your shoulder to see how far you have come, without even realizing it. Keep moving forward and I promise, your persistence and perseverance will give you your just reward!

Gemstone:
Clearing the Path

(for Jean-Claude)

"Make way, I step out on the path, of leaves and earth before me,

I breathe in deep and fill my lungs, with ambition, love and carefree...

Days...that start with morning light, my favorite time, you see,

for nothing more can fill my heart, than promise offered me.

That I can find the goals I seek, while treading on this trail,

as Birch and Cedar take a bow, like Willow's weeping veil.

I clear the path of obstacles, that tend to fall my way,

as I command the forest, yet again, another day.

But really, I am at the whim of branch and leaves that fall,

I truly have no power here, I merely heed the call.

The path has shown it takes control
but we can share the turn,

it's how we choose to handle it,
the real lesson learned."

~ Andrew Pacholyk MS L.Ac

Knowledge

We can never be to knowledgeable.

I know, for me, going to college was a great experience after high school. Yet, for most of it, all I seem to remember is going through the motions. I did do a double major and I did degrees in both Dance (BA) and Business (BS), so at some point, I must have been paying attention. But, when I went back to school for a Master's degree, it was a completely different experience.

> ### <u>Gemstone:</u>
> ### Your Window of Knowledge
>
> *"O, light of moon of wisdom thyn,*
> *Help to recall, O memory mine.*
> *Open and clear mental repose*
> *To help and study, recall and*
> *grow.*
> *O wisdom, great familiar when,*
> *Of knowledge, wise, insightful then*
> *When sun is high, energy strong,*
> *Please bring my concentration on.*
> *Now I absorb the wisdom here,*
> *And let go ~ unrelenting fear."*
>
> ~ Andrew Pacholyk MS L.Ac

If you are in the *"Fall of your life"* or whatever your time frame, heading back to school, as an adult, has new twists and turns to navigate. I now know, first hand, what it is like to go back to school. Going back to follow my second passion of medicine, after a very successful and passionate career as a dancer/choreographer, has been rewarding beyond belief.

The first day of school can be a scary prospect for anyone, but adult students confront special concerns and fears.

217

Adults are more likely to have multiple responsibilities, requiring them to juggle commitments to school, family, and employers. They may be haunted by earlier experiences with formal education or worried about being "rusty." Re-entry students may feel uncomfortable when surrounded by younger, technologically-savvy classmates. Previous drop-outs may be anxious about being able to complete the program this time around. While all of these concerns are legitimate, none are insurmountable.

Mind Games

Some of the best ways to engage your brain are by **using your memory functions and re-training your brain!**

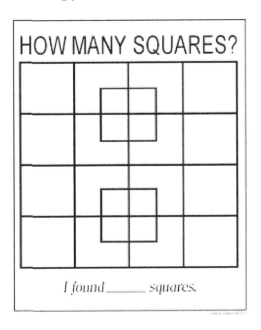

HOW MANY SQUARES?

I found _____ squares.

1. The number one rule is: Get off auto-pilot. Avoid brain shrinkage by expanding your emotional and mental capacity. Break up your routine. Switch it up. Do something different each day.

2. Memorize favorite poems, speeches, or famous passages.

3. Read challenging books or articles that encourage you to expand your interests.

218

4. Learn something new whether it is a new language, the words to a song or a new recipe. This helps stretch the brain.

5. Practice other-handedness. If you're right-handed, try brushing your teeth or writing your grocery list with your left hand.

6. Play word games like crossword puzzles, Sudoku, and Scrabble.

7. Test at your threshold. Testing yourself slightly beyond your capacity (80 percent right, 20 percent wrong) helps to increase brain neurons.

8. Get lost. Getting lost and then being able to find your way, by backtracking, reading a map, or deducing, helps to increase memory.

9. Choose one new thing to learn every day. You will greatly benefit your age/mind capacity, as you comprehend something new.

10. Stay optimistic, remaining so, enables higher cognitive function.

The Learning Process

1. Value your experience: Think of the significant lessons you've learned since you were last in school. No doubt you've learned a great deal about human relationships through a broad range of interactions. You may have learned about health and medicine through the birth of a child or the illness or injury of someone dear to you. Perhaps you've acquired technical skills through employment or home maintenance, repair and improvement. A love of travel could have exposed you to other languages and cultures. Certainly, you've learned the value of academic credentials, something your younger classmates may not yet realize.

2. Learning can happen ANYWHERE: Clearly, you don't have to be in a classroom to learn. Not only are your life and work experiences valid, they can sometimes give you an advantage over your less experienced classmates. Making connections between classroom studies and life experiences can enliven and enrich not only your own learning, but that of your teachers and classmates, too.

3. Get off on the right foot: Getting off on the right foot means managing your time effectively and establishing good study habits. Many "stressed out" people suffer from "an overbooked schedule or a greater number of responsibilities than one can reasonably handle." Don't let yourself get into this trap – learn to say "no" to responsibility overload. One of the first steps to establishing good study habits is understanding your learning style. Do you learn by seeing? hearing? doing? Try some learning style self-assessment steps below to help you decide.

4. Practice good study habits from the outset: Once equipped with an understanding of your learning style, brainstorm how to make the most of it. For example, if you are an audio learner, make sure to choose a seat where you will be able to hear clearly. Consider taping lectures and your own study notes for review purposes. Invest in tabbed binders to keep your notes organized by subject.

5. Stay organized: Many students start out all excited and have their materials together but lose steam through their course of study. Maintain a calendar of homework, assignments, test descriptions, and dates. Break up big tasks (e.g., writing a term paper) into smaller, more manageable targets (e.g., locate library and Internet resources; read and take notes; plan essay outline; write; proof-read; edit). Review materials regularly and consult a tutor. Ask your teacher when you encounter items you don't understand.

6. Use campus resources: The large number of adult students returning to school has prompted many institutions to offer resources and services to meet the needs of re-entry students. These services may include academic, financial aid and career counseling; child care; work opportunities; health services; housing; support groups and tutoring. Some schools even have a central office and orientation sessions to introduce their services to nontraditional students. Find out what supports your school offers and do make use of the ones you need.

7. Get comfortable with technology: Campuses have gotten increasingly wired in the past several years. Electronic student cards can be used for everything from making photocopies to signing books out of the library to buying lunch. Cell phones ring through the halls, and too often, unfortunately, in the classrooms. Library reserves are cataloged and searched on computer databases. Teachers may send and receive assignments by e-mail. You may be taking some or all of your courses online. Surrounded by younger, computer-savvy classmates, how can you narrow the "generation gap?" Look for free or low-cost computer orientation courses offered by your school. Most libraries help users learn to search their databases and Internet resources. Schools may also offer workshops in basic keyboarding and computer skills. A great deal of information and support can also be found online.

8. Develop a support network: Sometimes it helps just to know that you're not alone. Whether you are a career changer, a single mother, domestic violence survivor, recovering alcoholic, widow/widower, or "Baby Boomer", there ARE students like you, who share similar interests and concerns. If your school doesn't have an adult student support group, consider starting one up yourself or participating in an online community. If the going gets tough, think of the reasons you decided to return to school and keep your eye on the prize. Successfully managing the challenges of returning to school is a rewarding achievement.

9. Be flexible: If you are going back to school after college, you probably have a rigid, set schedule at work, with the kids, or in your daily routine. Learn a lesson from the willow tree and its ability to bend in the great wind. Whereas, when we are rigid like the old oak tree, we can easily break apart under the stress of change. Learn to relax and follow the path unfolding before you.

10. Become more mindful: Mindfulness is the act of being fully aware of what happens in each moment. Try living in the NOW. Be present. Pay attention in class or while doing homework. Do not get distracted with other life issues. Designate time for classes and time for study. Honor each moment you are given. Acknowledge each task you take on.

Prosperity

Prosperity is the state of flourishing, thriving, success, or good fortune. Prosperity often encompasses wealth but, it is not just about money. Prosperity encompasses those things which give us abundance, gratitude, appreciation, peace, happiness, and health. Prosperity is your right and reward. You have it and should always recognize it. Some important values about being prosperous include offering, compromising, accepting help, and recognizing new opportunities.

<u>Gemstone:</u>
Prosperity

"From east to south and west to north
I create safe space for me to work.

I add my hope in circle, round,
To bring prosperity, abound.

Abundance, gratitude and peace,
May health and happiness increase."

~ Andrew Pacholyk MS L.Ac

" Prosperity isn't about what you have or own, but what you feel about what you have or own."
~ Dr. Mehmet Oz

How to Achieve Prosperity

1. Prosperity is in your mind's eye. Another word, it is a state of mind. Most importantly, prosperity is about the emotional view of your life and how you feel about it. This is like a seed that must be planted in order for it to grow. A seed grows into a healthy plant when it is nurtured and cared for. When it is abused, forgotten, neglected, or not nourished it will never grow to its full potential. First, you must plant the seed of prosperity in your mind and then you must nourish this with positive thoughts, aggressive action, and keep it alive, always.

2. Energy follows thought. We create our own reality. We attract those things in our lives (money, relationships, employment) that we focus on. Focusing on having less, and that is exactly what you will experience. Focusing on having more and this is what we create for ourselves. Program your thoughts to be positive and this energy will follow through.

3. Give up the control. If you understand that not all things are in your control, you will be saving boundless amounts of time and energy NOT worrying about those things you have no control over. You can only do what you can do. A patient once said to me, "We are not driving the bus. We are passengers in the bus. Sit back and have a nice ride!"

4. If you are already resisting this thought... you are not trusting of yourself or anyone around you. This includes the Universe! Resistance slows all things. It is up to you to find the free flow in your life. If we can surrender ourselves, we can gain great insight, release more stress, and learn that vulnerability can be both enlightening and educating. It is time to let go and learn these lessons.

5. Pay attention to what you DO have NOW. Just wanting something isn't enough, because we still continue to think about what we don't have. Everyone is brought into this world with great gifts. Realizing what these are, can be found by appreciating what you have right now! Pay attention.

6. Appreciate all your life's abundance. You will realize just how much prosperity you do have. There is nothing worse than seeing someone who is ungrateful. Of course, it is human nature to want more, but not at the expense of your own happiness. Some people are so caught up in wanting more, they

223

miss out on experiencing the current abundance they have now. Only when this is gone, do they realize what they had…when it is often too late.

7. Get proactive. Since our jobs are our source of financial support, it is important to do your job well. It is even more important to absolutely love what you do. If you do not, you will never give the job the best you can give. If you do not absolutely love what you do, quit! You must do what you love in your life, as we spend the majority of our lives at work… it better be an inspiring combination of pride, creativity, and life-altering greatness. That choice is yours.

8. Find balance. The balance of work, play, family, friends, and self, are very important in achieving prosperity. They each equal the way we subconsciously honor a prosperous life. The minute one of these are out of balance, we begin a cascading effect of resentment, jealousy, and anger. Look at each one of these aspects. Are they balanced? If not, which one is overwhelming the other? Finding the balance between them will give you a better outlook. Make a "balance sheet" (see Gratitude Project below).

9. Be open to prosperity: When nothing else seems to be working, just simply try being open to endless possibilities without expectation. The greater you expect things to be, the harder it is to deal with things that do not go your way. Having no expectations is one of the greatest lessons we can learn. By allowing yourself to be open to ANYTHING that is new to you and giving it a chance, you can find your life going in the direction of new adventures and endless possibilities.

10. Our priorities of life. These are unique and individual. They are key to living a prosperous life, therefore, you must start aligning your thoughts, beliefs, feelings, emotions, and actions towards greater prosperity.

The Gratitude Project

This is a self-awareness exercise. I started this in my practice in New York City over 15 years ago. It has always been an offering to my patients who come in during the week of Thanksgiving for treatment. I would ask them to take home this handout and to fill it out in their private time. If they were interested in doing a little self-attunement exercise, this would be the ideal time, as we can be more conscious of the benefits we receive in our lives.

At this time in my life, things maybe going great or they may not be the best. Regardless, TODAY I am grateful for:

1. _____

My life is full of hidden blessings. I will name three of them I may have forgotten:

1. _____

2. _____

3. _____

I was able to eat today. I am thankful to have food to eat today because:

1. _____

I woke up in good health today. I am so grateful for this because:

1. _____

2. _____

3._____

I may not have woken up in the best state of health today, yet I cannot be more thankful because:

1. _____

2. _____

3._____

I am most grateful for two people in my life. Who are they and why?

1. _____

2. _____

There has always been a song or piece of music in my life that I have been very grateful for because:

Name of song: _____

Why?. _____

I have command of my senses today. I am eternally grateful for each one of them, as there are some who do not have the ability to use them. I am grateful for each one of them in this way:

Sight: _____

Hearing: _____

Taste: _____

Touch: _____

Smell: _____

My happiness depends on:

The path of my life depends on:

My choices determine my:

My final thought of gratitude is about:

I hope that this exercise in self-awareness has been a helpful one and I thank you for taking the time to be a part of it for yourself.

"Prosperity is not just having things. It is the consciousness that attracts everything. Prosperity is a way of living and thinking, and not just having money or possessions. Remember, poverty is a way of living and thinking, and not just a lack of money." ~ Eric Butterworth

Personal Growth

Within each *season of our lives*, we add to the experiences we've gained and hopefully incorporated these lessons into our psyche. Personal growth tools change as we age. We tend more towards fine tuning and utilizing the resources that serve us better at this point in life. We find it a little easier to let go of those things which no longer work in our day to day scenario.

Hopefully, throughout your life, you will continue to create and manifest what you desire and discard the old beliefs that no longer serve your purpose.

In the *"Fall" of our lives*, we tend to become more spiritually inclined. We contemplate bigger pictures of *who we are* and *where we've came from*. We tend to ask ourselves more questions.

Spirituality can be found anywhere. You can experience it in a church or temple, in the surrounding nature, in a yoga, dance or exercise class, in the darkest, most unlikely places. Spirituality is a state of mind. It is an experience that brings you closer to the realization of life's truths. It can be found when facing fear, enjoying simplicities or deeper contemplation.

Spirit Medicine: The Remedy Most Forgotten

Spirit medicine imparts the healing power on the entire body. This "trickle-down effect" can be seen repeatedly in many forms of Eastern medicine. The psychological root-cause of each person's belief system, which becomes the texture of how we live our lives, can be expressed in the subtle energies of the body, as well as, in the expression of disease.

The Western paradigm, compartmentalize these theories, not seeing any connection between them.

The Eastern paradigms of healing see medicine for the body, with a connection to the mind and a bridge to spirituality. It does not isolate one from the other. No matter what the means of therapy, (acupuncture, massage, exercise...) there is an arc, which leads you from the physical, through a path of mental processes to the connection of spirit at the other end.

No matter what form of therapy we use, we are only capable of balancing our lives by the beliefs we hold in our heart. By formulating a spiritual belief system, we lay the basic groundwork for a stronger foundation on which to build better health and well-being.

Our belief system is one of our most powerful assets. Instilling this message to a person can create the groundwork for change. The following is a look at both the Eastern and Western approach to mind-body-spirit practice.

Oriental Medicine Model

Within the traditions of Oriental Medicine, the connection between the mind, the body, and its spiritual components have been the basis of this holistic health system for centuries. Shamanism and incantations were the primary beginnings of this system, followed by well-known philosophers and their ideologies.

Traditional Chinese Medicine psychology bases the combination of Jing-Essence, Qi and Shen as the Fundamental Theory. The fundamental theories include:

1. The Integration of Body and Mind: The combination of Jing-Essence,Qi and Shen.

2. The Heart: Traditional Chinese Medicine has long looked at the heart as the dominant organ for mental activity. It is believed that all information is preserved and processed through the heart.

3. Five Zang Organs and mental activities: The visceral root of our emotions. Liver, Heart, Spleen, Lungs and Kidneys.

4. Individuality and Temperament: Every life begins with inherent strengths and weaknesses.

5. The Respect of the Soul: Deeper levels of the emotions affect our spiritual planes.

Eastern Minds

"Ru Jia" – Confucianism's "Doctrine of the Means" was how one would create a healthy balanced state between the mind, the body, and spirit. By nurturing the mind, the health of the organs would follow. The guidelines for achieving this balance would be to live with good manners, loyalty, honoring one's parents, the proper conduct, benevolence, and love.

Taoist guidelines for a healthy mind and body would be to "live with content." Be free in yourself and be close to nature. Lao Tzu, is regarded as the creator of the foundation of the Taoist philosophy. In the Tao Te Ching, Lao Tzu stated that "people should return to the original condition of nature's complete personal tranquility."

Buddhism teaches the benefits of deep calming and to be consciously aware. At the very heart of Buddhism are the Four Noble Truths, taught by the Buddha to his earliest disciples, in his first sermon. **The first Truth** is that life is dukkha — a word translated as suffering, dislocation. In other words, because something has gone wrong in the world, life is not as it should be, and there is pain. In order to relieve suffering, we must discover its cause.

The second Truth offers the explanation: The cause of dukkha is tanha, or desire — specifically, desire for personal gratification. A person ruled by Tanha is one who will ignore the welfare of every other being to satisfy his own desire. Since in reality all is one, shutting oneself off from that oneness through selfishness causes pain.

The third Truth identifies what must be done: If suffering is caused by selfish craving, overcoming that craving will eliminate the pain. The fourth Truth offers the solution:

The Buddha's Eightfold Path — follow its instructions, and one will find release.

The Western Psychiatric Model

1. The Bio-psychosocial Model

The bio syndromes, which include the syndrome, related to the anatomical pathology or disordered patho-physiology. This is where medicine blends with psychology. The psycho syndromes, includes the mental and emotional processes of the mind. This is the personality behind the medical illness.

The social syndrome, which intimately involves the person's family, environment, financial and educational backgrounds, expresses how no psychiatric patient exists in a vacuum.

2. The Perspective Model

Every psychiatric patient's disorder is viewed as being influenced by disease, behavior, personality, and life story.

Western Minds

Sigmund Freud remains one of the most influential figures of the 20th century. Freud's basic insight that our minds preserve memories and emotions which are not always consciously available to us, has transformed the way humanity views itself ever since. The tendency of people to trace their problems to childhood traumas or other repressed emotions begins with Freud.

One of Freud's more important discoveries is that emotions buried in the unconscious surface in disguised form during dreaming, and that the remembered fragments of dreams can help uncover the buried emotions. Whether the method is exactly as Freud describes it, many people have consequent insights into themselves from studying their dreams, and many people consider dreams emotionally significant, contrasting our ancestors who often saw them either as divine suggestion or as simply a side-effect of indigestion.

Carl Jung is one of the most respected and recognized psychologists of all time. Many people know Jung as one of Sigmund Freud's followers and co-workers. Jung's emphasis in the field of psychology had to do with dreams. Jung developed many theories about dreams, a lot of them disagreeing with

Freud. Jung was a great psychologist and psychiatrist that changed the ways of psychology today.

Jung thought that dreams were a tool to help us grow, not just to release extreme sexual desires. Jung felt that dreams were more than about sex, they were about life and spirituality. Jung said that sexual drive doesn't even motivate us as much as the fear of death and the unknown. Jung was an inspiration to all in the psychology field. His beliefs have become theories, which are now accepted concepts in the world of mind-medicine today.

Dr. Wilhelm Reich who discovered the "orgone energy" theory, emphasized that all diseases could ultimately be best understood as imbalances in the orgone energy system. Reich became convinced that a subtle biophysical energy permeates all living things and that the orgone is mass-free; permeates all of space in different concentrations; is responsible for all forms of life; is taken into the body through breathing; is present in all cells, and is especially drawn to water and forms units, both living and nonliving.

John Upledger DO. has been recognized as an innovator and leading proponent in the investigation of new therapies. His development of CranioSacral Therapy has earned him an international reputation. As an osteopathic physician, Dr.Upledger did extensive scientific studies from 1975 to 1983 at Michigan State University, where he served as a clinical researcher and Professor of Biomechanics. His therapy is a subtle, hands-on method of evaluating and enhancing the functioning of a physiological craniosacral system. This system is comprised of the "inner physician" as well as, membranes and cerebrospinal fluid that surround and protect the brain and spinal cord. In tune with the body's natural rhythm, the study of craniosacral therapy is continually utilized as a preventative medicine, as well as a treatment for psychological disorders associated with pain, neurological, intrinsic, extrinsic, and idiopathic disorders.

It is through the courageous and unique approaches of such Western minds as these, that allows for the mind-body model to be stretched and supplemented into new and innovative ways. These men have made great strides in allowing us to look at connections between the psyche and the physical body the mind inhabits. They bring closer the bridge between Eastern theories and Western advances in order to complete the circle of one ideal model.

The Realm of the Possible

In my approach to "Spirit Medicine", I use the power of my energy therapies I have studied along with a look at a particular person's belief in themselves and their surrounding situation(s). As individual as the cells that make up our systems, the process of healing each individual is as unique as this. It is inevitable as human nature dictates, to want to categorize and organize things. This is an innate function of the brain system itself. If you have this... then you do this... and so on.

As we learn...a system of healing, be it allopathic medicine or complementary and alternative modalities such as massage therapy, Ayurveda, Traditional Chinese medicine, color therapy and so on...there tends to be a set of tried and true rules to observe, follow, or be guided by.

As we practice... it is never as cut and dried! We would all like to see patients come in with classic textbook symptoms. This would make it so easy for us to treat. Unfortunately, those cases tend to be more the exception rather than the rule. This is what makes healing not only an art, but also a lifetime of discoveries. It is finally, a patient's belief in their healing that makes it so.

> This brings me back to spirit and belief. You can believe that you will get better and not be considered spiritual, and you may heal. But, when you have faith in your healing process, it seems that much more possible.

I feel, nothing in healing, is etched in stone. What method of treatment may help one individual may not help the next. This is why it is important to be open to and aware of as many possibilities in the healing arena as possible. I also do not believe that if someone has said or has proven that a form of healing MAY NOT work in general, that this is grounds for abandoning the treatment. What may not work for one may absolutely be appropriate in healing another.

In Western medicine, for example, we tend to only work with and accept the most recent medications; the most recent findings and the most current approaches...disregarding the rest.

In Chinese medicine, no theory or form of healing is ever thrown out but placed in the "tool belt of knowledge" and can be called upon when one path is not as efficient.

In any clinical setting where there is an interview, there is an exchange of energies. Through these energies, the practitioner and patient can observe the ability to relate to one another via intuition, creative hunches, the give and take of power, nonverbal and emotional insights and nonverbal forms of communication, which form a valuable source of knowledge about each other's personalities, and his or her transference.

In the clinical setting, the energies of transference and counter transference are always present. Trying to balance these energies that abound in a clinical interview are both challenging to recognize, as they are to cope with. The process of being aware, as well as being present, plays a major role in the recognition as to where an imbalance can manifest. As a practitioner, your "tool belt of knowledge" can be an imperative part of the process. As a patient, you can open yourself up to better understanding, trust and honoring the thoughts of the practitioner. These delicate energy levels, when balanced, can help both to maintain a level of strength and understanding.

Belief Becomes Substance

The belief in our recovery is probably the most important aspect of any treatment. When the patient and the practitioner are onboard, the healing process is brought up a notch. I see this time and time again, even with terminally ill patients. No matter what the dis-ease, as long as the patient retains the belief in their ability to sustain and maintain their level of health, it is their spirit, positivity, or energy of hope that can keep them going. Even threw some of their darkest hours. One of the greatest remedies about expanding our hope is that beliefs that used to seem impossible can now be a part of our everyday life. I want people to understand these guidelines:

* Energy follows thought. Program thought to be positive and our energy will reflect it.

* Our Belief System is one of the major factors that can get us through situations or can cause our life to crumble around us. I do believe that there is a lot of innate goodness and balancing that our minds create, subconsciously, in order to get us through hard times. The other portion of this is how we "program" ourselves to deal with any given situation.

233

* We have a conscious choice. We can choose to be beaten or choose to win.

* Our self-confidence and self-love are often the key to opening and strengthening our health.

* Really appreciating what we DO have as opposed to what we would like to have sometimes makes a significant difference. This is always an important element in healing that is often neglected.

With this foundation built, practically any healing modality will have an even better chance of taking root in the positive and strengthening all that it offers in return.

There are many factors in the healing process and the practitioner is only a part of the plan. The patient is the other piece of the puzzle. I had a wonderful teacher who once said to me:

"A doctor's job is not to heal a patient; it is to show the patient who they really are!"

This profound statement has stayed with me. It has given me the insight to offer options of healing for others. Steering a patient in a particular direction can allow them to heal themselves. It is good practice to constantly seek the reinforcing remedy of spiritual healing.

"Healing may not be so much about getting better, as about letting go of everything that isn't you - all of the expectations, all of the beliefs - and becoming who you are." ~ Rachel Naomi Remen

Gemstone:
Buddha's Thoughts

"He went through life a man of wealth, of power, lot, and privilege.

As time had passed, he found he could - no longer live in riches.

So off he went, forsaking all to seek a greater path,

a path of self-reflection, rediscovery, and wrath.

The wrath to turn life upside down and change collective thought,

*The way to liberation is by **middle way**, he taught.*

To remove the innate suffering and repetitive rebirths,

of spirit due to karma and the mundane path on earth

So follow now, the eighfold path, to find nirvana's light,

A light of truth, resolve, and bliss, your path of great insight."

~ Andrew Pacholyk MS L.Ac.

Fall Element: Earth

Earth is home planet. Yet earth doesn't necessarily always represent the physical earth, but that part of us, which is stable, solid, and dependable. Earth is the realm of abundance, prosperity, and wealth. Earth is a personality trait and Earth is an element, as well.

Earth represents traits of sensations, patience, stability, strength, health, grounding, and the centering of energies. Its associated with promoting peace, fertility, money, business, success, stability, warmth, comfort, and physical labor.

The element, Earth is associated with the late summer season, early Fall and with dampness. The element is associated with the spleen (pancreas) and stomach, where we process all that we take in emotionally and physically. The Earth is the source and provider of all our needs.

Emotionally, this element is associated with nurturing and with our survival instincts, as well as to our sense of grounding and connections with our bodies. Ideally, "earth" connects us to our health, prosperity, security, and dynamic presence. It is associated with our Root Chakra.

The Earth Signs of the zodiac are Taurus, Virgo, and Capricorn. Those who are "earthy" are considered disciplined. They think through their next move, are conventional, and dependable. They are often responsible, methodical, and concerned with details. They can count on being grounded, savvy, practical and good at following regulations and procedures.

Earth signs conform to established standards. Disciplined Earth signs follow protocol, seek standards, and obey orders. They agree with the social norm and conduct their lives in this manner. They work on being polite, accepted, and appreciated. Earth signs have a physical nature about them and are practical, prudent, and conventional. They make good business people, love buying, selling and trading, and are very socially oriented.

Emotionally, when earth is imbalanced, it can either cause excess worry or pensiveness. The trait of "over thinking" is a spleen/stomach issue and can affect our entire being. Worry can consume the body and express itself as stagnation. This is the case for anyone, but especially "earth personalities".

Physically, when the earth element is imbalanced, feelings that affect the stomach are common. The "knot" in the stomach or "plum pit Qi" (a tightening of the throat), nausea, vomiting, pain, ulcers (that eat away) are all the result of this imbalance.

Earth interacting with the other elements, is an ancient Mayan, Chinese, and Greek concept, which has been handed down through other cultures over time. In these ancient paradigms, especially the "5 element" concept of the Chinese and Ayurvedic theories, being "brought back down to earth" is earth's power over air. **Air** dries out earth and water turn earth to mud. Fire burns earth melting the metal.

The **earth** is composed of a wide variety of sand, soil, rocks, and minerals, which provides vegetation and supports life. All the elements are associated with earth.

Water supports this vegetation to grow. Water is considered the Universal solvent as it can dissolve more substances than any other liquid. Water flows and traveling through our body or through the ground taking nutrients, chemicals, and minerals along with it. Water turns to steam from the heat of the sun, evaporating into the air. This creates the rain water, which fills the clouds, along with a variety of gases and returns back to earth in a never-ending cycle.

The composition of these gases make **air** and is just right for life on Earth. When we breathe the oxygen in the air, we then expel carbon dioxide. Plants need to manufacture their food through photosynthesis, with help from carbon dioxide. Plants in turn give off oxygen during photosynthesis.

Fire is closely linked to air. Fire exists because of oxygen, fuel, and heat. Fire provides warmth and comfort. The earth provides natural fuel, such as coal and wood for fire to burn.

Therefore, **all these cycles** are a result of the elements we experience on earth and cannot live without.

Earth

December 21 to March 20

Abilities: Physical body, steadfastness, dependability, endurance, protection, realistic, practicality, sensuality, stored wisdom, growth, prosperity, nature, wealth, abundance, peace, fertility, money, business, stability, employment.

Stones: Moss agate, emerald, jet, jasper, salt, black tourmaline, agate, malachite, obsidian.

Plants: Corn, cypress, fern, honeysuckle, wheat, vervain, barley, buckthorn, sage, horehound, magnolia, mugwort, patchouli, rye.

Direction: North (South in the Southern Hemisphere)

Season: Winter

Colors: Green, brown, yellow

Cycle Celebrations: Yule/Winter Solstice

Number 3

Time: Midnight

Zodiac: Taurus, Virgo, Capricorn

Planet: Saturn

Angels: Gabriel, Uriel

Sense: Touch

Time of life: Maturity

Gemstone:
Earth

"This rich and salty ground we feel, with mud between our toes and heels
Grows grass as rich and fertile green, as mountains thrust so high we see,
The deep and blue celestial sky, which mirrors lakes and rivers, wide.
This precious ground for which we run, and play and work till day is done
And now another season comes, to show us now, that it's our turn,
to change, as we become anew, and thank the earth for lessons learned."

~ Andrew Pacholyk MS L.Ac.

Musical Landscape

Whether we know it or not, our lives are mapped out by the important moments we encounter. And most often, there is a song associated with it. Quite often, when we hear a familiar tune, it can take us back to the exact time and place, along with the experience that went with it! This "musical landscape" is the map of our lives.

From celebrations and ceremonies to proclamations and processions. Music marks the empirical reference we associated with time and place. Music is a magical medium that has always been a metaphor for our spirit.

Gemstone:
Fall Moods

*"When Fall comes round, we change our mood,
it's reflected in the somber tunes, we listen to and seem to hear,
round every corner, now Autumn's near.
So come along and listen in, we'll lift your spirits, take you in..."*

~ Andrew Pacholyk MS. L.Ac

Musical Playlists for Life's Journeys

Fall changes our mood. It brings a somber closing to the warmth and bright summer days and sets us on a path of introspection. It offers us a sense of deeper awareness as well as, the finalities of life.

On my walk through the woods today, I thought it would be a wonderful gift to share the songs of Fall, that make up my consciousness. These melodies cross several eras, yet they ring true for me as the seasonal mind set and the way Autumn can be expressed in song. I call this list:

Andrew's Fall Mood Play List

1. Metal, Daniel May
2. The Four Seasons (Autumn) – I. Allegro, Antonio Vivaldi
3. Darkness Falls, Philip Wesley
4. Autumn Leaves, Nat King Cole
5. Autumn In New York, Frank Sinatra
6. Autumn Of My Life, Bobby Goldsboro
7. Autumn Evening Breeze, Sound Providers
8. Color/Dance, George Winston
9. October, Autumn New England Players
10. Great Pumpkin Waltz, Vince Guaraldi Trio
11. Fugue in G Minor "Little", Virgil Fox
12. Conviction Of The Heart, Kenny Loggins
13. Yearning, Basia
14. Shine on Harvest Moon , Rosemary Clooney
15. Nella Fantasia, Sarah Brightman
16. Fall Leaves' Lullaby, The O'Neill Brothers
17. Last Rose Of Summer/Walking In The Air, Celtic Woman
18. Appalachia Waltz, Metamorphosen Chamber Orchestra
19. Thanksgiving Theme, Vince Guaraldi Trio
20. Fantasia (Waltz of the Flowers), London Philharmonic Orchestra

Soul Satisfying Journeys: Thanksgiving and the World Trade Center

This past Thanksgiving, by happenstance, I ended up home, alone in New York City. It was the first time, in a long time, that I had the opportunity to spend in my hometown on a holiday. This particular day was the first day, in a long time, that you could walk outside in a t-shirt, sans the scarf, hat and jacket and enjoy the sunny 75-degree weather!

I decided that it would be an ideal day to get outside and stroll through the city. Then, it dawned on me, that it would be the perfect time to go and pay homage once again at the World Trade Center.

I have three very special connections to this Sacred place. It was 1983 when I worked as a waiter at Windows on the World restaurant atop of the World Trade Center. It was here that I was schooled in the art of fine wine and service. It was my first encounter with the infamous legacy of chef James Beard, the steadfast maitre d', Mrs. Lee and two of my dearest waiter colleagues, Kimberly and Michael. In those early years of my dance career, it was the restaurant that fed me, educated me and helped me pay my rent!

On September 10th, 2001, my brother Steven, his wife Katherine and I, took our parents, John and Andrena to Windows on the World for a drink to celebrate their wedding anniversary. I recalled the swift ride up in the large elevators, recollecting back to my days as a waiter, traveling up and down in them for a year. In the bar, I remember looking out of the tall, floor to ceiling windows at the spectacular orange sunset, as we toasted my parents and their joyful union of 45 years together.

The next morning, September 11th, 2001, I was crossing Fifth Avenue early in the morning to meet my friend Antonio for breakfast. Striding across the street, I noticed everyone in the street looking south. As I turned to see what everyone's eyes were fixed on, I saw the first plane hit the North Tower. This lasting image, burned into my mind, will always be a part of my psyche.

Now, 10 years later, I was off to see the progress and reinvention of the World Trade Center. With music in tow, I walked along the waterfront down Hudson River Park. Hudson River Park is the largest park to be built in Manhattan since the completion of Central Park. The Park offers facilities for active and passive New Yorkers with tennis courts, basketball, jogging and cycling paths for the active participant along with ample space to layout and get sun. Stretching from 42nd Street to Battery Park, this landscaped, manicured and constantly evolving recreation spot on the Westside Highway has been an amazing transformation.

I was curious to see the brand-new children's playground, miniature golf, and skate park that just opened a few months before. What I also discovered on my walk to the World Trade Center, was an incredible new installation of a boardwalk that reminded me of Fire Island. Exquisitely landscaped with huge rocks and trees rising and falling over gently rolling hills, this wonderful passage was adorned with fragrant pines and juniper bushes. Strategic plantings of seasonal grasses and low ground cover added to its appeal. Benches were placed at the edges of the boardwalk, which made for very private spaces along with a wide-open area flanked by the Hudson River on the west and the Westside Highway to the east.

On a special note, the Hudson River Park's 400 acres of water area has been designated as the Hudson River Park Estuarine Sanctuary. Estuaries occur where fresh water from the land meets salt water from the ocean, resulting in a dynamic nutrient-rich habitat with high biodiversity. This designation acknowledges the importance of the sanctuary as an official New York State significant Coastal Fish and Wildlife habitat.

As I approached the area of the World Trade Center, I passed an entire block of fragrant jasmine trees in late bloom. The scent of this heavenly flower is one of the sweetest and most memorable fragrances on earth. I reached up and pick a bloom to take with me to my destination.

I walked along Warren Street and turned the corner trying to get my bearings. Landmarks I was so familiar with, now seemed to be either shadows of their former selves or gone entirely. It had been five years since I last visited the site and the borders around the area continued to change and morph as the construction progressed.

At that exact moment through my headphones, the song, *Night on Bald Mountain* started playing. Unaware of what I was listening to before this, the swirling strings and thunderous base caught my attention. It immediately brought me back to the confusion and horror of that day. I listened with great intent as I walked through the stone canyons. I could not help but think about those who endured the unspeakable. Tension rose up in my throat as I broke out in a cold sweat.

243

All of a sudden, I rounded the corner and a bell in the music started tolling. It resonated in my ear like a tranquilizer. The tone and rhythm of the music at the end of *Bald Mountain*, finishes with the redeeming sound of light and sunrise, clearly recognizable in the music by a choir.

In *Fantasia*, Disney's musical interpretation of several beloved classical masterpieces, *Night on Bald Mountain* is paired with its "yin counterpart", *Ave Maria*. This is one of the most influential musical pairings in history, which deserves high recognition for its relevance. As *Ave Maria* swelled in my ears, I burst into tears as my eyes became fixed on the new Freedom Tower. Standing at 58 stories (about 680 feet, less than halfway to its planned 1,776-foot height), the steel and glass figure commanded attention.

I was then made wonderfully aware of the resurrection taking place before me. I stopped to say a prayer and offered the Jasmine bloom I had picked, in respect for those who are now interred there. It will be a Thanksgiving that will remain ever important in my memory.

<u>Gemstone:</u>
Sacred Spirit

"When times so bleak and hard to know, there's often room for us to grow, To try and understand the "why", at times when hope seems far and wide, yet there can always be some light, in dark corners, a glimpse so bright…"

~ Andrew Pacholyk MS L.Ac

Music in Memorium

Compiled for a journey I experienced on Thanksgiving, 2011, this is a musical tribute to the World Trade Center. The music expresses the overwhelming sense of loss, love, and resurrection I felt when I went to pay my respects. Adding music and its therapeutic aspects to any situation, can bring together the power of heighten awareness, moving the healing process to another level.

I thought it would be a wonderful opportunity to share some of my most favorite musical inspirations. These melodies cross several eras, styles and themes and ring true for me through their message, rhythms and tempo. Discover how pain and redemption can be expressed in song. I call this list:

Andrew's Sacred Memorium Playlist

1. Mussorgsky: A Night On Bald Mountain
2. Ave Maria, Op. 52 No. 6, Schubert
3. Peaceful Light (Kiev Chant), William Knecht
4. The Immortal Fountain of Light, Johannes Andreasen
5. Voices of Light, Richard Einhorn
6. Light Out of Darkness, Randy Vader
7. Sarabanda in Memoriam, Aaron Jay Kernis
8. On the Transmigration of Souls, John Adams
9. Come Sunday, Duke Ellington
10. Adagio For Strings, Samuel Barber
11. Symphony No. 3, Beethoven
12. Hudson River Suite: The River, Ferde Grofé
13. Quiet City, Aaron Copland
14. Four Last Songs: III. Going To Sleep, Richard Strauss
15. Symphony No. 3, Symphony of Sorrowful Songs: Lento e Largo
16. Metamorphosen For 23 Solo Strings, Richard Strauss
17. The Lark Ascending, Vaughan Williams
18. Rachmaninov: Vespers (All-Night Vigil), Op.37 – 6. "Bogoroditse Devo"
19. Mozart: Requiem
20. Shall We Gather at the River, Santa Fe Desert Chorale
21. God Be With You Till We Meet Again, Mormon Tabernacle Choir
22. Benedictus (from The Armed Man), Karl Jenkins
23. A Hymn for the Lost and the Living (In Memorium 9/11/01)

Seasonal Landscape: Mountains

Metaphysically, mountains (and hills) represent challenges that will lead to growth once we overcome them. The steepness of that mountain is indicative of the degree of challenge or risk involved.

We all face "mountains" or uphill climbs in our lives. The approach to navigating this mountain demonstrates our ability to surmount the obstacle and eventually overcome it.

Soul Satisfying Journeys: The Middle of the World

I had the joy and privilege to see the center of the world at the equator in Ecuador. The journey started in Guayaquil, the coastal city. I have been coming here for over 20 years and still find it an exciting and fun city. It has changed dramatically over the last decade, mostly for the good. I have seen the impoverished city flourish in art and design, in commerce and industry, and become much more gentrified with time. With changing government, banks falling, and leaders rising, it has yo-yo'd up and down, but I would still consider its growth, steady and significant.

As a part of my own self-study, I come to Ecuador each year to study Amazonian herbs, visit with Shaman and healers, and search out amazing places, such as the European-like capital of Quito, the healing mountain town of Banos, and the sprawling discovery of Charles Darwin, the Galapagos Islands. One afternoon, I was approached by one of my Shaman teachers with a gift. It was more of an offering than a gift, I would say. It was a promise. He referred to this gift as the Cosmic Solstice Stones. A collection or "gathering" of sacred crystals from the four corners of the world, to be used as "tools for transition" in preparing for the 2012 Solstice. Knowing that I had a means of "getting them out to the world" as he put it, he thought I would be the one to make his gift available to everyone. I accepted his "gift" on the premise that the monies made would come back to his village in order to help them with clean water and the growing of new crops, in order to feed the village and their elders. He handed them over to me and said, "las herramientas estan en sus manos" (the tools are in your hands). So, off on my journey I went.

This particular visit took me to Quito. High in the mountains, approximately 16 miles north of the capital, marks the exact Middle of the World (Mitad del Mundo), latitude 0 ° where you can stand with one foot on each hemisphere. The Equatorial Monument is a statuesque block of iron and concrete covered with cut and polished Andesite stone featuring a globe perched at the top. Inside this monument is a museum paying homage to the indigenous Ecuadorian cultures including descriptions of the various ethnic groups, clothing, articles, and examples of their lifestyle. Within the area, there are other attractions such as a Planetarium, restaurants and a miniature model of Quito. There are often various musical and cultural groups performing in the Mitad del Mundo's Central Plaza. There is a town surrounding the monument replicating a colonial Spanish town and it is called Ciudad Mitad del Mundo (Middle of the World City).

My particular visit there came on the Winter Solstice, June 21, 2011 (This is the Summer Solstice in the Northern hemisphere). I was invited to a ceremony by the local Shaman to celebrate the Solstice on this day (just one year from the expected date of the lining up of the Earth with the center of our Milky Way galaxy). This most talked about event had the world preparing the planet for the end of the Mayan long count calendar. Known as *"End Time"*, it would take place on December 21, 2012. This date caused absolute fear and upheaval, due to its "gloom and doom" association with the Mayan's prediction as being the actual end of the world!

On a more metaphysical level, this time was looked at as a *simple awakening once again from a deep sleep and the beginning path of wisdom our ancient ancestors followed.* It was they who understood what it meant to live their lives in tune with nature and in a heightened state or another dimension of reality. As with any winter solstice, it is a time which signifies a rest period within the cycle of life. Looking at *"End Time"* could also be seen, not as *the end of the world*, but a time of transition. Astrologically, this time period was considered The Age of Pisces. At the turn of the solstice, this would become The Age of Aquarius or The "Golden Age".

Symbolically, a ceremony at this sacred and mysterious spot felt like ground zero, where the latitude is 0 ° where water flows both counter-clockwise and clockwise down a drain and balancing eggs on end seem possible due to the Coriolis effect. No matter what the truth might be, just the mere fact of being at the middle of the world on the Winter Solstice was incredibly fulfilling, humbling and sheer magic.

The ceremony started right before sunrise as myself and traveling companions were led to a location just beyond the great monument. A large circle of Andesite stone, created the ceremonial boundaries, straddling the north and south hemisphere line. The burning smell of pungent sage filled the air as we were each blessed on the forehead with a sacred blend of essential oils including sage, cedar, juniper, and lavender. Meditation and prayers were said and a form of sun salutation was performed. Music played a big part of the ceremony with local drummers and musicians accompanying the Shaman with soothing, hypnotic vibes as it turned into a rhythmic celebration of song and dance.

As the sun rose above the Andes mountains, we were all given the chance to have items blessed. We were given the opportunity to spend private time with the Shaman healers. I offered crystals in exchange for the blessing of my teacher's Cosmic Solstice Stones. As the sun lit the ceremonial circle, the start of a new and promising season began.

"I am here for a purpose and that purpose is to grow into a mountain, not to shrink to a grain of sand. Henceforth will I apply ALL my efforts to become the highest mountain of all and I will strain my potential until it cries for mercy." ~ Og Mandino

The Mineral Kingdom

Crystals are profound gifts and a great integrative therapy that can be used in conjunction with any other form of health care for personal pleasure, meditation, stress relief and healing.

Top 10 Crystals for Fall

Fall is a time of transition. A change in the amount of light we get and changes in weather conditions can all have an effect on our mood and emotions. Crystals can play a part in making changes, improving transitions, and helping us to move forward gracefully. They are a great tool to meditate and contemplate with. Here are my top 10 choices for Fall.

Amber: Warm and inviting this actual resin from tree sap is an excellent choice for Fall. It is great at detoxification and protection from other people's energies. Due to its strong connection to nature and the earth, amber is a great stone for grounding your higher energies. Amber can add stability to your life. Helpful in clearing up mental chatter it can bring about a positive mental state. Also useful as a memory booster, it a good stone for studying. Amber is used for past life work, divination, and scrying. It aligns mental and emotional bodies via its deep orange and yellow color.

Amethyst: The stone of spirituality and dream recall. Used for contentment and meditation. Provides common sense and flexibility in decisions. Native Indian cultures have used this to strengthen and enhances psychic abilities, imagery, and mind quieting. Wear when sleeping or when awake to reduce anger, impatience, and nightmares. Most effective on the Third Eye and Crown Chakra. Amethyst contains the grounding color of red with the energy of blue, which is expanding, spacious, and flows with peace. Amethyst is the color that you see in the sky as twilight transitions into night. Amethyst takes you on this transition from the magic time of dusk to a conscious shift into a different place. Crossing this threshold is the lesson of humility, which amethyst can teach us. This stone can show us how to let go and trust; so that you may see beyond the cycle that consumes our attention. Amethyst is considered a Master Healing stone.

Carnelian: This stone represents confidence, boldness, initiative, dramatic abilities, assertiveness, and outgoingness. Used for precision, analysis, stimulating appetite, encouraging celebrations, and brings awareness of feelings. It is the stone of passion and sexuality and is associated with the

Sacral/Spleen Chakra. This stone helps you feel anchored and comfortable with your surroundings. It provides a connection to the past or to historical events. Carnelian can improve motivation. Helps one achieve greater success in career or personal matters. Carnelian is one of the most helpful crystals for healing trauma, stress, and emotional wounds that have accumulated in the etheric body or the Aura and manifesting as physical symptoms.

Copper: Excellent energy conductor. It sends and amplifies thoughts, healing, and electrical energy into the wearer's energy field. Worn next to skin, copper is known as a detoxer and soothes arthritis, rheumatism, and other inflammatory problems. Use to improve exhaustion, poor circulation and balancing energy levels. Helps stabilize the metabolism and heightens the immune system.

Hematite: This crystal is the most recommended stone for grounding and is associated with the Root Chakra, by encourages one's survival instincts. Hematite condenses scattered feelings, turns fuzziness into mental clarity, enhances concentration, memory, practicality, and helps those who study. Considered the symbol of life energy, hematite allows for more confidence, will power, and boldness. Helps us adjust to being physical. A protective stone that helps bolster low self-esteem, Hematite is known to deflect negativity. In Renaissance times, it was used to restore equilibrium, bring stability, and for astral protection. It brings our awareness back to the body and helps one maintain their sense of self. If worn, magnetic hematite can be placed on any traumatic injury to increase blood circulation.

Jasper: This stone is a methodical and meticulous worker of practical, down to earth solutions. It has the ability to foster and nurture. Its energy is used for grounding and protection. Considered more effective if it is used for long periods of time because it works slowly. Each color of Jasper has additional, specific qualities when used alone. Jasper is very effective when use on the Root Chakra.

Kunzite: Kunzite was discovered by George Frederick Kunz, the former vice president and buyer for Tiffany's. This stone is used against negative energy and empowers positive and loving thoughts. Most effective on the Heart Chakra, it opens the emotional heart and spiritual heart. It represents unconditional love and compassion. Used for healing abuse/loss/addictions. Helps empower confidence, connection to our higher self and unity. Kunzite is also used for the reason that it deepens altered states, emotionally and spiritually.

250

Petrified Wood: This "stone" is most noted in helping us to investigate past-life experiences. Makes the user more aware of nature, which India's shaman used at the Root Chakra, encouraging one's survival. Petrified Wood is also believed to energize the Heart Chakra. In mythological times, petrified wood was believed to possess divine power and to this day, stands as a symbol of man's true connection to the natural world. This stone helps with mental longevity, helping to soothe emotions, generating calm and relieves stress.

Sodalite: This stone is most recognized for healing, meditation, and wisdom. This is a good stone for general communication, for the self and writing. It is used for expressing logic and ideas due to its connection with the Throat Chakra. It is also used at the Third Eye Chakra due to the fact that it can access levels of intuitive information and promote the understanding of these concepts. It is also known to enhance community relationships. Sodalite can strongly affect changes in your attitude about yourself. It helps you be more objective and less critical about ways of dealing with existence. It is a stone associated with studying.

Sunstone: This stone is a kiss of sunshine, crystallized. Honoring God, this stone brings good luck and fortune. It energizes and empowers one's self. Historically used to warm the heart and lift/rejuvenate the spirit. Sunstone is used for protection, life force energy, and grounding. Sunstone is a great stone to use with "energy vampires", or those who drain your energy from you. This includes parents, children, lovers, patients, bosses or anyone who is possessive, aggressive, or overbearing. Sunstone breaks these bonds and allows light, separation, and clarity from these energies. The Mayan used Sunstone by placing it on the power center or Solar Plexus Chakra. Sunstone is a great stone to relieve stress and overcome fear. This stone is so brilliant that it can bring optimism, happiness, and joy to anyone. Use this stone to help bring awareness to your spiritual realm and encourage the priorities of life. This is one of my favorite stones for depression. A good stone to strengthen the psyche as it promotes cheerfulness, good humor and a benevolent temper.

Shaman Stones: Special Energy Crystals

This is a very special collection of some of THE MOST amazing energetic stones from some of THE MOST incredible places on EARTH!

Sedona Vortex Stones: famous for its energy centers or vortex, Sedona has become a magnet for those seeking powerful enlightenment and a spiritual presence. These amazing stones pulse with energy. These are stones gathered from near area vortexes. These stones are said to embody compassionate, nurturing, energy that engulfs you when you work with these stones. Vortexes are famous for sacred Native ceremonies held to honor the heart, mind, spirit and body.

Moqui Balls: are sacred stones from the Navajo Sandstone formations. They are made of iron and sandstone. These stones offer insight, as they are able to sharpen the eye of its owner, bringing knowledge of what is natural and right. They bring inner peace and harmony to those who embrace them. Said to be used to contact extra-terrestrials, they are used for visioning and for journeys. They act as a protector when placed in one's environment. They synthesis male/female duality, liberate one's nature and help to recognize and understand the self. Used to realign the energy centers, relieve energy blockage, stimulate Qi energy, and ground, center and balance.

Shaman Stones of Ecuador: these stones are used in healing ceremonies by local Shamans. Andesite is the stone for grounding and focusing. They can help in prevention of any physical or mental injury. If you have a low threshold, then this stone can help you to become more understanding, allowing for a grounding stance, a patient outlook and forgiving heart. Therefore, this stone can assist in helping us to detach from old thoughts and beliefs, encouraging the opportunity to look at attaining new beliefs and goals.

Marble Wish Stones: from the quarries of India. These smooth, tumbled marble "gems" provide both clarity and states of "suspension in both meditation and tantric activities. Provides for strength of self-control and mastery of thought. It enhances the powers of serenity. Marble can provide the "good common sense" in matters of the home, heart and one's constitution. Allows for total recall of dreams as well as, provides protection, stability and structure both in the physical and emotional mind. Called "wish stones" because they would be found, made a wish upon and then tossed into the sacred waters. These stones have been tumbled smooth and picked at dawn along the banks of India's Ganges River.

Gratitude Stones: The power of positive thinking creates positive energy. Gratitude stones are a reminder of all the good things we have in our life that we should be grateful for. These smooth and powerful stones from riverbeds all over the world, are usually agate, jade, basalt or granite tumble stones. It is usually a Sacred stone or pebble that fit in your pocket. It acts as a touchstone, so whenever you reach into your pocket or purse and come in contact with the stone, you think about how grateful you are.

Magic Eye Stone: These rare, natural occurrences in the crystal world are the "watchers" of the Mineral Kingdom. Each one is a unique formation that happens in all types of gemstones. Their layers will form the image of an eye at one end of the stone. Their properties are as special. These crystals are a symbol representing the capacity of human consciousness to see beyond the obvious or perceive beyond the outwardly visible and tangible; to reach that inner source of life which is the font of divine energy and power. This symbolism says that all human beings who use their unique powers, can, in the silence of their inner-selves, seek the sanctuary of truth and purity. Magic eye stones have been used in many cultures.

Food for Thought: Eating for Fall

When eating along with the seasons, there are two elements that should be taken into account. The "nature" of the food and the "flavor" of the food. The nature of the food refers to the foods innate temperature ie: cold, hot, warm, cool or neutral. Eating a moderate amount of all flavors sweet, salty, pungent, bitter and sour can help to keep your body balanced and regulated.

In Fall, we should be concerned with tonifying the lungs and large intestines. Pungent taste is attributed to the lungs. Moderate amounts of pungent foods like garlic, onions, ginger, horseradish, and mustard are beneficial to the lungs.

To help tonify the large intestines, concentrate on eating fiber rich fruits, vegetable and psyllium. Consider chlorophyll rich foods such as spirulina, chlorella, barley grass, wheat brass, Klamath blue green algae Other green foods that are beneficial are kale, parsley, and collard greens.

What we eat greatly affects the health of our lungs. Eating excess cold and raw foods creates dampness or phlegm which is produced by the spleen and stored by the lungs. Dairy products, such as milk, cheese, cream, and butter also create phlegm. Consider eating these foods for Fall:

1. Fruits and nuts: apples, cranberries, grapes, energy-rich nuts and seeds (including walnuts and sunflower seeds)

2. Cereals, grains, and legumes: brown rice, corn, millet, oatmeal, sorghum, soybeans, black gram, adzuki bean, red kidney bean, broad bean.

3. Meat, poultry and fish: chicken, turkey, shrimp, carp, eel, chicken eggs.

4. Vegetables such as the root vegetables (including garlic, onion, carrot, potato, sweet potato, yam, and burdock), as well as squashes and gourds (including winter squash, acorn squash, and pumpkin) cauliflower, broccoli and all types of cabbage.

5. Herbs, spices, condiments, oils such as perilla leaf, peppermint, dandelion, honeysuckle flower, basil, parsley, wolfberry (gou gi berries), fleece-flower root, licorice, astragalus, rhubarb, ginger, pepper, honey, sesame oil.

In Ayurveda, your diet is a powerful tool to help your body cope with the change of seasons. Have a solid basis of good fats, such as olive oil. Eat high protein foods. Enjoy an array of warming, stimulating herbs and spices (ginger, cardamom, anise…) and food that is served warm to hot. This will go a long way toward sustaining and maintaining your internal energy and keeping your energy grounded through the Fall season.

Fall foods should favor a slightly sour, sweet, and salty taste combination. Breakfast with cooked grains, congee porridge, oatmeal, tapioca, cream of rice, and cream of wheat can be the perfect warm cereals for this time of year. Lunches and dinners that include hearty soups, steamed vegetables, rich grains and stews are grounding, softening and moisturizing. This is one of the best times of year to enjoy meat and eggs, if it is in your diet. Adding a little more dairy can also be beneficial, as long as there is no issues with phlegm.

In the Fall, it is recommended to reduce your consumption of raw vegetables, cold and frozen foods, as well as the bitter, pungent, and astringent or drying tastes. These include foods such as broccoli, cabbage, cauliflower, sprouts, leafy greens, white potatoes, beans, popcorn, crackers, millet and dried fruit. Consume them in moderation, well-cooked and drizzled with olive oil or warm spices.

You may find that, during the course of the Fall, you'll naturally want to increase your intake of food, but be careful not to consume excess amounts of drying, starchy carbohydrates.

Essential Oils for Fall

Fall, like Spring, is a time of extreme change. The air becomes drier and the climate starts getting wetter and cooler. We now become more confined to the indoors because of the weather. This time of year, is when we also see cold or flu symptoms increase. Emotional stress tends to be stronger in the Fall as we tend more toward reflection. To assist in staying healthy, there are a number of things you can do using essential oils in your environments.

The air becomes drier in the Fall. Our skin, as well as our mucous membranes, can become dry and irritated. This lack of proper moisture can result in germs and bacteria easily finding their way into the body, causing allergies, bloody noses, colds, flu and cracked, dry skin. You can create a better surrounding with essential oils.

Fall can also be an emotionally uncertain time for people. With shorter day, due to less light and the temperature dropping, we sometimes experience SAD, or Seasonal Affective Disorder. Also known as "the blues". Essential oils can be very uplifting and mood changing so that it may help us on both a mental and physical level. You may want to consider these other essential oils for your Fall medicine chest:

Bergamot (Citrus bergamia): is a powerful citrus oil that is a strong antiseptic. This delightful oil is helpful with headaches and irritability. It enhances vital energy and is uplifting. When massaged into the abdomen, it can assist with gastrointestinal spasm and flatulence and gentle abdominal massage can bring relief from constipation and colic. Bergamot oil can soothe inflammation and can help with symptoms of cystitis. Inhalation or massage can be done to treat respiratory infections, sore throats and bronchitis. Bergamot can also be used on the hair to control dandruff.

Cedarwood (Cedrus atlantica): has a rich warm, woody, sweet fragrance. The oil is extracted from wood by the process of steam distillation. This rich, soothing oil can be used in the treatment of respiratory issues. It has antiseptic properties and is effective against coughs, bronchitis and beneficial in the treatment of dandruff, eczema and acne. The oil is particularly useful in treating stress and tension.

Cinnamon (Cinnamoma Cassicia): There are two different oils extracted from this tree. Cinnamon leaf oil has some use in aromatherapy, but cinnamon bark oil is a strong oil that should be used sparingly. Cinnamon leaf oil is extracted from the leaves and young twigs of the tree by steam distillation. Helpful with massage on the stomach for digestive disorders. It is a stimulant and is used to treat circulatory problems. In Traditional Chinese Medicine, Cinnamon is used to warm the interior as well as used for exterior conditions such as a common cold or flu.

Clove (Eugenia aromatica): This essential oil is extracted from the buds of the tree. Heating the oil creates vapors which open sinuses and breathing passages. This oil is uplifting, used as an aphrodisiac and is a reviving, mental stimulant. It can be used to improve mental clarity and memory; improve digestion; and reduces pain by numbing an area, particularly the gums of the mouth. Clove bud oil can irritate the skin and should either be avoided or used with extra care by people who have sensitive skin.

Lavender: (Lavender cassia) is one of the most accepted and most notable essential oils in the Materia Aromatica. This flower oil is used as an antiseptic, antibiotic, anti-depressant, and immune stimulant. It helps with issues of sleep or anxiety due to its sedative properties. Best known for treating burns and blisters, wounds (cell regenerator, minimizes swelling and scarring) insect bites. stings and heat exhaustion. Avoid during the first trimester of pregnancy.

Patchouli (Pogostemon cablin): Essential oil of patchouli is obtained by the process of steam distillation from the leaves of the plant. The oil has a distinctively sweet and earthy smell that is long-lasting. Patchouli is an antiseptic and anti-inflammatory oil used in skin care to treat acne, oily skin, weeping sores, and skin that is reluctant to heal. It has been used for athlete's foot, chapped and painful skin and eczema. Patchouli is particularly beneficial to aging skin and will also help prevent scars and stretchmarks. Patchouli can be used to strengthen the spirit when exhaustion has set in and will help restore a sense of calm and determination in stressful times. The oil is considered an aphrodisiac and can benefit those whose desire or sexual performance has been adversely affected by stress and fatigue. Patchouli oil can also be used as an insect repellent.

Tea Tree: (Melaleuca alternifolia) is a camphorous, pungent, woodsy scented essential oil and is considered a "first aid kit in a bottle". Its properties are antiseptic, antiviral, antibacterial, antibiotic, antifungal, insecticide and is one of the best wound healing oils. It has been used historically to fight infections, ringworm, athlete's foot, sunburn, irritation from shaving, bruises and cuts, warts and acne. May irritate sensitive skin.

Autumn Elegance
Used for: scenting the kitchen/any room with aromatherapy, inviting Fall, honoring Halloween, or as a love potion.

-Blend 2-4 cups of apple cider or apple juice with:
-1 apple cut into small pieces
-1 pinch of nutmeg, cinnamon oil or 1 cinnamon stick

Slowly simmer on the stove. Allow the smell to permeate the room.

Walk In The Woods
This is a nice recipe for an essential oil diffuser.

Add water to the diffuser and light the candle underneath
- Add 3 drops of Clove
- Add 2 drops of Patchouli
- Add 2 drops of Cedarwood

A Spicy Fall Blend
This offers up a crisp, tart scent of the season.

-Add 9 drops of clove
- 7 drops of ginger
- 5 drops of lavender
- 2 quarts of water.
Set your stove on extremely low to allow the steam to diffuse into the air. You can also do the same with a tea pot without a whistle. Remember to always watch the stove and turn it off when no adults are present.

Fall Citrus Delight
Sweet and firm, this season scent combination is uplifting and sacred.

- Add 10 drops of Bergamot
- 4 drops of Clove
- 3 drops of Cinnamon
- add to water in a diffuser.

Light a tea light under the oil to gently diffuse the scent into any room.

Cycle Celebrations

The celebration of the seasons and the passing of time have been celebrated since the beginning. Before there was a monotheistic religion, or the worshipping of one God in our culture, there was polytheistic or the worshipping of nature and many gods.

The process of claiming and adopting styles, religious beliefs and rituals has been repeated over and over again throughout time. Like the cultures before them and every culture after, our celebrations for life and the seasons have evolved over centuries with a history and folklore rich in myth, mystery and magic.

Lammas

Celebrated all over the world and in different cultures, Lammas includes the festival of Lleu, Calan Awst (Wales), Lugudunum (Lyons), Lammas (Christians), Garlic Sunday (Ireland), Lughnasadh (Ireland, Scotland). Lammas, also called Lughnasad, is an ancient festival celebrated as the beginning of the harvest season that was historically observed throughout Ireland, Scotland and the Isle of Man.

The celebration is named after the Celtic god, Lugh, "The Shining One", who was skilled in many arts, smith craft, and was considered a champion warrior. In mythology, Lugh overpowered a primitive Earth god to conquer the harvest time for his people. This day is honored by religious ceremonies, athletic contests, feasting on foods from the first harvest, matchmaking couples, and trading goods. Homage and respects would be paid by climbing to tops of hills and mountains, visiting wells and springs, and offering the first corn, bilberries, and baskets of wheat in thanks. When the Christians adopted this holiday and called it Lammas, the festival shifted slightly to align with the harvesting of potatoes.

This is typically around the last Sunday of July (Garlic Sunday). By the early Middle Ages, the Christians essentially replaced the god Lugh, with the patron saint of Ireland, St. Patrick.

Even now, on the last Sunday in July, a mass pilgrimage climbs Croagh Patrick in County Mayo. The devoted trek up a 2 mile path along the rocky mount (many with bare and bleeding feet) as a testament to the power of this holiday.

When: August 1st (varies)
Season: Cross Quarter: (Mid-way point between Summer Solstice and Autumn Equinox)
Represents: 1st Harvest, Luck, Food Blessings
Virtues: Good Luck, Prosperity
Symbols: Lammas bread, bundle of grain stalks (Sheaf), grain
Gemstone: Ammonite, Carnelian, Copper, Flint, Jasper Mookaite, Petrified Wood
Color: Green, Brown, Yellow
Essential Oils: Eucalyptus, Patchouli, Sandalwood, Vetiver
Remedies: Bilberry, Chives, Dill, Mint, Marjoram, Oregano, Parsley, Rosemary, Tarragon, Sage, Thyme
Flowers: Alstromeria, Cone Flower, Dahlias, Hydrangeas, Hibiscus, Lilies, Sunflower
Element: Earth
Direction: Southwest
Life Event: Change, Healing, Decline
Lunar: Dispute Moon or Sturgeon Moon
Body Healing: Exercise
Mind Healing: Change and Transformation
Spirit Healing: Sacred Spirit

Lammas Bread Recipe

Ingredients

2 cups whole wheat flour
2 cups bread flour, plus more if needed
1/4 cup toasted sesame seeds
2 tablespoons active dry yeast
2 1/2 teaspoons salt
2 cups milk, scalded
3 tablespoons smooth peanut butter
3 tablespoons honey

Prepare Your Dough ~ Mix all the dry ingredients in a large bowl. Add the peanut butter and the honey to the hot milk and stir to combine. ~ Cool milk mixture until it is temperate to touch ~ Stir milk, mix into flour mixture. ~ Knead for 15 minutes, adding more flour if necessary, to make a smooth, elastic dough. ~ Oil the dough's surface, then cover with plastic or a damp towel. ~ Let it rise in a warm spot until doubled in size.

Prepare to Bake ~ Push down the dough, then shape into 2 rectangle loaves or one large braided loaf. ~ Let rise again until doubled in size. ~ Bake at 375ºF until golden. It should make a hollow sound when tapped.

Blessing of the Fruit

Gather together a host of herbs, spices, and fruits. Place them in a basket or cornucopia and place them on your table, altar, or in the Westerly direction. Sprinkle with water or salt (the element of Fall) to anoint them.

Give thanks for the abundance you have been given this year and honor those who may be less fortunate than you, (as there is always someone less fortunate, who could use your prayers.)

Corn is the food of the harvest and it is ready at this time. For centuries, corn has been used in rituals for growth and transformation. One seed brings a stalk plentiful with more corn to enjoy. Corn is associated with being self-sustainable and correlates to the seeds of fertility, growth, and prosperity.

Gemstone:
Sacred Spirit: Blessing of Abundance

"We shall eat the labor of thy hands:
Happy thou shalt be,
We bring these gifts from nature's land
that we have grown by seed.
We honor and give thanks to thee,
for all that you have shared
We bow in great humility
for joys that are most fair.
In times like these we must be proud,
for sometimes it's not so,
as harvest wax and wanes, you see,
you often may not know,
just how lucky each day is,
so with that we must say,
We're grateful each and every day,
as blessings come our way."

~Andrew Pacholyk MS L.Ac.

Mabon

This is also the **Autumn Equinox**. This is the time of the completion of the harvest started at Lammas. Day and night are equal once more as the God prepares to travel toward renewal and rebirth from the Goddess.

Mabon, a Welsh son of the Divine Mother, was captured as a child and taken to the Otherworld. He was ultimately rescued and this sun festival celebrates the second harvest (or second chance). Autumn is a season of shadows and a time of waning light, but it is also a season of abundance, giving thanks and harvest.

Traditions from this season include long walks through the wilderness or fields, gathering dried plants to be used for decorating or for ,future use in herbal decoctions. The altar can be adorned with acorns, pine cones, corn stalks, and various colored Fall leaves. This is the time for completion of tasks, the act of forgiving, and the fruition of long-term goals. Celebrated all over the world as the Autumn Equinox.

When: September 22, 23
Season: Autumn Equinox
Represents: 2nd Harvest, Completion of Tasks, Observing Abundance
Virtues: Forgiveness, Prosperity
Symbols: Cornucopia
Gemstone: Agate, Amethyst, Azurite, Copper, Flint, Lapis Lazuli Sodalite
Color: Gold, Brown, Orange
Essential Oils: Cedarwood, Ginger, Myrrh, Pine, Sandalwood
Remedies: Chives, Dill, Fennel, Garlic, Marjoram, Mint, Oregano, Parsley, Rosemary, Thyme, Sage
Flowers: Aster, Chrysanthemum, Dahlia, Marigold, Zinnia, Dried Leaves
Element: Water
Direction: West
Life Event: Success, Harvest
Lunar: Singing Moon or Harvest Moon
Body Healing: Meditation
Mind Healing: Gratitude Project
Spirit Healing: Sacred Spirit

A Gratitude Stone

Gratitude stones are a reminder of all the good things we have in our life that we should be grateful for. I suggest you carry any small stone in your purse or pocket.

Remove the stone from your person in the evening and place it back in your pocket or purse at the beginning of the day. Whenever you touch the stone, tell the stone (and essentially the Universe), something you are grateful for. **This simple reminder** is a powerful and effective way to bring gratitude, humility, and positive thoughts into your life.

An expression of gratitude gives you a greater sense of purpose in life. Those who reflect a grateful attitude are less depressed, less stressed, and realize all the good things that keep coming their way. This is the **Law of Gratitude or the Law of Cause and Effect.** Your thoughts are the Cause and reality, the Effect.

If you want to change your reality, you must change your thoughts. The principle of thought creation is the expression of sheer gratitude. Gratitude attracts the same gesture of gratitude, which always comes back to you. It is truly up to you to pay attention. Make the **"Gratitude Project"** a part of your life.

The Wreath of Relevance

A Wreath of Relevance is an honorary tribute to the harvest and can be created and given to those who have shown you kindness or have played a significant part in your life.

Start by winding grapevines around a large bottle or pot. Remove the vine wreath from the bottom of the vessel and then start to decorate it. Tuck the ends of the vines into each other. Start filling the wreath with beautiful colored leaves, vines of berries and grapes, twigs with leaves on them, and charms representing the season. The circular shape or the wreath represents eternity, for it has no beginning and no end. From a Christian religious perspective, it represents an unending circle of life. The evergreen, most frequently used in making wreathes, symbolizes growth and everlasting life.

Corn Dollies

From the Native Indian to the Celtic culture, the corn doll or dolly is associated with the "spirit of the harvest." Corn dolls, poppets, or corn dollies were often made at the end of harvest, Mabon or Autumn Equinox in order to "capture the spirit of the crops." They were then brought indoors for the winter.

These blessing dolls are often placed on your altar, fireplace or sacred space, hung in the kitchen, or over the inside of the front door. They are used to protect the "harvest spirit." On farms, they were taken back outside and plowed back into the ground at the start of the Spring season. The dollies were often made into the "old crone" representing the aspects of the Harvest Goddess

Decorate her as the Crone for Autumn harvest, abundance, and good fortune (Harvest Mother). Place your Harvest doll in your home for Lammas or Fall Equinox, near a place of love and prosperity, like your kitchen or hearth.

Gemstone:
Sacred Spirit: Mabon Blessing

"O harvest mother, bring us near,
a place of love when Fall is here.
To bless and honor hearth and
home,
when chill comes round and changes
so,
so much to bring abundance in,
and keep us well, till Spring begins.
Oh harvest dolly, blessing dear,
we thank thee for our season's
cheer.
So bring around a basket full,
for all to have and share by Yule."

~ Andrew Pacholyk MS L.Ac

Season of the Moon: Moonrise

The moon is symbolically found in all cultures and religions throughout history.

The moon represents the deeper emotional state of Fall, the beginning of the moon's reign over the dark half of our years.

The Moon is associated with a person's emotional make-up, unconscious habits, rhythms, memories and moods, and their ability to react and adapt to those around them. It is also associated with the mother, maternal instincts or the urge to nurture. It represents the home, the need for security, and the past, especially early experiences and our childhood.

The Fall season represents the cardinal direction of West. The West offers more conclusions in our lives along with mature stability, actuality, physical wisdom, the "root connection" or grounding of spirit and our interpersonal achievement of goals. As the sun sets, we are made aware of the precious moments we may have left, in accordance with the time we have been given. This realization helps with understanding, thoughts of completion along with reminiscent thoughts, as we make that revolution around the wheel of life.

<u>Gemstone:</u>
West

"When day is done, Sun slowly parts,
To leave in contemplative thoughts.
Like water's waves, sun ebbs and
flows,
We trust you'll return another show."

~Andrew Pacholyk MS L.Ac

Our Twilight Years

Between sunset and moonrise is the magical time of twilight. This magic can be felt as you watch the sun transition in the Western sky. Amethyst is the color that you see on the horizon as twilight crosses over into night. This time takes you on a transformation from the mystical hour of dusk to a conscious shift into a different place. Crossing this threshold is the lesson of humility.

But, as the moon rises, the feeling of another opportunity rises with it. A feeling of a renewed chance comes your way. It is like a second wind or second chance at life! The moon rises every day in the East and always sets in the West, due to the Earth's continuous rotation.

The moon orbits the earth about every 29 days, and this first cycle is the one most people are familiar with. The moon is illuminated by sunlight, the giver of all warmth, light, and life in our solar system, but we can't always see the part being lit. As the moon goes around the earth, we see the moon from different angles. When we see a full moon, the moon is directly opposite the sun. When we see a new moon, it's because the moon and sun are in the same direction.

"As within, so without." Knowledge of the basic cycles of the moon are an understanding of the forces that motivate and drive us. They are the constant changes we see as our life mirrors the lunar phases. The lunar lesson suggests that we pay attention to our insight, our bodies, and our emotions. For what we feel inside, we tend to express outside.

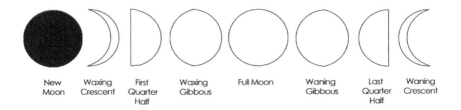

| New Moon | Waxing Crescent | First Quarter Half | Waxing Gibbous | Full Moon | Waning Gibbous | Last Quarter Half | Waning Crescent |

Gemstone:
Moon Power

"O' magic of the moon reveal,
and move through phases,
that which heal ~
our body mind and spirit health ~
to start anew, empower thyself
To grow our wishes, hopes and
dreams,
to full fruition and extremes."

~ Andrew Pacholyk MS L.Ac

*When the moon is NEW, this is considered the time of birthing. Birthing new ideas, intentions, and seeding new ventures. This is also called the **dark of the moon**. This time marks the beginning of a major new cycle in your life. It is not yet a definitive separation with the past, but it is a time when you instinctively feel an impulse for creating new beginnings. This is the right time for setting your intentions.

*When the moon is WAXING, this is when it is growing towards a full moon. It is the time to do empowerment work in manifesting, expanding, and growth. Use this time for developing a clear, practical plan, lose all hesitation, and move forward. Nurture the intention and ideas you started at the new moon. This is the time to be conscious of your new venture, as you work to manifest it.

*When the moon is FULL, this is considered the highest time for manifesting goals, nurturing your passions, full attention to healing, encouraging strength, power, and love. Employ knowledge and legal undertakings, work to manifest money, and bring dreams to fruition. It is the most potent time for rituals for prophecy, protection, divination, and any manifesting work that needs extra power and letting go. This is the time when the seed you planted at the new moon may have developed and released.

*When the moon is WANING, this is when it is shrinking after a full moon. It is time to do empowerment work in diminishing, decreasing, and dissipating. This is a time to complete old projects and let go of strategies and situations that aren't working. This is an important time for reversing circumstances, releasing old ways of thinking, removing unwanted negative energies, along with addictions, illness, or oppressive belief systems. This is the process of letting go.

Crystals Associated with the New Moon

Meteorite: Usually solid, dull, mottled, brownish to black in color, these space stones amplify thoughts/telepathy, sending/receiving, greater awareness, or have some connection to extraterrestrial life. They often have odd/unusual energy, best used by those drawn to them. Some Native Indian tribes believe that since meteorites are in tune with the energies of the cosmos they are more capable of raising our energies to a Universal level.

Black Moonstone: India's culture used this stone for finance and prosperity Believed to help attract a gradual increase in your finances and helps you to feel more financial security. Like a new moon, changing to a full moon, black moonstone is symbolic of a "new moon beginning" and the ideal time to plant the seeds of good intentions in order to watch them grow.

Black Obsidian: Obsidian is actually natural glass that is formed when hot lava is submerged in water. This is a strong grounding stone and is known as "the protector." It is said to "mirror one's soul. This stone brings about objectivity, dis-attachment, and is grounding. According to traditional Celtic lore, obsidian reduces fantasy and escapism. A stone used for scrying.

Black Onyx: This stone is believed to help one retain memory of the physical occurrences surrounding a person. A strong stone to use in psychometry because it tells the story of the wearer. Onyx is a strength-giving stone. A good stone for athletes or people under extreme mental and emotional stress. It brings balance to mind or body, as well as strength of spirit. Good stone for those who are flighty by nature. A strengthening stone that can help you approach a lesson or task with greater self-confidence.

Smoky Quartz: Smoky Quartz is a grounding stone. It is used most often to overcome depression, soothing nightmares, or stress. Quartz stimulates the natural crystal in body tissue and fluid to resonate at the highest healing frequency. Because it is associated with the Root Chakra, it helps to alleviate fear, anxiety, and associated emotional issues.

Tektite: This is a type of natural glass, chemically and structurally unique, to meteoric origins. Tektites are found on earth within narrow equatorial belts. Tektites usually have a heavily pitted surface. Many have the appearance of being stretched while in a molten state. They assist one in attaining knowledge and learning lessons throughout the travels of life.

New Moon Meditation

A new moon meditation is a journey into your deeper self. It is a way to connect with your spiritual resonance. A new moon is the spark of new beginnings. Our subconscious emotions connect with this moon.

When you are ready to start fresh, begin a new task, or start a new project, consider starting it on a new moon A new moon meditation is a self-healing and self-discovering journey. It empowers you with the knowledge and fact that once you can pay attention to yourself, you can attend to others by giving them your full awareness. A new moon is a tool used for renewing yourself, birthing new ideas, and activating creative energy within yourself. It is a very rejuvenating meditation. It is the act of setting the ground rules and beginning your path to dreams, ideas, inspiration, affirmation, incantations, missions, or a goal or vision.

This meditation is for your "spiritual intention", to grow into fruition.

Moon Meditative Space

The best place to perform this meditation is within the sight of a new moon. Your next best place would be your meditation space. This is a clear, peaceful space where you can meditate deeply and freely of disturbance.

Intention Tool Options

If you prefer, prepare your meditation space with incense, crystals and/or gentle music. Consider lighting a candle.

Monday happens to be the day the Moon was assigned to "rule", signifying intuition and a time to bring about creativity in your work.

Take a look at *Crystals Associated with a New Moon*. For example, obsidian stone represents the new moon. This is a strong grounding stone and is known as "the protector." It is said to "mirror one's soul." According to the infamous "seer", Nostradamus, this unusual black stone is known to absorb darkness and converts it to white light energy. Smoky Quartz is a good grounding stone, while black moonstone is often used to encourage financial security or prosperity. Consider holding one of these stones for meditation.

Crystals can represent nature, one for each element – fire (red stone), water (dark blue or black stone), air (green or blue stone), earth (brown or grey stone.) The elements are also related to a direction and intent. Here are some to consider:

Fire – South – Fire element empowerment is related to consumption, heat, entropy, fuel, energy transfer and thermodynamics. Element: heat. Signs of Aries, Leo, Sagittarius. Candles can be used here.

Earth – North – Earth element empowerment relates to grounding, cultivation of energy and energy stability. Elements: metal, earth. Signs of Taurus, Virgo, Capricorn. A vase with dirt, stones or rocks, plants or herbs can be used here.

Water – West – Water element empowerment relates to flow, forms, cycles, combinations and manipulations. Elements: water, ice. Signs of Cancer, Scorpio, Pisces. A vase with water or ice can be used here.

Air – East – Air element empowerment harness the wind, kinetic forces, static energy, free form energy and directed movement. Elements: lightning, wind, spirit. Signs of Gemini, Libra, Aquarius. Incense can be used here.

How do these apply to your intention? They are tools to enhance energy.

Use 4 similar stones, or different colored stones to represent four elements. Place them in your meditative space in 4 directions. You can also use any of the new moon stones, listed previously OR place the stones on the floor, so that you are able to sit in the middle of them.

A Master Stone: You can then use a 5th stone, or a master stone (a crystal that is your favorite to work with or one which calls to you.) Trace the outline of the crystal circle with your master stone (either on the table or sitting within your meditation circle.) Then place your master stone in the center of the circle. (If it is on your table place it in the center. If you are meditating on the floor, hold it with you – in your dominant hand – sitting in your circle.)

Your Intention on paper. If you place your circle of stones on a table or altar, you can write down an intention on a piece of paper and then place it under your master stone in the center of that circle. If you are sitting in your circle, you can hold the paper in your hand or place it in front of you. At the end of your meditation, you may choose to burn the intention paper by touching one end of it to the candle light and letting it burn in a dish or bowl in front of you. The same holds true with your candle. When you are done with your meditation, extinguish the flame, by covering the flame. In many spiritual practices, it is believed that these actions release your intention outward to the Universe.

These are different ways to incorporate "tools of intention" into your meditation. You can choose to do none of these and just close your eyes.

Working with your Moon Intention

Once your meditation space is set, get into a comfortable seated position and close your eyes. NOW, spend time with your circle, your intention, and your crystals.

Gentle breath work can be done by breathing in deeply and slowly exhale out. On the inhale, take in your intention... on your exhale, release the energy that is blocking that intention.

Your intention and purpose for this meditation should really be focused around growth. Think about achieving, gaining, improving, and the introduction of a new idea. Meditate on how you would like this to manifest. Think about the reasons why you want this to happen and how it will serve you.

Focus on your intention. Bring that thought to behind your eyelids. Sense how you can make this work. Slowly move that intention up to your Third Eye (between your eyebrows.) "See" your intention grow, taking all the time you need to empower your dream. Spend the time you desire to feel grounded, calm, and relaxed. You will know, instinctually how much time you need.

Gently move your intention back to behind your eyelids. Allow yourself a positive, peaceful place to feel safe. When you are ready to finish your meditation, you can end with a deep breath, a prayer, or just a large sigh... open your eyes. Your positive (wish) intention has been set.

Chapter 8

Winter

Winter is our time of introspection. It is our fourth quadrant of development from our late 60's, early 70's and onward. This period in our lives represents the coming of age of life's lessons learned. Winter represents our collective thought and knowledge gained through our experiences.

The Chinese Medicine paradigm offers practical advice for adjusting to seasonal changes. The season of winter is associated with the element of water. The emotional aspect related to winter, is fear. The predominant taste is salty. The cold and darkness of winter urges us to slow down. This is the time of our lives to reflect on our health, replenish our energy, and conserve our strength. This is a good time of year to be more conscious about and take care of the kidneys, urinary bladder, adrenal glands, ears, and hair.

Strengthening the immune system should be a part of any seasonal ritual. Simple tips include moving regularly, walking more, standing more frequently (instead of sitting) and improving your sleep habits.

This is the astrological season of the zodiac signs of Capricorn, Aquarius, and Pisces. Capricorn, the ambitious Sea Goat, is duty bound, ambitious, serious with single-minded focus and drive. Aquarius, the knowledgeable water-bearer stands for independence inventiveness, and ingenious behavior. This unique nature makes them progressive, unpredictable, detached, and logical. Pisces, the mysterious dreaming fish is known for being an escapist, self-sacrificing, and a highly idealistic person. Together, they are the most connected, psychic and spiritually in tuned signs of the zodiac.

In the winter of our lives, a contemplative thought is central to our focus. At this time of our lives, we tend toward reason, rational and logical thinking. We are more analytical and aware, as we try to bring order to our lives.

It is the time to reflect and ponder as we connect. That connection is a full circle retrospective of our lives. It should be considered a collage of the best experiences we have made for our lives and these experiences should be honored.

Although "winter" represents the longest night, it also represents the dawn of new light. The priorities in our life tend to focus on finding peace, protection along with self-balance, self-healing, and self-power.

If we have not been spiritual throughout our lives, this period tends to force us to pay attention to the inevitable. It opens our eyes to the subjects of healing, empowerment, and death. We look deeper into the "watery" depths of our soul and try grasping and understanding some opportunities we may have lost. We can also choose to see the incredible times that brought us the greatest happiness.

Gemstone:
Dawn's New Light

~ *"O darkest night of Yule's light,*
I come to honor in circle, bright
To contemplate in winter's glow
This time when new beginnings grow.
To reach as sunlight does each day,
And cast-way shadow, dark and grey"

~ Andrew Pacholyk MS. L.Ac.

The Priorities of Life

In each aspect of our lives, there are certain "priorities" we find important and tend to focus more on. This is often based on our age or need to fit in, our self-discovery or need to be recognized. Our priorities of life are the cornerstones we use to define ourselves, better understand who we are, or are sometimes forced to recognize out of circumstance.

Peace

Peace is a great gift. Peace is something that we are constantly seeking. Its idealism runs parallel to seeking the ultimate truth. It is within our own hearts that peace is found. Seeking peace on external levels can only bring temporary joy. Once we have a better sense of peace within us, we can remain calm a little easier, even in the most chaotic of external situations.

Peaceful Meditation

Focus on the quiet within you. Fold your hands gently in your lap and close your eyes. Take a few deep breaths. Then just sit. If you have never meditated before, you will probably feel as if your mind is full of thoughts. Don't try to stop the thoughts, just watch them.

Imagine that you are on the bank of a river and that your thoughts are the river going by. Don't try to stop the river, just watch it. Within time, and the more you meditate, you will see the river begin to slow down. Do this for 5 to 10 minutes.

You may find that you fall asleep because you are so relaxed. That's good because, in many ways, you have begun to let go. Your goal is to become relaxed, yet present and aware of the practice. Continue at this pace. Each day allow just a little more time for yourself to meditate. Doing this allows you to relax, let go and forget about time.

Gemstone:
Angel's Song

"I close my eyes and breathe deep
down to my inner core.
I'll breathe away the stressors,
even those I can't ignore.

I'll visualize an ocean,
or a feather on a breeze.
I'll see myself just praying,
in a forest, on my knees.

I can't control what's happening,
around or in my way.
I can control what's happening,
deep in my heart, today.

I'll breathe and let go sorrow,
or chains or ties that bind.
This moment I'll discover,
a way to be more kind.

To myself and to my loved ones,
to friends and family, too.
I'll allow myself no judgement,
That's when I knew - I grew.

Live-in each peaceful moment! "

~ Andrew Pacholyk MS, L.Ac

Tenants of Peace

√ Conflict is the antagonist of peace. Internal problems that you allow, create blocks. These conflicts are governed by fear, insecurity, and a sense of feeling scattered.

√ When we feel peace, our mind is clear and our spirit is calm. Our heart senses joy and we are at ease with everything around us. Of course, this fluctuates like a barometer, but the real test of ease is finding more times that we are at peace, than our heart is in turmoil.

√ A peaceful mind comes with trust. Trusting has a Universal purpose. It allows spiritual guidance. Peace is allowing your heart to sing without the ties that bind it to earthly issues or material traps.

√ Peace can be built by letting go. When we hold on to worry and create a wall of anxiety, we become weighed down by its burden. Only you can lift this wall. Only you can see beyond what you are standing in…. often a pool of doubt, a river of thoughts, or an ocean of impossibilities.

√ Let go. Trust. Start to honor yourself. Begin to be good to yourself. Reframe your situation. Open your heart to all that is possible. See past the wall. Step through the door. Give in. Let go.

Protection

Protection looks at our core feeling of fear, anxiety, and lack of security. **Letting go**. By giving this fear up to the Universe to handle, you are allowing yourself to release this fear, and strip away any kind of meaning or significance it may have upon you. By letting go, this allows us to move to the next level in our lives.

Protection always comes by letting go of the fear.

~ "On life's journey, faith is nourishment, virtuous deeds are a shelter, wisdom is the light by day and right mindfulness is the protection by night. If a man lives a pure life, nothing can destroy him." ~ Buddha

Gemstone:
Protection

*"Insight into my familiar,
enfolds me in my fearless
nature.
Faith, security, protection,
fill my heart with trust,
reflected.
That I'm deeply sound,
connected,
guided safely and protected."*

~ Andrew Pacholyk MS L.Ac.

Tips on Protection

1. Be Grounded: Physical identity, oriented to self-preservation, being grounded represents the element of earth and is therefore related to our survival instincts, and to our sense of grounding, connection to our bodies and the physical plane.

2. Be Aware: Ideally, being aware allows us the understanding of fear, which allows us the comfort to feel protected. Being aware can keep us healthy, secure, and allow us a dynamic presence.

3. Be Familiar: When we are familiar, we are comfortable and we feel connected with our physical body and the space around us.

4. Be Open: Being open, gives us the ability to be conscious and secure in ourselves and determines how we look at life around us. This roots us in the survival of both the physical realm and spiritual body.

Create A Worry-Free Journal

The Worry-Free Journal is a book or record you create to chart progress, make steps to follow, or create a journey to building security. It can be used for writing down experiences you have, words that give you power, and help you to work toward your protection. This journal is a good place to record your information so that you can go back and look at it later.

Protection is about alleviating fear and worry. Upon waking, pick up your journal and write down any dreams (or nightmares) that may appear to be related to your lack of security and protection. Worry can only serve you well if you worry and recognize that a plan of action is needed, in a stressful situation and then you act on it. But, when worry becomes overwhelming, this is considered fear. No matter what type of fear you are experiencing, there are many techniques to move forward. Let's elaborate:

1. By slowly taking away the "layers" of what covers this fear, we discover what is truly at the root of this fear. It enables us to deal with it from a higher point of view and opens up a path in which to rebalance. Write down your main fear that threatens your protection.

2. Look at it on paper. Be honest with yourself when you write them out. Go with your immediate intuition. Fears have a tendency to dissolve when we are looking at them head on.

3. Re-balance. As a holistic individual, you know that your body is continuously in a state of re-balancing itself. This is how we function. This is how we grow. By holding on to a fear, we are not allowing these processes (your intuitive state) to flow freely. This block can be the cause of a much bigger problem. Write out the possible solutions to relieving this fear.

4. Letting go. By giving this fear up to the Universe to handle, you are essentially allowing yourself to release this tension, and in turn, strip away any kind of meaning or significance it may have upon you. By letting go, this allows us to move to the next level in our lives. The next natural process. Often times, this is a fear in itself. The fear of "what will happen when I DO move to my next stage in life?" Feeling protected always comes by letting go of the fear. Write down 5 ways you will let go of this emotion that does not serve you.

5. Let your guard down. Let it go. This is not a fear. This is a great journey. Allow yourself to follow it.

6. Being Grounded. Being grounded is related to our survival instincts, and to our sense of connection to our bodies and the physical plane. Choose a few crystals that appeal to you. Lay them in a circle on the floor and lay within the circle. Anoint your wrist, neck, and forehead with your favorite essential oil. Make this your safe place. Breathe and relax into your safe place. Allow the stones to work by dissolving your negative, unhealthy fears.

7. Being Aware. Ideally, being aware allows us the understanding of fear, which gives us the comfort to feel protected. Once you know what your fear is, you can take steps to address it. Being aware can keep us healthy, secure, and allow us dynamic presence. Use the **white light protector exercise**.

8. Be Familiar. When we are familiar, we are comfortable and we feel connected with our physical body and the space around us. What makes the fear familiar to you? What do you recognize within this emotion?

9. Deep Breathing. Learn to breathe deeper. This is very helpful in stressful situations. It allows for the release of carbon dioxide (stress) and room to take in fresh, soothing air (calm). Close your eyes and imagine your breath as an ocean wave. As you breathe in, imagine the ocean wave rolling onto shore, as you exhale, imagine the ocean wave moving back out to sea taking all the debris on the beach with it. This is your breath cleansing your mind and body with every breath.

10. As you inspire yourself and build your confidence and self-esteem, you inspire confidence in others. This natural progression is one of the most rewarding gifts you can receive. Write down 10 items, people, places… which inspire, empower, and give you a feeling of a protective life. How do these inspirations figure into your life? How will you use these tools to bring out the most potential and radiant you? Write them down now.

Your worry-free journal will show you your particular path to overcoming fear and gaining a feeling of security. At the end of the day, write down everything that you are thankful and appreciative of in your life.

White Light Protector Exercise

White color or white light is protective. Objects that REFLECT all wavelengths and DOES reflect everything, is white. As reflective as the snow in winter or the starkness of a white room, white energy offers us a canvas to paint on or a light energy to bathe in.

Culturally, in Europe or in the West, when there is a death, it is associated with wearing black or by honoring the "dark times" of someone's life. In China, it is the opposite. Wearing white to a funeral or for an ancestral death ceremony is a tradition. This is because white is considered the color of winter when all things return to earth in a dormant state.

White is considered the color of purity and innocence and white light is encompassing. Therefore, cleansing or purifying yourself in white light is a century's old tradition.

Attracting and retaining people's energies is a very common occurrence. The best way to protect yourself from energies (negative), which make you uneasy, is with white light.

Sit, or lay on the floor and close your eyes.

Imagine white light warming and engulfing first, your Crown Chakra and bathing your eyes in light.

Let the white light warm your mind and relax and release all thoughts...

Move the white light down the Chakra and let it bathe each energy center.

Allow the white light to massage each center of energy. In your mind's eye, allow the light to stay in each area of energy for as long as you need. You will instinctually know when it is time to move the light downward through your body until you finish at the Root Chakra.

Then allow the white light to engulf your entire being. This protects your aura from negative energies, environmental assult, and allows your "psychic defense" to come into play. This can be done at any time, in any place. Just close your eyes and visualize this White Light Protector.

Self-Balance

The Balance Within ~ Each of us seeks to find something new, which will take us to the next level in our lives. As humans, we constantly need something to believe, find faith in, or have hope for. It could be from the simplest pleasures of having a good day to the beginning of a new relationship, good health, or self-awareness. Believing, hoping, and having faith that we will find what we seek is the life-thread which keeps us going to the next minute, the next day, the following year.

Balance is the bottom line. We strive all our lives to keep in balance. Our emotional, mental, physical, and spiritual being is constantly striving to stay balanced. When we are balanced, our "whole-self" works in conjunction with all our other beliefs. When we are not in balance, we allow ourselves to be more susceptible to doubt, even illness or dis-ease. Keeping this delicate balance is up to you.

<u>Gemstone:</u>
Balance Within

"I seek to find a steady frame,
and believe that life is but a game,

of finding focus, setting stakes,
to reach or fail then reach and make,

a goal or certain set of rules,
that, I set ~ and then re-tool.

for balance comes and then it goes,
to find its way back where it knows."

~ Andrew Pacholyk MS L.Ac

Everything works in a delicate balance. Yet, balance is constantly fluctuating. Moving in and out of balance is a natural process. The Universe is always re-balancing itself. It is an on-going recalibration of the elements from the largest mass to the smallest atom. Balance is literally seen as standing on a see-saw or teeter totter and consistently keeping the ends from tilting too far to one side or the other.

We can find the "strive for balance" within ourselves and everywhere we look. Consider how our bodies re-balance as the seasons change. A women's menstrual cycle is the body constantly rebalancing. It is related to the moon and how our birth, life, and death cycles are similar to the cycles of nature. It is important to realize that we are never, fully in balance all of the time.

The proponents of Yin and Yang, our Circadian rhythm, and the energy of the Chakra are ancient paradigms used to understand balance. These theories show how life finds a point of equilibrium and constantly works to stay within this balance. When factors are introduced to sway this balance, the energies surrounding them push back to find that point of equilibrium once more.

"Balance... comes from your vital engagement in, and personal striving toward, goals that give your life a sense of meaning and purpose." ~ Ellen Ostrow

Yin and Yang

Yin and Yang exist in everything in the Universe in relation to each other. The duality of the Universe and the world around us is expressed in this "Tai Chi," symbol (often, mistakenly called the Yin/Yang symbol) a circle created by a light and a dark side, positioned end to end with one small circle of yin in yang and yang in yin. This is the presence of its complement.

This has been accepted for several thousand years in Chinese philosophy, but the acknowledgment that every male has a feminine aspect, and every female has a male side, is new to the Western mind and medicine. Together, yin and yang comprise a whole, and yet there is an element of each in the other.
Sometimes we have too much yang, and other times, we have too much yin. It is up to us to find and maintain the balance between the two in our physical, mental, emotional, spiritual, sexual, and intellectual selves. Achieving this balance helps us become grounded and centered.

Biorhythms

Biorhythms are the body's cycles that fluctuate on a regular and predictable schedule. It was developed by Wilhelm Fleiss in the late 19th century and popularized in the late 1970s. According to a NASA study on circadian rhythms, *"The theory of biorhythms is a theory that claims our daily lives are significantly affected by rhythmic cycles. The theory is built on the idea that the biofeedback chemical and hormonal secretion functions within the body could show a sinusoidal behavior over time."*

A biorhythm chart can measure four distinct fluctuations: physical, intellectual, emotional, and intuitive, based on the daily changes of each. Each fluctuates at its own speed, but all start off at zero on the day you were born. *"Most biorhythm models use three cycles: a 23-day physical cycle, a 28-day emotional cycle, and a 33-day intellectual cycle."* Therefore, simply by calculating how many days you have been alive, the biorhythm chart can map out your readings for any given day. Knowing the high and low points of the rhythms and the "critical periods" where they cross over from positive (active) to negative (inactive) and vice versa just might give you an edge on what kind of activities to plan and avoid for certain days.

The Keys to Achieving Balance

You need to find the right balance that works for you. Take the time to enjoy your successes and remember, what you consider failures are usually just choices that did not go your way in the moment. Life is a process, and it changes, minute by minute. Striving for balance in your life will come and go and then return. The most important aspect to remember is how you choose to deal with these moments.

1. Be Patient: We live in a world that is "immediate gratification" driven. If we cannot have something we desire, right this minute, we become impatient. As we become more spoiled by having "life at our finger tips" it makes it more difficult to accept the fact that we may not be able to have everything we want when we want it. This is where learning the art of patients is imperative.

2. Slow Down: This is probably the first step in understanding patience. If we did not multi-task 50 things in one day, we feel like we have wasted time. Take time to stop and enjoy situations and people around you. Schedule more time between appointments or meetings. Do not make plans for every evening or weekend. Learn to accept situations as they come and take time to deal with them. Appreciate what is right in front of you at that very moment.

2. Learn to Delegate: This comes back to the issue of trust. You cannot do everything yourself. I know that there are some of us who feel that way, but in the end, you tip the scales to the point of saturation, leaving yourself overwhelmed, over-worked, and fully stressed. Start by giving simple tasks to those who are willing to help you.

3. Don't Get Caught Up: The minutia of life can bog us down. Our minds can get wrapped around details that may not be necessarily important in the moment. We can spend hours in a day looking for the right color to match our curtains, dealing with customer service on the phone, getting angry over things we cannot control. Try to learn how to move past these issues that waste time and create imbalances in our life.

4. Learn Time Management: You will be surprised when you learn how to work smart and efficiently. Try delegating less time to a project that needs your attention instead of over-extending yourself. Procrastination is the cause of much strife in our lives. Make time for everything. Create a schedule. Schedule time for work, exercise, play. You will find that balance will make you feel much lighter, happier, and powerful.

5. Daily Balance: When choosing which area of their lives they are most imbalanced with; most of my patients will say "work." We devote more time to our work and deadlines, than we do with any other facet of our lives. Because of this, our family, home, exercise, play schedules all fall prey to this imbalance. By the time we are able to actually spend time balancing the other areas of our lives, we are too tired, too stressed, or too late. Whatever area of your life you are the most out of balance with, consider regulating your time, schedule, or routine.

6. Open Yourself Up to Other Possibilities: There are always other possibilities. If you are feeling overwhelmed with your responsibilities, find other options. Balance comes when you understand there is another way of doing something. It may take some time to see, but the possibilities are there.

7. Make Things Easier: Simplify your life. Make priorities happen. Change your lifestyle choices. Begin looking at ideas which cut corners, give you relief time or ask for help if you need to. Organize your life in ways that allow time for the most important aspects of that day and stick to your plan.

8. Declutter Your Life: If you were to strip away everything in your life, what would be the top 3 things you would add back into this "empty space?" If you only had 3 options, consider how you would make these 3 options work for you. Keep in your life, only the things you love and make your heart sing!

9. Find Gratitude: Really appreciate when you have achieved some balance in your day. Acknowledge it. Be grateful. When things are really working in your life, accept and observe this balance. Recognize what made this come together.

10. Learn What You Want: More importantly, learn to recognize what you don't want in your life. These are usually the things that take up a large percentage of our time and block the real desires we want to bring into reality. Balance comes from knowing what you want and engaging in them.

An Ancient Look at Balance

The Doctrine of the Mean

The Doctrine of the Mean or "Zhongyong" is the name of one of the Four Books on Confucianism, as well as a doctrine of his beliefs. The mean is also described as the "unswerving pivot" or zhongyong. Zhong meaning "bent neither one way or another", and yong represents "unchanging." The Doctrine of the Mean explains how the tenants of moderation, honesty, objectivity, sincerity, rectitude, and propriety are the core beliefs. The doctrine includes 3 guidelines:

Self-watchfulness: This guideline requires self-education, self-questioning, and self-discipline during the process of self-cultivation.

Leniency: This guideline requires understanding, concern, and tolerance towards one another.

Sincerity: Sincerity contributes to a close connection between Heaven and human.

The Doctrine of the Middle Way

In the Pāli Canon of Theravada Buddhism, the term **"Middle Way"** was used, which the Buddhist tradition regards to be the first teaching that the Buddha delivered after his awakening. In this sutta, the Buddha describes the Noble Eightfold Path as the "middle way" of moderation, between the extremes of sensual indulgence and self-mortification.

The Noble Eightfold path refers to Buddha's doctrine of the: right understanding, right thought, right speech, right action, right livelihood, right effort, right mindfulness and right concentration. By finding this middle way, one could be avoiding the extremes by understanding that the middle ground or path helps us on our life journey as it gives vision, gives knowledge, and leads to calm, insight, enlightenment and Nirvana.

The Doctrine of Dharma

Dharma stands for the ultimate moral balance of all things. Dharma belongs to the Universe and to the individual as well. So, just as there is a divine order of the natural and cosmic realms, there is the same order within a personal life. However, each one has the responsibility to balance his or her own dharma.

A Hindu's dharma is played out in all areas of life: religious, social, and familial. If a person makes a promise, the promise must be kept at all costs. Likewise, the faithful maintain their religious rituals while attending to their family's needs.

When these responsibilities are not met or taken seriously, the outcome is equal to your lack of commitment and follow through. Reaping what you sow, is the result failing to follow your Dharma. This is your Karma.
Karma stands for the belief that a person experiences the effect of his or her actions that every act or thought has consequences. Living in a balanced Universe, if an individual disturbs this order, he or she will suffer commensurately. But, an ethical and moral life, with undisturbed dharma, will lead to happiness.

Self-Healing

Our health is a balancing act.

Our health. It is our greatest gift and is often the one thing we take for granted. Our health is always changing. The basis of our health is a combination of genetics, lifestyle, and environmental choices. We tend to only be aware of our health after we are ill. The issue of prevention is often neglected due to the fact that we take our good health as something we will always have.

Combining awareness of all three levels of our mind, body, and spirit health can make the person you seek in yourself, a better one. It will allow you to love, honor, and enjoy who you are. It will help you to understand what makes YOU tick. Embracing all three aspects really creates an energy or vibration that resonates with your higher self. You will feel different. You honor yourself more and know why.

Gemstone:
Self-Healing

*"Anoint myself for healing sake,
to release the binds and make the break
from illness, ill will, broken ties,
O' show me honest, good allies.
Let health and wellness show and tell,
my soul where rainbow colors dwell.
And bring a path for those to heal,
With open arms and heart gentil."*

~ Andrew Pacholyk MS L.Ac

Your Healing Journey

What shift does it take for someone to find that road to feeling well again? The path to wellness must include a sense of freedom and enjoyment within that journey, and we have to be true to ourselves. We have to believe in the recovery process.

Whichever form of therapy you are working with, these practices should reinforce the belief in the recovery and the transformation to wellness and balance. What stops us from getting better?

"Life is designed by our soul and spirit as our moment-by-moment opportunity to expand our consciousness." ~ unknown

We get sick for a reason. There is the germ and virus explanation that is the basis of Western medicine. There is also another way of looking at it. When we catch a cold, it is because our immune system is low (often due to stress) and makes us more vulnerable to these bacteria or viral infections. When we are stressed and the adrenal glands are working over time, we set ourselves up for an even bigger fall. We leave the door open, when we do not take care of ourselves.

Once we are ill, this becomes another mind set. We become more aware, more sensitive to our bodies, to our emotions, to our mortality. Our perceptions create our reality. When we realize that we are ill, we can become overwhelmed. I have seen it with myself and I have seen this with my patients.

There is a mind medicine that must be taken along with all your other treatments. That is to reprogram your consciousness to create the perception that you are on the road to recovery. I have seen this work with someone who has had a cold, as well as those who have been terminally ill.

When a positive belief is taken alongside any other remedy to fight the illness, the healing process accelerates. Your belief in your recovery is the first and foremost therapy that should be applied.

Again, it is our mindset. There are those who actually enjoy being in their illness. They get the love and attention they may not feel they have. They may find this a great excuse to miss work, step out of life for a bit, or simply to slow down. Perhaps, it is a sign their bodies are telling them that it is time to slow down.

Some people are just not ready or willing to be on the recovery path. Even if they say they are. If they have not made the conscious effort to truly believe in their recovery, they are only half way there. Your belief in your recovery is the first and foremost therapy that should be applied.

Top 10 Ways To Improve Your Health Now

Would you like to improve your health? Better your life? Be who you are supposed to be? We sometimes stray from these very simple facts that can make our lives the most fulfilled. Consider these ideas:

1. Visit your Alternative healthcare practitioner at least once a month.

Alternative medicine is one of the most comprehensive medical systems in the world today. This medicine looks at the entire individual on a functional systemic basis that integrates all components of our mental, visceral and emotional bodies. See your local practitioner for prevention and maintaining good health as well.

2. Eat Nutritionally Sound Food.

A balanced diet with the appropriate amounts of protein, carbohydrates, fats and water are essential for sustaining a well fueled body, which will allow you to do everything in your life to its greatest potential.

3. Exercise and Move Your Body.

Movement has been shown to ease depression, increase flexibility, keep muscles toned, and help us to gain better balance. Movement also increases endorphins. This is the "happy" chemical in our brain that allows us to think clearer, function optimally and feel great.

4. Get "good" sleep.

Everybody is different with the amount of sleep they need. The one thing that is most important is not necessarily the quantity of sleep but the quality we get. A sound night's sleep allows our entire body to regenerate, replenish, and rebound back into a day that is full of life and energy.

5. Welcome the Power of Nature.

"Going back to our roots" can also mean becoming in touch (again) with nature. The power of the sea, sun, trees and plants have an energy they are willing to share with us. All we have to do is pay attention.

6. Learn to Love!

Take the time to pay attention, appreciate, and love the one you're with. Be them friends, family, or your partner. Learn to love unconditionally and without expectation.

7. Strengthen your Support.

Your family and your friends are the ones who are there for you when you need them the most. Take the time to listen to them, share stories, show appreciation for what they do for you and what they do for people around them. Tell them. Let them know they are appreciated. Learn to love them for who they are, not for what you want them to be.

8. Stay Spiritual.

Giving thanks to the Universe/Ultimate Power/Godhead is powerful. Religion is a bridge to spirituality. You don't have to go to a church or synagogue in order to be spiritual. Spirit is everywhere. Spirit is energy and it is in all things. The best part is being aware of it.

9. Keep Growing and Laughing.

Keeping the brain stimulated is one of the best ways we can fight off the signs of aging. Stay curious, creative, and learn something new about the world. It is essential to keep maintaining a playful spirit and to keep the mind sharp. Find laughter throughout the day. See things on the lighter side of life. I promise, it will bring great joy.

10. Honor Who You Are.

You are the most powerful, successful, and happiest. You deserve all that you desire and should honor all that you are. Find the complete and satisfied soul inside yourself. You are without a doubt, an amazing person. Take time to honor that.

Self-Power

Power is a broad reference to the ability to effect change or exert control over people, subjects, or objects. Self-power or self-empowerment is the ability to "enlighten", "enhance" and "educate" yourself in order to become a better human being.

This is one of the highest forms of spiritual consciousness we can give ourselves. Improving our way of communicating, appreciating, and honoring who we are, gives us special gifts such as gratitude, self-esteem, and a sense of being grounded.

As empowered beings, we have the opportunity to remind ourselves of our selflessness, our humanity, and our endless source of energy we can tap into. Here you can discover the building blocks of self-power. Refuse to be the victim.

<u>Gemstone:</u>
Self-Power

"O sacred soul of ancient roots,
Your energies of those which suit,
me, help me understand myself.
To further grow and be myself,
With wisdom wise and truth be told,
I seek to be empowered, bold"

~ Andrew Pacholyk MS L.Ac

Change Creates Power

If we choose to focus our attention on the negative around us, we will be that negativity.

If we choose to focus our attention on doing what we can't do, we will surely not do the things we can.

If we choose to focus our attention on being a victim, we will remain a victim.

To empower your spirit and create your true self, you must change your thoughts and the feelings around them.

Change is inevitable.

Our lives are made up of the building blocks of change. Change creates the person we must grow to be. Change happens for a reason. That reason is to allow us possibilities we may not have seen in the first place. This can be traumatic or it can be less so.

The single most important point you can make about change is that in most cases it's not what faces you that's the problem, it's how you react to it.

How you react is determined by how you perceive a particular change. The Chinese word for crisis is "weiji". Two characters that separately mean danger and opportunity. Every problem we encounter in life can be viewed that way. It is a chance to show that we can handle it. Changing the way, you think, can change a life of stress and discomfort to a life of challenge and excitement.

Change shows itself in many forms. The move to a different career, by choice or not, the loss of a loved one, the loss of a relationship, the move to a new home or simply the change in the weather and how we feel.

It is important to embrace the transition. Struggling, kicking and screaming, and dragging your heels will only prolong trying to control the uncontrollable. Learn to recognize strengths you may have overlooked. Embrace optimism and reform your old belief system. Honor the new you, which you are transforming into. Here are some ways to embrace change:

1. Often, in any situation, we must take the quiet time to be with ourselves to observe this change. How is it going to affect me? Better yet, how am I going to let it affect me? What am I going to do to get through this? Allow the answers to come to you in your quiet time.

2. Take Everything one day at a time. Sometimes situations can become overwhelming when looking at the big picture. Again, take your quiet time to observe the moment. Allow yourself to take all the time, take all the space, and to grasp the change.

3. Breathe. Deep breathing allows us to open our chest and expand. It clears our minds and bodies of toxins and should be used as a tool for change. Allow the breath to cleanse you and make room for change. Make room for something different.

4. Support. We are always put at ease when we have support behind us. In these vulnerable moments, we can find strength in others. If you have a good friend, a family member, a loved one, or a community group that you can turn to, do so. Be sure that this support comes from a positive, unbiased source. Otherwise, it can be more damaging than good. Rest assure, there have been others who have gone through what you are experiencing right now. See if you can take away with you some of their positive pearls of wisdom.

5. Love Yourself. You are the true source to your own happiness. You have to live within yourself. You have to be at peace within yourself. Only you can do that. Only you can make that happen. We each have our own way of being with ourselves, but there is only one way to be at ease with your soul. That is to love yourself, always.

6. Our Belief System is one of the major factors that can get us through situations or can cause our life to crumble around us. I do believe that there is a lot of innate goodness and balancing our minds do subconsciously to get us through hard times. The other portion of this is how we "program" ourselves to deal with any given situation.

7. Let go of Ego. Embracing peace of mind, optimism, the ability to forgive, and a sense of humor are all good ways to allow the ego to step aside and make room for some humble pie.

8. Allow Emotional Release. Identifying, expressing, experiencing, and accepting all of our feelings is your doorway to accepting all change in your life.

9. Be Flexible. You have a rigid, mind set about work, relationships, kids or your lifestyle. Life will bring us challenges we do not see coming. It is important to be able to adjust and learn as we grow. Our adaptability needs a sense of willingness in order to let go. By lowering our expectations, it reveals an openness to accept.

10. There Is No Security in something that is irrelevant or no longer has meaning. When we let go of the familiar, we have the power to embrace the new. Embrace it.

Personal Growth

Within each *season of our lives*, we experience the highs and lows life sends our way. We either learn to cope with them or we don't. It is always a challenge to face those situations we do not understand or do not wish to look at. When we accept the opportunity to look at them more closely, we open ourselves up to better comprehending and perhaps, spiritual understanding.

Hopefully, throughout your life, you will still continue to embrace them. They are the lessons that can help you to cope, understand, and appreciate circumstances that find their way to you.

In the *"Winter" of our lives*, we seek a spiritual path. We wish to further understand our place in the Universe. We tend to ask ourselves more questions. Our facing the inevitable is our greatest question.

In winter, our thoughts are deeper. With shorter days and longer nights, we become much more introspective. These metaphors for the end years of our lives are profound. We know just who we are and make no excuses. We honor who we are as we look at life now, through a much more mature set of eyes. We understand and we reflect. We have gained perspective and bring to the table a greater need to connect with those from our past and feel as though we still have hope for a long future.

This does not have to be an unhappy time, but truly a time to love, honor, and respect ourselves, even more. More for what we have learned and accomplished in life, as well as to appreciate all that we have been given. This can be a time of great revelation and pride.

Coping with Death

Death has been very close this year. From the sudden loss of my dearest mentor and friend Zachary Selig, the passing of my young cousin Nancy Pacholyk, my cousins Paquito and Lucita, my aunt Betty, my adopted godmother, Justina Gomez, to the greatest loss of all, my father, John Pacholyk. Death has made its presence known.

I have learned this year, that there are really no ways to prepare yourself for the moments when it occurs. You can tell yourself it is forthcoming or try to envision what life would be like without them. You can even prepare your will and estate for such a day, but when the moment arrives, there is no preparation.

On the Holmes-Rahe Stress Scale, death of a spouse and death of a family member are number 1 and number 5, respectively. In the case of my father, he was ill for over 4 years, so in many ways, my mother, brother and I had time to "prepare", in some way. With the loss of my mentor, it was all very sudden. I felt that we were going to grow much older together and yet, he left this world as quickly as he came into it. This too was the case of my cousins, Paquito and Lucita. They were both taken in a flash. In the case of my cousin, Nancy, her death from breast cancer was a long and painful one. Her death at a young age, made me feel life as unresolved and unfair. For my adopted godmother, her Alzheimer's diagnosis left her bed ridden and speechless for years. So, in some way, death was a welcomed relief.

In each case, I found my heart and mind going through an entire range of emotions. Fits of crying one day, then laughing the next. Some days, it would be a conglomeration of both. I also watched as my mother, brother, and family expressed their grief in many different ways.

I have learned that there is no right or wrong way of coping with death, only awareness. This awareness has shown me how to understand the process better. By observing how people react and bringing attention to my own responses, I have learned to be conscious of the events, objects, thoughts, emotions, or sensory patterns that present themselves each day.

Grieving such losses are an important part of moving forward. Until we grieve in our own way, we are likely to find the present, a difficult place to live in. The end product of our grief is peace. Getting there does not mean having to drown yourself in tears, feel guilt or anger around the loss, or feel like you need to forget in order to move forward. Getting to a place of peace with someone's transition comes with awareness.

Realization can bring to the forefront, a hard reality. But it is through this realization that we must rally to its truths. My mom is now alone on a large farm, by herself. I am now made aware of the fact that I have to be there for her, even more. My cousin left a wonderful husband and two children behind. I found it important to try and understand how they must now cope with their loss. My mentor only left his books, work, and intellectual properties behind. Helping to keep these projects alive, are now my mission.

With someone's passing, expectations become evident. But it is the letting go of these expectations, which will allow you to let the "natural" grieving process unfold. We are geared to handle this process, yet our need to control it, often steps in. We may think that we are supposed to "feel" a certain way or grieve for a certain amount of time. If we release these expectations, observe our own processes, and be more aware of them, we will find that grieving is an active process. Grief is ever-changing and constantly evolving.

This active "unfolding" of emotions must allow us to accept the finality of the loss. No two people grieve exactly the same way, but it is important to acknowledge the full range of emotions we experience and to express them in a healthy and balanced manner. This "balance" also gives us a way to adjust our own life, after our loved one is no longer with us. We tend to pour all our efforts into finalizing our loved ones' wishes and consequently, we do not give ourselves adequate nourishment, attention, or self-love.

Accept help when it is offered. Talk about your situation with someone you trust. Give yourself time with things you love. Try to maintain healthy eating and sleep habits. Journal about your experience or help someone else with a project or plan. These acts of self-balance will help you to grieve naturally without control, expectations, or feeling you have to grieve by any set of rules, other than your own.

Gemstone:
O' to Death

*"Death is a part of life, they
say,
It has the power to make its
way,
into our lives when we least
expect.
Or come around in time to
connect our corporeal selves to
spirit light
and pray relief from earthly
plight.
So, fear not, this continued
walk through time and space, a
journey not,
-unlike the one we started from.
So as we pass, the spirit
soars...
We simply walk through
another door.*

~ Andrew Pacholyk MS L.Ac

Winter Element: Water

Water is associated with the Winter season and with cold. **The mysterious and amazing healing power of water** has been utilized for centuries. Water cleanses, refreshes, and restores all life. We are always drawn to water. Water is a carrier. It flows. It moves along the line of least resistance to find its way to the ocean where it comes and goes in the ebb and flow of tides and waves. The appeal is inexplicable. We crave water, maybe because our bodies are made up of a large percent of it. Maybe because we instinctively know how it can heal us.

In the Chinese Medicine paradigm, the element is associated with the kidneys and the bladder, which regulate water metabolism and the reproductive system. There is also a strong relationship with the immune system and the ability of the body to lubricate, repair, and protect itself.

The Water Signs of the zodiac are Cancer, Scorpio, and Pisces. These signs run the gamut of our emotional rainbow. Since all life forms consist of water, we all have these extremes. They involve healing, compassion, reconciliation, friendship, de-stressing, insightfulness, peace, sleep, dreams, intuition, psychic power, and beauty. Yet, these astrology signs tend to encompass these emotions in full spectrum. A positive water person is sensitive, caring, and nurturing. A negative water person can be a little over emotional and over dramatic in certain areas of life. They find it hard to make a decision and change their mind often. They go back and forth, like a wave. When the "water personalities" are balanced, they are able to share their true gifts.

Emotionally, water represents taste, which is experienced on the tongue. It also represents one's taste, in general, and one's desire to taste or experience the world. Therefore, excess water is often equated with sensuality, possessiveness, and greed.

Psychologically, water represents a good memory. This can manifest as dwelling on the past. But, the ultimate experience of water is remembering that we all share life as a common denominator. This manifests as peace, love, and compassion.

The Sacral Spleen Chakra, is found below the navel and above the pubic bone. Historically, it is associated with our emotional strengths and deficiencies, our sexual connection (in relation to our sex organs) and connect to the element of water. It is the root of our feelings and how we process our emotional issues. It is the center that helps us to move forward with grace and fluidity. It is the area which helps us to accept change and to what degree we are able to "let go and let flow."

Water has played a role in areas of worship, as a tool for blessing, anointing, and spiritual baptism.

Water is the most nourishing element on the planet.

Water

September 23 to December 20
(Autumn equinox to the eve of winter solstice)

Abilities: Fluidity, acceptance, tolerance, emotion, love, mercy, compassion, erosion, empathy, sleep, meditation, purification, healing, friendship, fidelity, prophetic dreams, mystery, feelings, fertility, subconscious mind, reconciliation.

Stones: Aquamarine, Chalecdony, Jade, Pearl, Lapis Lazuli, Moonstone, Sugilite, Amethyst, Chrysocolla, Rose Quartz, Coral.

Plants: Apple blossom, lemon balm, camellia, catnip, daffodil, elder, geranium, grape, heather, hibiscus, jasmine, orchid, birch, blackberry, thyme.

Direction: West

Season: Autumn (Spring in the Southern Hemisphere)

Colors: Blue, Green, Turquoise.

Cycle Celebrations: Mabon (Autumn Equinox) (Spring Equinox in the Southern Hemisphere)

Number 7

Time: Twilight

Zodiac: Cancer, Scorpio, Pisces.

Planets: Moon and Venus

Angel: Raphael

Sense: Taste

Time of life: Death

Musical Landscape

Whether we know it or not, our lives are mapped out by the important moments we encounter. And most often, there is a song associated with it. Quite often, when we hear a familiar tune, it can take us back to the exact time and place, along with the experience that went with it! This "musical landscape" is the map of our lives.

Musical Playlists for Life's Journeys

From celebrations and ceremonies to proclamations and processions. Music marks the empirical reference we associated with time and place. Music is a magical medium that has always been a metaphor for our spirit.

> **Gemstone:**
> **Winter Play**
>
> *"Oh winter blush, can blow in strong, with hush of dark and night's so long ~ so here's a soundtrack just for you, to play on days when winter's blue, when cold and harsh come down your way, just buffer it with songs you play..."*
>
> *~ Andrew Pacholyk MS L.Ac*

Winter Playlist

Winter expresses a host of emotions and desires. Within this framework, we are brought to places of solemnity and isolation, holiday celebrations and joyful times and the contemplation and iconic images of seasonal snow, angelic beings, the promise of heaven, and the remembrance of loved ones who have passed.

At the turn of this season, I thought it would be a wonderful gift to share the songs of winter that make up my consciousness. These melodies cross several eras, yet they ring true for me as the seasonal mind set and the amazing way winter can be expressed in song. I call this list:

Andrew's Melodic Winter Play List

1. Claire de Lune, The Philadelphia Orchestra
2. Violin Concerto In F Minor, Op. 8/4, RV. 297, The Four Seasons: Winter
3. Moonlight Sonata, Ludwig Van Beethoven
4. The Skaters Waltz, Manhattan Pops
5. Canon in D Major, Pachelbel Orchestra
6. Night / Part One: Snow, George Winston
7. Thankful, Josh Groban
8. Angels Blush, Basia
9. Skating, Vince Guaraldi Trio
10. Nutcracker Suite, Tchaikovsky
11. Welcome Christmas, Dr. Seuss – How The Grinch Stole Christmas
12. We Need A Little Christmas, Glee Cast
13. Christmastime Is Here, Vince Guaraldi Trio
14. Grown-Up Christmas List, Amy Grant
15. Ding Dong Merrily On High, Celtic Women
16. Have Yourself A Merry Little Christmas, Judy Garland
17. Breath Of Heaven (Mary's Song), Amy Grant
18. The Most Wonderful Day Of The Year, Glee Cast
19. Jesu, Joy Of Man's Desiring, Amy Grant
20. Carol Of The Bells, Celtic women

Gemstone:
Angelic Music

"The lilt of soft angelic airs,
bring joy and truth and songs of care,
to honor those etheric lights,
who protect and guard throughout the night.
Now listen well, they'll let you know,
when they are close, you'll feel their glow..."

~ Andrew Pacholyk MS L.Ac

Angels have been the heavenly source for songwriters and singers, poets and painters, writers and authors for thousands of years. Compiling a musical tribute is virtually impossible without leaving out someone's favorites. I have attempted to list some current standouts, as well as a list dedicated to entire recordings compiled and dedicated to the winged messengers.

Melodies for Angelic Enlightenment

1. Addio, Aria 2 New Horizons, Paul Shwartz
2. Angel, Sarah Brightman
3. Angel Standing By , Jewel
4. Calling All Angels , K.d Lang, Jane Siberry
5. Songs Of Angels: Christmas Hymns And Carols, Robert Shaw, Choir
6. Flower Duet from Lakme , Opera Angels
7. A Dance With Angels (Antoinette's Song) , Fort Million
8. Lullabye (Goodnight, My Angel) , Billy Joel Angel , Jon Secada
10. Angels , Jessica Simpson
11. Borrowed Angels , Kristin Chenoweth
12. Angel's Lullaby , Richard Marx
13. Angel of Music, Phantom , Emmy Rossum, Gerard Butler
14. Undercover Angel , Alan O'Day
15. Send Me An Angel, Real Life
16. On The Side Of Angels , LeAnn Rimes
17. Where Angels Fear To Tread , The Worship Crew
18. Angel Of The Morning , Juice Newton
19. Heaven Must Be Missing An Angel , Tavares
20. Angel , Rod Stewart
21. Touched By An Angel , Stevie Nicks

Most Notable Complete CD's

1. Music From The City Of Angels , Soundtrack, Various
2. The Voice of Angels , Various
3. Touched By An Angel , TV Soundtrack
4. Angels & Demons , Movie Soundtrack
5. Archangel , Two Steps From Hell
6. Gifts of the Angels , Steven Halpern
7. Song of Angels Vol.1 , Freddy Hayler
8. The Truth About Angels – The Original Score , Enrico Sabena
9. Angels In The Outfield , Randy Edelman
10. Classical Angel – Classical Masterpieces, Various

Seasonal Landscape: Valleys

Valleys are the low-lying areas between the hills or mountains. Sometimes, in our lives, we find ourselves "in between" the hills and mountains, searching for answers or ways to move upward and closer to the sun. In a spiritual sense, being in a valley represents "an elongated depression" or times in our lives that are fearful or uncertain.

Like the bio-rhythms of our emotions, we all experience peaks and valleys and this is a very normal journey. Of course, walking along the mountain crest would be ideal, but if we did not experience these valleys, we would never know true joy. It is ok to be low and in solitude, as this offers us greater time for reflection and reconnection to ourselves.

Soul Satisfying Journeys: Full Moon Over Ojai Valley

This was a surprising journey initiated by my dear friend and mentor Zachary Selig, one of the foremost theosophist and metaphysical painters of the Chakra Codex. Zachary and I took the day and headed for the mystical town of Ojai.

Ojai, California is a vibrant place with so much natural beauty that it gained fame decades ago when the area was photographed to represent Shangri-La for the 1939 movie, *The Lost Horizon*. Nestled in the Ojai Valley, the town is surrounded by peaks that give off a glow in the evening light known as "the pink moment."

Since Ojai is lined up with an east-west mountain range, it is one of the few towns in the world to have a "Pink Moment". This magic moment occurs as the sun is setting and fading sunlight creates awash of brilliant shades of pink, lavender, peach, and purples for several minutes over the Topatopa Bluffs at the east end of the Ojai Valley. If you tour the mountains, visit the Secret Garden, or see the Chumash Indian's sacred places, you could understand why Ojai offers special meaning to all who visit time and again.

The exceptional climate of the Ojai Valley has drawn many who wish to rejuvenate their health and wellness, enjoy the dry, comforting air and take in the seemingly never-ending sunshine. It was early on in the discovery of this energetic place that settlers established the reputation of Ojai as a center of physical and mental health. Well known for its new age gurus, metaphysical institute, and the coexistence of Protestants, Catholics and yoga practitioners, this rich and diverse blend of spiritualism has evolved with room for all.

Driving through this quiet little village, I was introduced to the tall lemon-eucalyptus trees, the weeping pepper trees, and fragrant sage and lavender bushes. Ojai is literally dripping with orange groves! The sweet scent of citrus fills the air as you drive through the verdant valley and rolling hills.

Our first stop was the energetic vortex of the Krotona School of Theosophy. We followed the winding road past the stone gates to the very top of the hill. Krotona was one of three important Theosophical "colonies" in the U.S. during the early part of the 20th century. Originally built in Hollywood during 1912, the colony was eventually relocated to Ojai, California in 1926, where it operates today as the Krotona Institute of Theosophy.

I had always heard about the famous Krotona Library, filled with the teachings and writings of Blavatsky, Leadbeater, and Olcott, to name a few. Dedicated to the **search for truth**, the library was founded in 1926 and is a part of the Krotona Institute of Theosophy. The library emphasizes the ageless wisdom and traditions of Theosophy and spiritual teachings of East and West. There are over 10,000 books with new titles added each year.

In the front of the library stands a plaque which represents the energetic vortex. The plaque is in a geographic opposition of its yang counterpart, The Meditation Mount. The plaque reads:

The Three Truths

*The soul is immortal, and its future is the future of a thing whose growth and splendor has no limit.

*The Principle which gives life, dwells in us, and without us, is undying and beneficent, is not heard or seen, or smelt, but it is perceived by the one who desires perception.

*Each of us is our own absolute lawgiver, the dispenser of glory or gloom to ourselves, the decreer of our life, our reward, our punishment.
These truths which are as great as is life itself are as simple as the simplest mind of man. Feed the hungry with them. ~The Idyll of the White Lotus

Inside the library, Zachary introduced me to one of the library's curators, Lakshmi. Lakshmi, named after the Hindu goddess of wealth and prosperity (both material and spiritual), was a lovely Indian woman, small in stature but rich with knowledge. Her peaceful, quiet demeanor captured attention and respect as she quickly educated me on the history of the school and library. Taking my hand, she leads me into a large, sunlit music room to tell me the story of the paintings by Sarah Eddy hanging on the walls. As I thanked her for the brief history, she leaned into me and said, "Tonight, the moon is full like the almond blossoms in Ahmed's love garden." I thanked her for the insight and promised I would make an effort to see it.

Since its founding in 1967, the Krotona School of Theosophy has been helping students deepen their understanding of theosophy, the ancient wisdom, in its many forms, and has encouraged them to live a spiritually-oriented life. The school emphasizes "transformative education" which focuses on spiritual renewal. Such studies lead students to orient themselves to eternal truths in a changing world. The school, an integral part of the Krotona Institute, supports the work of The Theosophical Society and its three objectives, which are concerned with: 1) The unity of all people; 2) The study of comparative religion, philosophy, and science; and 3) The investigation of unexplained laws of nature and our latent powers.

Our next visit was to have tea with Ingrid Boulting. Ingrid, an open, enterprising, and endearing spirit, was a very famous, world-class model in the 60's and 70's. Now, living in Ojai, she is the proud owner of a beautiful yoga studio called, *Sacred Space Studio*. We had a wonderful afternoon, as her and Zachary, childhood buddies and friends for over 40 years, reminisced and caught up. One of Ingrid's passions is her love and care for stray dogs. We were greeted by the joy and barking of several of her canine house guests as we enjoyed tender jasmine tea in her garden.

Our next stop was Meditation Mount. This sacred site sits on 32 acres of land at the east end of the Ojai Valley. It is a remarkable place of peace and beauty. It is comprised of five separate buildings in and among extensive gardens. The premier structure is the auditorium featuring a mostly glass facade overlooking the Valley. The International Garden of Peace is a spectacularly groomed meditational path filled with fragrant herbs and flowers, beautiful Asian sitting structures, stone seats, and a blissful water pond. The path leads you to an open field that overlooks the most breathtaking view of the entire Ojai Valley! What better place to experience the power of the full moon?

Some call Ojai a vortex of positive, feminine energy that complements Sedona, AZ, known as the masculine vortex. Men seem mellow and happy visiting Ojai, where there are more female businesses launched per capita than any place in California. People love to escape, re-energize, and have a Pink Moment in Ojai.

Ojai, the Chumash Indian word for "moon", is honored each evening when the Pink Moment fades and the moon comes into view, often lighting up the valley with its own unique glow. My Full Moon Meditation (see, end of chapter) was done with Zachary and myself, along with several new friends we met on the Mount. We decided to create a grid or meditation circle using selenite stones. We then placed at the pinnacle of each selenite, a very special mother of pearl, to represent the moon's energy. We used tumbled moonstone to create an inner circle. The Full Snow Moon was huge. The light of the moon bathed the valley floor embracing all it came in contact with. This truly gave me a sense of gratitude and a feeling to want to continue to learn and keep my heart open to receive.

The Mineral Kingdom

Crystals are profound gifts and a great integrative therapy that can be used in conjunction with any other form of health care for personal pleasure, meditation, stress relief and healing. This season is associated with stones and crystals that represent snow and snowflakes, have opposing associations and represent the sun, especially when we need it the most. These crystals also represent celestial icons, images, and the flavor of the holiday season.

Top 10 Crystals for Winter

Winter is the time for being introspective and meditative. Winter is our time to rest and replenish. Because winter is a time of less light and colder conditions, it can also be a difficult time for many people. Crystals can play a part in brightening our nights, improving our outlook, and encouraging us to look within, peacefully. Here are my top 10 choices for Winter.

Angelite: This stone is excellent at balancing, polarizing and aligning the physical body with the Aura or ethereal network. It is very calming and its shade of blue refreshes the eyes and spirit. This crystal helps us to be in touch with angels and animal guides, as well as assisting in distant communication with other humans. Most effective on the Throat Chakra, Angelite helps in self-expression, communication and allows us to speak our mind, helping us to become more assertive. Its soothing effects on the Throat Chakra works beautifully in calming and soothing anxiety or overactive children. Use this stone to call your Angels for guidance and support. Angelite is often used for psychic connection to oneness with the Universe, the angelic realm and for spiritual guidance.

Azurite: Referred to as the jewel of wisdom or Stone of Heaven, azurite symbolizes insight and discovery. It is said to increase psychic abilities. Azurite activates the Third Eye and Throat Chakra for more assertive communication and alertness. It is a great stone to assist in astral travel. This great balancer helps those who talk too much and allows for those who need to be expressive when they have a tendency to hold back. This opens our psychic intuition and gets us acquainted with our inner selves. It is a stone that stimulates creativity, giving access to a fountain of ideas, images and awareness of things around us. This is a wonderful stone for decisiveness and decision making.

Black Onyx: This stone was used to promote fidelity. Excellent for centering/aligning the total person with higher powers. Used by Indian tribes to banish grief, enhance self-control, make wise decisions, encourage happiness, and find good fortune. Onyx will retain memories of the physical occurrences surrounding a person. It is a strong stone to use in psychometry because it tells the story of the wearer. This strength-giving stone is for those who are flighty by nature. The Greeks used this stone to help approach a lesson or task with greater self-confidence.

Blue Chalcedony: A type of Quartz that heads a family which includes Agate, Carnelian, Jasper, Tiger's Eye, and Onyx. Chelcedony helps ease self-doubts and makes one more reflective. Indian tribes in the Southwest used this stone to eases bad dreams. Cleansing in nature, this stone will promote healing. Blue is used to open the Throat Chakra and helps with communication and self-expression.

Citrine: This stone is very versatile and is used for mental and emotional clarity, problem solving, memory issues, will power, optimism, confidence and self-discipline. It reduces anxiety, fear, and depression. They can guide you to harness and utilize your creative energy. Citrine helps us analyze events and steer us in a positive direction. They work to develop inner calm and security and makes us less sensitive and more open to constructive criticism. It can dispel negative feelings and helps us to accept the flow of events.

Petalite: also known as Castorite, is highly spiritual stone. It has been called the "Stone of the Angels" (not to be confused with Angelite) and will help one connect with one's guides and enhances your angelic connection. It is also said to dissolve negativity. Petalite has been used on vision quests for strength, protection, and peace. It will balance one's yin/yang qualities, as well as one's mind, body, and spirit. It can enhance one's ability to feel energy in stones. Known as an aura calmer, this stone works on the Throat, Third Eye, and Crown Chakra in particular.

Quartz: Quartz is the Master Healer and the "stone of power." This crystal has the appearance of frozen water and clear quartz appears to look like ice. The natural tendency for quartz is for harmony. Quartz can both draw and send energy therefore it is effective for sending/receiving guidance. Quartz is used for transformation in healing and in all levels of change (mentally/emotionally, physically and spiritually). Quartz stimulates the natural crystal in body tissues and fluids to resonate at the highest healing frequency. Quartz works with All Chakra and master glands for balancing, cleansing and healing. It is the perfect stone for complete Aura balancing.

Selenite: This crystal is Gypsum. This white/clear striated crystal can look like snowy mountains or tumbled snowballs. Selenite is wonderful for mental focus, growth, luck, immunity, kundalini. These are centuries-old recordkeepers of events and information. Holding this crystal can help with visualizing and bringing white light/energy (higher ideas/consciousness) from a transpersonal point above your head down through body, out through feet into the earth/physical plane. Mexican Shaman have used this to help physical and emotional letting go. This stone helps to send healing to the earth, expands your sensitivity and field of awareness.

Snowflake Obsidian: This obsidian stone, which has inclusions of phynocryst, gives it a snowflake pattern on its surface. This stone allows us to recognize unnecessary patterns in our lives. Indian shamans have used it to promote self-esteem and confidence among their warriors. This is a strong grounding stone and is known as "the protector." It is said to "mirror one's soul." This stone brings about objectivity and detachment. It reduces fantasy and escapism. Known to absorb and dissolve anger, criticism, fear, and darkness, native healers saw it as a tool to convert this negativity to white light energy. This stone can be used at the Root Chakra to encourage one's survival instincts. This stone is an ancient tool used for transformation, scrying, and changing what you do not like in your life.

Snow River Quartz: This amazing quartz crystal is used for seeing into the future and discovering our congenital past. These clear quartz balls are incredible in their clarity on the inside and covered with a beautiful white frost on the outside. The ends are sliced off so that you can see into its deep translucent center. These "picture window" crystals are originally from the riverbeds of Brazil. The crystals are washed down out of the mountains and tumbled over and over by violent surging waters. This natural process gives the crystals their frosted look. They are the "gazing" stone, also called "seer quartz." These stone evoke clarity, clear thinking, and renowned insight.

Food for Thought: Eating for Winter

Within the Inuit tribes of the Arctic, the hunting, cooking, and sharing of food was not only necessary, but a spiritual act as well. Buddha expressed, "to keep the body in good health is a duty, for otherwise we shall not be able to light the lamp of wisdom or keep our mind strong and clear." According to Chinese Medicine, eating a moderate amount of all flavors including sweet, salty, pungent, bitter, and sour help to keep the body regulated.

The Ayurvedic school of thought is similar. The source of fuel you find to nourish you on a daily basis changes as the seasons change. The demands for a healthier diet make your journey more important. The Ayurvedic science of food is based on incorporating the 6 flavors (pungent, salty, sweet, bitter, sour and astringent) into each meal.

Salty taste is attributed to the kidney and urinary bladder, therefore adding some salty foods in your diet during Winter can improve the kidney and bladder function. Consider burdock root, eggs, fish, miso soup, nuts, tofu, and sea vegetables such as arame, hiziki, kelp, kombu and wakame.

In winter, it is important to eat foods that warm the body's core and keep it nourished. Use cooking methods such as steaming, roasting, stir frying, or poaching in order to heat the food all the way through.

Avoid raw foods, which are cold in nature such as salads, cold fruits, ice (especially in drinks), ice cream, and raw vegetables as these tend to cool the body. Consider eating these foods for Winter:

1. Warm hearty soups and healthy lean meat and root vegetable stews, whole grains, and roasted nuts.

2. Cereals, grains, and legumes such as brown rice, corn, millet, oatmeal, sorghum, soybeans, black gram, adzuki bean, red kidney bean, broad bean.

3. Meat, poultry and fish such as chicken, turkey, shrimp, chicken eggs.

4. Root vegetables such as yams, sweet potatoes, yucca, potatoes, beets, turnips, ginger, ginseng, taro, burdock, carrots, parsnips, as well as, onions, chives, scallions, garlic, leeks, common mushrooms, shiitake mushrooms, mitake and reishi.

5. Herbs, spices, condiments, and oils such as perilla leaf, peppermint, dandelion, honeysuckle flower, basil, parsley, wolfberry (gou gi berries), fleece-flower root, licorice, astragalus, rhubarb, ginger, pepper, honey, sesame oil.

6 Fruits and nuts (at room temperature) apples, clemetines, cranberries, red grapes, grapefruit, kiwi, kumquats, passion fruit, persimmons, pomegranates and rhubarb.

Essential Oils for Winter

Aromatherapy brings us the aromatic energy of living plants in the form of essential oils. These fragrances are a natural antidote to the emotionally debilitating effects of winter. Aromatherapy is supportive in the winter season of quiet regeneration. Winter essential oils cleanse and freshen the air in our homes, help with aches and pains, and bring peace and special memories back to us. Essential oils for winter include woody, evergreen, citrus, spice and resin oils.

Christmas cookies, pine trees, and spice tea are "scent-filled memories" that essential oils such as clove, cinnamon, allspice, ginger, and nutmeg bring to mind. Fresh citrus oils including bergamot, sweet orange, lemon, and tangerine recall memories of old- fashioned citrus pomanders. Pine and cedarwood remind us of Christmas trees and holiday wreaths.

Bergamot (Citrus bergamia): Bergamot is uplifting and sweet with a fruity fragrance. Helpful for depression. Refreshes a room. Avoid sunbathing and sunbeds when using this oil.

Black Pepper (Piper nigrum): Hot, dry, spicy oil with a deeply warming effect. Relieves muscular aches and pains. Stimulates the digestive, circulatory,and lymphatic systems. Can irritate sensitive skin, use sparingly.

Eucalyptus (Eucalyptus globulus): was utilized by the Australian aborigines, to treat such disorders as fever, cough, and other respiratory disorders. European travelers also used it as medicine. Use a few drops of eucalyptus oil in boiling water in a bath or as an inhalant. Eucalyptus is often used for sore muscles, as an insect repellent, for tension headache, cold, cough, sinusitis, rheumatoid arthritis, and strains/sprains. Warming and antiseptic oil with a strong camphorous smell.

Juniper Berry (Juniperus communis): essential oil contains mainly pinene, myrcene, sabinene and limonene. These constituents are also found in other winter season oils including pine, cypress, and fir needle. Juniper berry oil blends especially well with these oils. Juniper oil is refreshing, clarifying and uplifting to the spirit. Its physical actions are cleansing, astringent (for oily complexions) and toning. Detoxifying, cleansing, and antiseptic. Do not use if pregnant or if you suffer with kidney disease. Not suitable for children.

Lemon (Citrus limonum): is a fresh sunny scent that is cold pressed from the rind itself! Lemon has antiseptic-like properties and contains compounds that have been studied for their effects on immune function. It may serve as an insect repellent and may be beneficial for the skin. Diffuse it in your house for a fresh alternative to air spays. It complements the Oil of Oregano to neutralize the over growth of candida. Put a few drops on a tissue and vacuum it into your vacuum bag to freshen the smell of your carpets and furniture coverings. 1 drop is also very refreshing and purifying when taken in a glass of water.

Neroli: (Citrus aurantium): is distilled from bitter orange trees. It has a refreshing, spicy aroma and is known for its sensual, exotic effect. Neroli oil is emotionally unifying and soothes with harmonizing effects. Described as both sensual and spiritual, Neroli helps to re-establish the link between a disconnected mind and body. Neroli paves the way for a gradual release and allows us to recall hope and joy.

Orange (Citrus sinensis): Orange essential oil is obtained from the rind of the fruit and used principally as a flavoring agent. Warming, orange oil is an antidepressant, antiseptic, antispasmodic, carminative, digestive, febrifuge, phototoxic and sedative tonic. Orange oil helps spreads sunshine on gloomy depression. It has a very comforting and warming effect and dispels tension and stress helping to revive us when feeling low on energy. Orange oil calms the stomach both for constipation and diarrhea. It stimulates bile which helps digestion of fats. Rubbed on the chest, it has a beneficial effect on colds, bronchitis, and fever. Helps with the formation of collagen, vital for tissue repair and hair growth. Also helpful with muscular pains, anxiety, and insomnia. Orange oil helps dry skin conditions softening wrinkles and dermatitis. An excellent skin tonic. Orange oil can make the skin photosensitive to sunlight.

Peppermint (Mentha piperata): Peppermint oil is the most extensively used of all the volatile oils, both medicinally and commercially. The characteristic anti-spasmodic action of the volatile oil is more marked in this than in any other oil and greatly adds to its power of relieving pains arising in the alimentary canal. From its stimulating and carminative properties, it is valuable in certain forms of dyspepsia, being mostly used for flatulence and colic. It may also be employed for other sudden pains and for cramps in the abdomen.

Rosemary (Rosmarinus officinalis): Rosemary is stimulating and refreshing, and is an invigorating pick-me-up. It is helpful to refresh and open nasal passages and assists in easy breathing. Excellent for hair and scalp problems including hair loss and dandruff. This herb has been used as boutonnières for both weddings and funerals, as this herb represents the passing through of life's transitions. Do not use if pregnant, have high blood pressure, or suffer with epilepsy.

Tea Tree (Melaleuca alternifolia): Tea tree oil was first extracted from Melaleuca alternifolia in Australia, and this species remains the most important commercially. In the 1970s and 1980s, commercial plantations began to produce large quantities of tea tree oil from Melaleuca alternifolia. Many of these plantations are located in New South Wales. Tea Tree is a powerful antiseptic, anti-bacterial oil, which helps boost the immune system. Excellent for treating cold sores and fungal infections such as thrush. It is used to treat dermatitis, insect bites, warts, cuts and grazes.

Winter Warmth Blend
Combine the following oils:
10 drops of cedarwood
25 drops of bergamot orange
15 drops of fir needle
30 drops of juniper berry
20 drops of sandalwood

Make a wintertime aromatherapy massage oil blend. Dilute 12 drops of this "mother" blend in 4 ounces of vegetable oil. To diffuse into the air, use a tea light candle diffuser or electric style diffuser. Add a few drops of "mother" blend to your diffuser.

Sinus Congestion Blend
To relieve sinus congestion, respiratory problems, and to clear a stuffy head.
5 drops of Eucalyptus
3 drops of Lavender
2 drops of Tea-Tree
2 drops of Pine.

Add drops to a bowl of hot water and inhale. Makes a great cold remedy. This is a powerful decongestant for those unwanted colds. Add a few drops to your diffuser and inhale.

Seasonal Affected Disorder (SAD)
Many people are affected in the winter months by this disorder which is associated with a reduction in sunlight, as the days get shorter, and the weather is frequently overcast. Symptoms can range from depression, fatigue, lethargy, weight gain, and food cravings. The following essential oils can help to relieve the symptoms associated with this disorder. The oils can be used in a diffuser, either individually or in combination.

Pick Me Up Blend
7 drops of Bergamot
5 drops of Grapefruit
3 drops of Rosemary

Sunshine Blend
5 drops of Lemon
5 drops of Orange
3 drops of Geranium
2 drops of Peppermint

Cycle Celebrations

Each celebration of the season we enjoy has roots from the past. Each religion has borrowed from the cultures of our ancestors to create new traditions and ways to honor the season.

The process of claiming and adopting styles, religious beliefs, and rituals has been repeated over and over again throughout time. Like the cultures before them and every culture after, our celebrations for life and time have evolved over centuries with a history and folklore rich in myth, mystery, and magic!

Samhain

Celebrated all over the world and in different cultures including: the festival of All Hallow's Eve (Ireland, Galic, Britain) Halloween (US) All Saint's Day (Christian) Day of the Dead (Mexico).

October 31 – November 2 is considered All Hollow's Eve, All Saints Day and All Souls Day (The Triduum of All Hallows). This 3-day holiday event is a magical representation of the suspension of time when it is believed a thin wall or veil between earth and the Otherworld is lifted.

These are considered the most powerful days to communicate with spirits, ancestors, and our departed loved ones. This time marks the end of the pastoral year and the beginning of the next year's cycle.

In Ireland, it was the celebration of the fermentation of grains and the consumption of alcohol. Bonfires were built on the hill of Tlachtga, to honor "the crone", the first funeral site, (which honored divination), and a time to honor the dead. It has also been referred to by the Celts as the "wild hunt" of the fairies that would ride the land and wreak havoc and mayhem on crops and unsuspecting farmers.

When: October 31 – November 2
Season: Cross Quarter: (Mid-way point between the Autumn Equinox and Winter Solstice)
Represents: "Summer's End", 3rd Harvest, Death and New Beginnings and the New Year.
Virtues: Divination, Intention, Intuition
Symbols: Cauldron, Protection Charms, "Dumb Cakes", Pumpkins, Ghosts, Candles
Gemstone: Agate, Copper, Flint, Obsidian, Onyx, Selenite, Clear Quartz
Color: Black, Orange, Indigo
Essential Oils: Cinnamon, Clove, Pepper, Pine, Patchouli, Vetiver
Remedies: Cinnamon, Garlic, Ginger, Marjoram, Oregano, Pepper, Rosemary, Thyme, Sage
Flowers: Aster, Chrysanthemum, Gerber Daisies, Dahlia, Marigold, Roses, Sunflowers, Zinnia,
Element: Air
Direction: Northwest
Life Event: Divination, Harvest
Lunar: Harvest Moon or Hunter's Moon
Body Healing: Self-Healing
Mind Healing: Divination
Spirit Healing: Sacred Spirit

All Hallows' Eve

All Hallows' Eve, most often called Halloween, is the eve of All Hallows (All Saints' Day) and is the first day of the Hallowtide. According to some scholars, the Christian Church absorbed some of the Celtic practices associated with Samhain and Christianized the celebration in order to ease the Celts' conversion to Christianity. Halloween originated from the Pagan festival, Samhain, and celebrated among the Celts of Ireland, Great Britain, the Irish and Scottish immigrants.

Samhain is a time to remember, honor, and commune with our ancestors. It is their wisdom and history which enriches our lives and gives us a clearer path to follow and emulate. This is a time to let old habits die and to meditate on who we wish to become. These months are times spent looking inward, seeking one's self. Spend this time self-reflecting, meditating, and using gentle self-care so that, come Spring, you may rise - renewed, rejuvenated, fresh, and whole.

All Saint's Day

The second day of Hallowtide is known as All Saints' Day, All Hallows or Hallowmas. Occurring on November 1, it is a principal feast of the church year and one of the four days recommended for the administration of baptism in Anglicanism. In some denominations, All Saints' Day is a holy day to honor all the saints and martyrs, both known and unknown.

All Saints' Day observances focus on saints and angels recognized in the canon of the saints by the Catholic Church. All Saints' Day was formally started by Pope Boniface IV, who consecrated the Pantheon at Rome to the Virgin Mary and all the Martyrs on May 13 in 609 AD. The feast of All Saints, on its current date, is traced to the foundation by Pope Gregory III (731–741).

In his book, *"Stations of the Sun: A History of the Ritual Year in Britain"* author, Ronald Hutton, says, *"this fell on the Celtic holiday of Samhain, which had a theme similar to the Roman festival of Lemuria, but which was also a harvest festival. The Irish, having celebrated Samhain in the past, did not celebrate All Hallows Day on this 1 November date."*

All Soul's Day

The final day of Hallowtide is known as All Souls' Day and is also called the Commemoration of All Faithful Departed. All Souls' Day focuses on honoring all faithfully departed, especially family members and friends. In her book, *"Italian-American Holiday Traditions"*, author Lori Granieri wrote, "observance of All Souls' Day was spread throughout Europe by Saint Odilo of Cluny in the late 13th century. Like All Hallows' Eve and All Saints' Day, family members often attend mass and visited the graves of their deceased loved ones, placing flowers and lighted candles there.

Many of these traditions from All Souls' Day, have been traced back to a number of ancient rituals from several different cultures including Pitru Paksha from India, the Bon Festival from Japan, the Roman celebration of Lemuria, the Day of the Dead in Mexico, and the Ghost Festival from China.

Gemstone:
Sacred Spirit: Samhain Blessing

"O memory dear, of loved one passed,
I come to honor in circle, cast,
O _____(honoree's name), I come to
ask for care,
that you will come through humble
prayer,
I pay respect and honor here.
that you will always be so near,
to guide, protect and hold me close,
let danger always be disposed.
So with this gesture, loved one dear,
please know I'm with you, every year."

~ Andrew Pacholyk MS L.Ac

Yule

This is also the Winter Solstice. This is the time of the rebirth of the Sun God. It is the longest night (or shortest day) of the year, but yet it is filled with the promise of lengthening days of light to come.

The winter solstice has long been celebrated as the birth of the sun, the gleaning of light, and of life itself. It is a time for introspection, contemplation, and planning for the future.

Yule means "Yoke of the Year", celebrated as the "restful time of year", the longest night, and birth time of the new Sun King OR Son of God. On this darkest time, the archetype of mother, is honored and loved. She gives birth to the sun (child) who will lead and offer great hope for sun (son) to return.

Celebrated all over the world and in different cultures including the festival of Winter Solstice and the Christian festival of Christmas (US, Ireland, Britain, Europe), Yule (North Germanic, Scandinavians).

When: December 21, 22
Season: Winter Solstice
Represents: Rebirth "Sun standing still"
Virtues: Intention, Peace, Contemplation, Introspection
Symbols: Boughs, Trees, Mistletoe, Yule Log, Green Man
Gemstone: Quartz, Clear Quartz, Snow White Quartz, Snowflake Obsidian
Color: Gold, White, Violet
Essential Oils: Cedarwood, Frankincense, Ginger, Myrrh, Peppermint, Pine, Sandalwood
Remedies: Angelic Root, Cayenne, Lemon, Ginger, Juniper Berry, Peppermint
Flowers: Holly Berry, Mistletoe, Narcissus, Pine, Paper White, Poinsettia
Element: Earth
Direction: North
Life Event: Peace, Self-Power
Lunar: Oak Moon or Cold Moon
Body Healing: Peace
Mind Healing: Mindfulness
Spirit Healing: Sacred Spirit

Yuletide

Yule or Yuletide ("Yule time") is a festival observed by the historical Germanic people. Scholars have connected the celebration of the Wild Hunt, the god Odin, and the pagan Anglo-Saxon Mōdraniht to this holiday. It later underwent Christianized reformulation resulting in the term "Christmastide."

Within the Nordic, British, and Irish countries, the equivalent of Yule has been celebrated and adorn. Yule has become synonymous with Christmas, incorporating rituals such as the Yule log, singing of carols, roasting the Yule pig or goat, decorating and lighting of the tree, and the hanging of stockings on the hearth.

Candle Ritual

The winter solstice focuses on the return of light, joy, and happiness. It is the celebration of the longest and darkest hours and the promise of more sunlight to come. It is also a very special time of reflection and introspection. It is the time to banish or dispel the darkness, in order to make room for more light.

We all have shadows to varying degrees. Our shadows come from our personal beliefs, taboos, and cultural upbringings. We too, create our own shadows out of personal feelings based around our beliefs on death, birth, marriage, aging, youth, and love.

Place 5 candles in a circle. On a piece of paper, write down three "shadows" you wish to banish from your life. Light your candles. Now, take the paper and touch it to the center candle flame to light the paper. Place the burning paper in a bowl to continue burning (and banishing) your shadows.

Making A Yule Wreath

Make a Yule wreath by winding grapevines around a large bottle or pot. Remove the vine wreath from the bottom of the vessel. Tuck the ends of the vines into each other and then start to decorate it. Have approximately 8-10 pine boughs (branches with green needles and cones) and weave them or wire wrap them into your grapevine base. Position the boughs outward so they show off the green.

Now start filling the wreath in with beautiful pine cones, red holly berries, or even red cherries. Use twigs with leaves on them and charms representing the season.

The circular shape of the wreath represents eternity, for it has no beginning and no end. Within many religions, a wreath represents an unending circle of life. The boughs of the evergreen tree, which are most often used in making wreaths and garland, symbolize redemption, growth, the promise of renewal, and everlasting life.

Gemstone:
Sacred Spirit: Yule Night Miracle

"Of all the times we need some light,
it seems it's at the darkest night...

When all the worlds asleep and lost,
suffering from unconscious thought,

It's time to make yourself aware,
of deep connections, if you dare.

To honor self, and give more love,
to those who look to high above

for answers, they cannot impart,
it's best to look within your heart.

For here is where the answers lie,
your greatest source and best ally."

~ Andrew Pacholyk MS L.Ac

Soul Satisfying Journeys: Miracles at Medjugorje

Medjugorje is a small mountain town located in western Bosnia and Herzegovina, in the Herzegovina region, close to the border of Croatia. Since June 24, 1981, it has become a popular spiritual pilgrimage site due to reports of apparitions of the Blessed Virgin Mary to six local children.

This entire journey was a miracle from the start. Flying to Medjugorje was no easy task. Tonio started to call the airline for tickets several months in advance, always running into obstacles. Finally, after numerous phone calls, scheduling attempts and extremely expensive ticket prices, Tonio felt it just might not happen. Weeks would go by and occasionally, he would pick up the phone and call the airlines. The later it got to the day we wanted to go, the more difficult (and unavailable) the tickets became. Then, on a Saturday (the day of the Virgin), Tonio called the airline and got a representative who happened to be originally from Croatia. She said, "I will help you to get there." She recommended the best route to go and was able to use all our frequent flyer miles to travel.This was the first miracle.

The easiest route was through London and then Dubrovnik, a spectacular city on the Adriatic Sea of Croatia. It is one of the most prominent tourist destinations on the Adriatic. Dubrovnik is among the 10 best medieval walled cities in the world and among the 10 best places in the world for a fairytale proposal on Valentine's Day. Although in 1991, after the breakup of Yugoslavia, it was besieged by Serb-Montenegrin forces for 7 months and received significant shelling damage. Following the end of the war, damage caused by the shelling of the Old Town was repaired. Adhering to UNESCO guidelines, repairs were performed in the original style. Today, peace reigns over this region and being there, you would never know there was such turmoil.

Dubrovnik is a beautiful jewel, perched on the azure Adriatic Sea. The waters are spotted with over 175 islands and watercraft of all kind. We spent the first day of summer, swimming in the buoyant and healing salt water along its rocky coastline. Later, we made our way to the Old Town where we had a fantastic seafood dinner alongside the ramparts of Fort Lovrjenac.

The City Harbor of Dubrovnik is a vibrant, bustling attraction filled with boats of all shapes and sizes. Cargo and recreational vessels still traverse these waters. Built on sea rock at the foot of Mount Srd, the City of Dubrovnik is a perfect example of medieval construction and the harbor has brought life to this merchant republic for over 700 years.

Croatia has many varieties of flora and wonderful vineyards, as well as lemon and orange plantations. Rich in predominantly pine, palms, agaves, cactus, and olive trees, there are also striking cypress trees that stretch skyward, giving this Mediterranean landscape a unique look.

The following day, we wanted to leave for Medjugorje. The problem was that the public bus only left at the end of the day at 5pm. The local tour buses only went to Medjugorje on Wednesday and Sundays and this particular day happened to be Thursday and my birthday! After some investigating, we had the luck and the pleasure of a private car and driver to take us to Medjugorje. The two-and-a-half-hour journey was a wonderful way to see the countryside as we traversed through three of the seven countries that were once Yugoslavia. The winding coastline of Croatia allowed us to see the precious beaches, steep cliffs, and beautiful bays.

On our way through the Peljesac Peninsula, our driver suggested we stop in the town of Ston. This small, quiet town in Croatia has a well-kept secret – a Great Wall, hundreds of years old which is the longest, complete fortress system around a town in Europe, as well as the second in the world next to China. Yet very few seem to have heard of the Walls of Ston. When they were built, beginning in the fifteenth century, they were heavily fortified not only to serve as the first line of defense for the city of Dubrovnik but they were constructed to protect a precious commodity of Croatia – sea salt and the salt mines. Nestled alongside this unique structure and town, is Mali Ston Bay. It is here that the famous Ston Oysters are farmed.

Crossing the border from Croatia into Bosnia and Herzegovina happens twice, as the road between them is in part, split between the countries. The border between Bosnia and Herzegovina is only recognized by a sudden change of scenery. In Bosnia, you pass through hilly, wooded terrain. The soil is black and the mountains rolling and green. Passing into Herzegovina, we found ourselves surrounded by white limestone mountains, dusty brown soil, and low ground covering, brush, and tumbleweed. It is here that the Dinaric Alps, the southernmost reaches of the Swiss Alps, become a wave of tall, jagged rock, that then spills into the sea. This younger mountain range is an emphatical karst area (made up of chalky limestone) with stretches of limestone expanses, coves, basins, and funnel shaped holes in the limestone formation. As we drove a little further into Herzegovina, we turned up into the hills following a small dirt road, eventually leading us up a mountain pass into the town of Medjugorje.

The car dropped us off at a little hotel on the edge of town, about a 15-minute walk from the St. James Parish Church. We quickly washed up as we were eager to discover this holy place. 10 am in the morning and the sun was already scorching hot as we walked through town. The new St. James Church is a simple parish church. The construction of the old parish church was completed in 1897 but soon after, it started to develop cracks in the foundation, due to it being built on unstable ground. Shortly after the end of the First World War, the parishioners began to think about building a new church. Construction lasted from 1934 until January 19, 1969, when it was consecrated. Today St. James Church is the focus and center of Medjugorje, not only for the parishioners, but also for the millions of pilgrims that come each year. Because of the new needs of the parish, an exterior altar was built behind the church in 1989 and the surrounding prayer area extending outward with 5000 seats. It is a place of gathering in the summer time for big feast days, reciting the rosary, or prayer services.

Behind the church, a promenade was built. Named, the Via Domini (the Way of the Lord). The path starts with the Mysteries of Light and connects the old town cemetery to the newest addition, *the Risen Christ statue*. The statue is the work of a Slovenian artist Andrej Ajdic given to the parish on Easter, 1998. One of the many beautiful gifts of Medjugorje, standing 15 feet tall, this statue of the crucified Christ has been exuding a unique oil from one knee, continuously since the 20th anniversary of the apparitions in 2001. Although the nature of this oil is mysterious, the fact is, it has begun to increase and now the unknown substance flows from both knees of this bronze sculpture. Here, Tonio and I stopped to pray in the garden. We walked up to the statue and stepping up on the wooden steps, wiping the endless flow of liquid on to handkerchiefs we bought in town. This was the second miracle we encountered.

Crnica Hill is several hundred feet above the Bijakovici town called Podbrdo, but today it's called Apparition Hill. It is here, that the Blessed Virgin Mary or Gospa, as the locals refer to her as, has been appearing to six children, (the visionaries), since June 24, 1981. Ivan, Jakov, Marija, Mirjana, Vicka, and Ivanka had first began receiving messages from Our Lady on a daily basis. Then, Our Lady began to give weekly messages on Thursdays to the parish community via the children, and through them to the rest of the world. Since some of the events that Our Lord desired were fulfilled, from the 25th of January 1987 onwards, Our Lady would then appear to the children and give a message only on the 25th of each month. This has now continued up until the present.

Early the following morning, just before sunrise, we took a taxi to the base of Apparition Hill. The journey to the top was a dangerous path of sharp and jagged limestone. This porous rock dissolves relatively easily due to rain, winter ice, and the thousands of pilgrims that climb the mountain, wearing down the stone over time. This action creates holes and sharp edges. As we climbed the mountain at dawn, there were several people who were barefoot. In 1989, beautiful bronze statues, (the work of artist Carmelo Puzzolo), were stationed going up the mountain, representing the joyful and the sorrowful mysteries of the Rosary. In June 2002, bronze statues representing the glorious mysteries of the Rosary were stationed on the path descending Apparition Hill. At the foot of the hill is the Blue Cross, placed there in 1985. It is one of the sites where Our Lady appeared to the visionaries when they were hiding from the Communist police in the beginning days of the apparitions. A blue cross was erected to mark the spot, which led to the naming of the site, as "Blue Cross." Going up the mountain, we stopped to admire the fine craftsmanship and say a prayer. On the way towards the location of the apparitions, a large wooden cross was also erected, denoting the place where visionary Marija, on the third day of the apparitions, Our Lady gave the call to peace for the first time. "Peace, peace, peace – and only peace. Peace must reign between God and man and between men."

At the very place of the apparitions, honoring the 20th anniversary, a statue of the Queen of Peace was placed. It was here that Tonio and I knelt on the rocks to say the rosary. Looking out from the top of the mountain, the town and parishes of Medjugorje stretch out through the blissful valley. There was only a handful of people on the hilltop that morning and it was very quiet. The sun pierced the top of the pine trees in the East, splashing warm and peaceful light across the rocky mount. For myself, my first encounter with Apparition Hill was an encounter with Our Lady through my personal prayers and praying the rosary.

On the morning of the annual apparition, thousands of people flooded the little town of Medjugorje. Even before sunrise, we woke to see people of all ages, on foot, walking into Medjugorje from every surrounding town and village, over the mountains and across borders. That was a very special sight to see.

My second visit to Apparition Hill was the evening of the annual apparition and message. The mountain had, what seemed like thousands of people gathered around the statue. You could hear a variety of different languages that night. The air was hot and damp and the absolute sense of desperation was palpable! I remember trying to sit there on the rocks in peace, yet all I could feel was an overwhelming sense of angst as people scrambled all around us, just to be close enough to the experience. Instead of taking in the beauty of nature and the opportunity to be there in the first place, people's sense of need, hopelessness, and despondency made me very sad. Regardless, Tonio had a very different experience. At one point, he was on his knees saying the rosary and later, he described his experience as if no one else was on the mountain and he was simply floating. It dawned on me then, that it was perhaps my empathic nature that picked up on other's despair and my own lack of feeling grounded that made me so uneasy. According to the visionaries, the June 25th, 2012 message from Our Lady was:

> *"Dear children! With great hope in the heart, also today I call you to prayer. If you pray, little children, you are with me and you are seeking the will of my Son and are living it. Be open and live prayer and at every moment, may it be for you the savor and joy of your soul. I am with you and I intercede for all of you before my Son Jesus. Thank you for having responded to my call."*

This was the third miracle!

On our way down the mountain that night, Tonio slipped and fell forward on to the dangerous rocks. He happened to have a piece of rubber in his hand that we had bought earlier, as a kneeling pad. When he stood up, the pad had a huge hole in it. I could only imagine the damage he may have suffered, had he not had that pad in his hand. He was in pain from the fall and a little shaken up. I was so terrified that he got hurt and his biggest concern was that it would ruin the rest of our trip. I did some gentle acupressure on his hands and knees. The next morning, he had absolutely no pain and no bruising. This was the fourth miracle!

The following day, we had one more journey to take and that was to Cross Mountain. This mountain above Medjugorje stands 1,710 feet high. It is here on March 15, 1934, the parishioners constructed a concrete cross, 28-foot-tall, built in remembrance of the 1,900 years since the death of Christ. On the cross is written: *"To Jesus Christ, Redeemer of the human race, as a sign of their faith, love and hope, in remembrance of the 1900 years since the death of Jesus."* Relics received from Rome for the occasion were embedded in the cross itself. Since then, the custom was established to celebrate Holy Mass at the foot of the cross in commemoration of the Exaltation of the Holy Cross, on the 1st Sunday after the Feast of the Nativity of the Blessed Virgin Mary. According to the visionaries, in the message of August 30, 1984, Our Lady said *"The cross was also in God's plan when they built it."* With Our Lady's message, the faithful started to pray the *Way of the Cross* on Cross Mountain. This journey was even more perilous than Apparition Hill. Extremely treacherous, the path was not only difficult because of the rocks but navigating around the sheer numbers of pilgrims was also dangerous. Yet, the view at the top was unparalleled and the climb was very spiritually rewarding.

The Miracles

From the beginning, the Medjugorje apparitions were accompanied by many unusual phenomena, both in the sky and on the ground, especially with miraculous healings. We witnessed many from the beginning of our journey right up through our last days there. From the weeping statue of Christ to the amazing sun and cloud phenomena that occur (we saw two) to the Cross on Cross Mountain that shines at night as though it was covered with lights yet, there is no electricity on the mountain! Amazing images captured in photographs and incredible videos of (un) natural happenings are just too many to ignore. Yet, overall, I think the biggest miracle is the millions of people that come from the farthest reaches of the world to see a place that is still being graced by the powers of heaven for over 30 years. Even though, Medjugorje has not yet been sanctioned officially by the church as an authentic Marian apparition site, the innumerable amount of prayers, pilgrims, and penance is incomprehensible.

Miracle in the Clouds

On our way out of town, we took the local bus to the airport. I remember as we were leaving Medjugorje, many people sitting in front of us, were pointing to the sky and taking pictures. As we looked out the window, we saw a single wisp of a cloud in the bright blue sky. It was clearly a cloud formation that looked like the Virgin Mary. She was standing behind the cross of Christ as an offering of her son to the world. People on the bus were in shock, not speaking but only pointing in amazement! Again, as we were crossing the Croatian border, in a cloudless sky, there was one single cloud formation with the image of Mary surrounded by four angels. Even people outside of the bus were standing and pointing upward to this incredibly spectacular site! This was the fifth miracle. (Many of these cloud formations are now documented online. See what you think)

The Secrets

In addition to the messages, the visionaries have each received a total of ten "secrets" from Gospa. Only one secret has been revealed by the visionaries. Our Lady promised there would be a great sign on the mountain in Medjugorje, where She first appeared. There are also three warnings our Lady said She will give. The warnings will be warnings on earth. The Blessed Virgin Mary warned that, *"there is not much time for conversion. After the three warnings, the permanent visible sign will be left on the mountain in Medjugorje."* The ninth and tenth secrets talk of a chastisement for the sins of the world. The chastisement can be lessened by praying and doing penance, but it cannot entirely go away.

The "5 Stones" or Messages

In one of her messages, the Virgin Mary, suggested that *"you put five stones into your sack in order to overcome the atheism that surrounds us, for that paganist mentality that is being disseminated, and seems invincible."* In his article, Father Jozo Zovko, said "neither we nor the Church are capable of conquering materialism on our own. Our Lady has appeared in Medjugorje to declare that this is possible."

Here are her five stones: **prayer, fasting, the Eucharist, the bible, and confession.** With these simple weapons we can overcome the world. In the book, *Medjugorje, A Testimony*, published by Misma Notebooks, 1989, the gifts, (the five stones), have not been given to us as a gratuitous perfection, but in order to develop our spiritual potentialities, to cause the growth of the seeds, which will sprout forth if they fall upon fertile soil.

Prayer: Our Lady insists upon prayer. She wept when she appeared upon the hill, because Christians no longer pray. Her tears are a medication for you; they fall upon your heart made of stone in order to transform it. Our Lady tells us that to pray means to live as the Church lives.

Fasting: The second gift, another stone in your sack, is fasting: from cigarettes, from television, from an evil thought, from a negative project, and from food. Fasting demonstrates your individual capacity to love and affirms that you are important for everyone. Our weakness is nothing if we possess the ability to love. Even our own physical sufferings, if offered to the Lord, are a gift.

The Eucharist: The Eucharist is the third stone. In May, Our Lady admonished us, "You do not know how to live the Mass." The Mass is not simply a rite; it is a mystery and a gift of the Lord. It is a sacrament which cannot be comprehended without humility.

The Bible: The Bible which illuminates the path in the dense fog of ideologies is the fourth stone for the believer of today. It must be the source of our prayer. The Bible illuminates a person's walk amid doubt and conflicting ideologies today.

Confession: Confession is the fifth stone. Our Lady requests monthly confession of us. The purpose of confession is a sacrament and a source of peace with oneself in the meeting with the Lord. A proud person does not know how to confess; humility leads to confession and conversion.

Physical Stones and Crystals

It is also no coincidence, that stones play a central role in Medjugorje. They are the main attraction on the mountain and because of this, the stones and soil of Apparition Hill are handpicked and made into beautiful rosaries, peace chaplets, and decade bracelets from this holy ground. Real pieces of stone are available along the streets leading to the parish church. These healing tools can all be relevant in order to help one bring themselves closer to their heavenly goal or a new spiritual path.

Limestone: This is an assisting stone used to enhance healing properties and encourages purification. It reminds us of our innocence, grounds and centers us and entices positive thoughts. Due to its grounding make-up of clay, sand, organic remains, iron oxide and other materials, many limestones exhibit different colors, especially on weathered surfaces. Therefore, the color of the limestone can help assist with colors of the Auric field and Chakra centers. Red and tan stones for the Base or Root Chakra, orange for the Sacral/Spleen Chakra and so on. Limestone is the root of many crystals including, agate, calcite, dolomite, lapis and Septarian, just to name a few. Therefore, it takes on the metaphysical properties of its additional minerals. This is why limestone is such a multi-dimensional stone.

Dolomite: The Dinaric Alps or Dinarides is a mountain chain which spans from Italy in the northwest, over Slovenia, Croatia, Bosnia and Herzegovina, Serbia, Montenegro to Albania in the southeast. Dolomite is the one of the most prominent stones here. This stone soothes hurt, loneliness, and crushes anxiety. It facilitates giving and receiving, generosity, spontaneity, creativity and an energy uplift. This stone encourages charitable actions. It is used for energy alignment, balance and energy blockage. The lesson this crystal teaches is that "everything happens for a reason". This is one of my favorite stones for encouraging original thought, therefore, it is wonderful for inventors, writers, artists and those looking for creative spark. On an emotional and spiritual level, it brings stability (due to its calcium content) and is a great stone to use to help soothe grief and sadness on every level.

Blue Quartz: This is sited in Judy Hall's wonderful book, *Crystals and Sacred Sites*. Blue Quartz is colored by several minerals including Boulangerite, which happens to be a rare mineral found near Medjugorje. Judy also chose this stone for its spiritual connections. It helps you discover or increase your understanding of your spiritual nature. It has a calming effect upon the mind and stimulates hope. This beautiful blue stone helps to transport you to a peaceful, tranquil space of inner contemplation and soul knowledge.

Blue Lace Agate: This is my choice for this wonderful association with Medjugorje (or any Marian site), as the white lines or veins of this stone represent the veil of the Virgin Mary as does the blue coloring representing her girdle. Blue Lace Agate helps to focus on the inner source of love within you that transforms and heals all wounds. Contains the qualities of flight, air, movement, and grace. Highly inspirational when working with the inner self. Works well with not only the Throat Chakra, but the Heart, Third Eye and Crown Chakra. This nurturing stone connects us to any powerful, feminine energy.

Azurite: This is considered the "stone of heaven." This jewel of wisdom symbolizes insight and discovery. It is said to increase psychic abilities. Azurite activates the Throat and Third Eye Chakra for more assertive communication and alertness. It allows for quiet, deep access to the subconscious and as a "seeing stone", offers access to other times, places, and lives. Therefore, it is a great stone to assist in astral travel. It is a stone that stimulates creativity, giving access to a fountain of ideas, images, and awareness of things around us.

Gemstone:
Magnifica

*"La Reina, dear, the Queen of Peace, you
gather your children near,
With blessings strong and light abound, your
power is now here.*

*Your foretold wisdom has the strength to
nourish us each day,
and teach us how to love ourselves and those
so far away,*

*from you and your eternal Son,
who sent you here to be,*

*a guiding light, endearing force for all the
world to see.*

*You bring your messages and teach us just
how we should pray,*

*and honor, love and cherish those whose
hearts are filled with hate.*

*Your grace, humility and right to offer up
such love…
in such a way, that we can see, the favor
from above.*

*O Magnifica, you reign, with subtle powers
be,*

*We simply ask for your sweet light, while
praying on our knees.*

~Andrew Pacholyk MS L.Ac

Season of the Moon: Moonset

The moon is symbolically found in all cultures and religions throughout history. The moon represents the deeper emotional state of Winter, the closing of the moon's reign, as it sets in the West.

The Moon has a metaphysical connection to our deepest emotions. It connects us to our ability to interact, envision, and employ our emotions on a more conscious level. The moon is associated with the power of our intuition and unconscious insight. The moon taps into our autonomic response. It is also associated with "the mother" archetype, maternal instincts and the urge to nurture. The moon rises every day in the East and always sets in the West, due to the Earth's continuous rotation.

Although we lose the powerful light, reflecting off the moon, we are still able to see the North star as it allows us its final twinkling, before a new dawn rises once more.

Winter represents the cardinal direction of North. The North represents a stage in life, as well as, our mental attitude. North progresses us into the improvement of our mental wisdom, our need for discovery and logic in a way that excites us and illuminates our path.

Knowledge, accumulated through our years, is looked at more clearly now, as a wakeup call for this quarter of our lives. We sense more intellectual illumination and more positive awareness. We embrace these flashes of enlightenment with better knowledge and improved intellect in order to actually connect with this form of "knowing."

Gemstone:
North

"Thou dark of night we see in thee,
The way that it was meant to be,
As earth rotates and grounds us too,
Another day is finally through."

~Andrew Pacholyk MS L.Ac

Crystals Associated with the Full Moon

Moldavite: is a great stone for bringing change in short periods of time. This stone is used for accessing the higher self as a catalyst for the inner spirit. It is used to align yourself with the power of the divine. Its divining spiritual nature is believed to come from it extraterrestrial roots.

Moonstone: honors the Goddess in all women. This stone helps women (and men) to be more comfortable with their gentler feminine/yin receiving side. It is a stone for accessing your intuition and emotional self. Its connection to the moon has been documented for centuries.

Pearl: is in tune with emotions, water, and women, especially pregnant women. Pearls are a symbol of pure heart and mind; innocence and faith. Because it is from the sea, it has watery and lunar connections, therefore it is used for balancing emotions, especially for water signs. Absorbing by nature, this mineral absorbs thoughts and emotions and because of this helps us on a more spiritual connection.

Quartz, Clear: thought to amplify both body energy and thoughts, this stone can assist in the creation of power, clarity of thinking, meditation, cleansing, clearing the aura, spiritual development and healing. Clear Quartz is considered the "stone of power." Pure white light passes through it easily, leaving all the colors of the spectrum unaltered and gives substance to the argument that Clear Quartz crystals can help balance all the elements needed to make us whole and fulfilled.

Selenite: this is the mineral gypsum. Its white/clear striated crystalline body is a sheer source of calming, spiritual light. It works with the higher spiritual Chakra in accessing our higher consciousness, spirit guides and the angelic realm. Because of its striations, like tourmaline, it works along the spinal column grounding and anchoring our Earth vibration and utilizing kundalini to rise freely up our light body stimulating each center as it vibrates.

Silver: this metal is excellent for mental, emotional, and physical releasing and cleansing. Works on mind/emotions to see life's overview, our emotional balance and need for patience. Like the moon's energy, silver has a gentle, cool, smoothing effect. Therefore, it reduces stress through meditation.

Snow White Quartz: also known as Snow Quartz or Milky Quartz, is a variety of Rock Quartz crystal with microscopic water bubbles and inclusions of carbon dioxide. This gives the stone its "snowy", white, or "milky" appearance. Snow White Quartz is the "Observation Stone". Like the introspective and contemplative time of winter, this unique stone allows us to notice more of the actions around us.

Full Moon Meditation

The reflective light of the full moon gives a wonderful and magical sense of harmony and peace of mind. Meditating in its light, gives an etheric and positively enchanting feeling of unity with nature and sky.

Meditating with A Crystal

When you sit in your meditation pose, cross your legs and place your hands on your knees. You can sit with your palms open and place a crystal in both of them. You can also place your stone in front of you.

Moonstone is a beautiful translucent stone which is right for both men and women. It honors the Goddess in all women. It is suggested for awareness and meditation. It soothes stress, anxiety, enhances intuitive sensitivity via our feelings and makes us less overwhelmed by our personal emotions. It helps with greater flexibility and flow in life.

Step by Step

In the glow of a full moon, find a peaceful place, either indoors, perhaps where you can view the full moon, or outdoors when the moon is high in the heavens. Make yourself comfortable.

Slowly take three deep breaths. With each one, consciously release the mental, emotional, and physical tensions. Visualize our radiant light reaching out and connecting with every object under the light of the full moon. Know that we are connected with each individual through the collective emotions we all share by the wonder of this lunar light. Feel this radiant light reaching out even further as we realize that we are all joined by the human experience. Give thanks for the abundance in your life and feel the connections created by our own emotions. Recall that we are all in this struggle together, that we are not alone, and that we live by the law of Universal love.

Sit quietly with your mind receptive and open to receive spiritual energies. Do all that you can to feel the light of the full moon upon you. Feel how your crystals vibrate in your hands.

Make mental notations on thoughts or ideas that come to you. These can appear as knowledge, wisdom, understanding, or inspiration. Whether you are conscious of it or not, you are planting the seed of intention that will manifest with time. From this point forward, it is time to release the old beliefs that no longer serve you. Let go of the pain and suffering you endure. Forgive those around you who have hurt you. It's OK.

Develop the ability to listen within, as you go about your expansive meditation. This is a similar process as remembering an important dream. The full moon brings ideas and dreams to full fruition. Meditate on the image presenting itself. See what is in front of you. Glow with the realization of who you are and the full potential you can become.

In this meditation, you can become part of the Universal flow that brings peace, compassion, love, humility, and gratitude into your human consciousness. As you become more spiritually grounded, you can become more of your true self.

Use the light of the full moon to "see" all that is before you. It is your journey to find the best parts of "you" and enhance these special gifts. It is also within your journey to learn and let go of those habits we may have acquired that block us or keep our minds closed.

This miracle of light is the sun reflecting on the moon. Therefore, this combination of two heavenly bodies, offers both an opportunity and a choice. An opportunity to change the parts of us, we wish to better and a choice to make it truly happen.

When you are ready to take control, you can slowly open your eyes. Be sure and journal about this experience so that you can look back on your insights gained through this meditation.

Gemstone:
Total Eclipse

"When sun turns black from moon's dark side,
in total cover, a halo glides,
just like a ring around its edge, a loving couple
who make their pledge.

The sun and moon in brilliance shine,
their energies are intertwined.

Imbued with love and leadership, this new
beginning, starts its trip
in Universal synchrony, just like a fine-tuned
symphony.

Now take advantage of this tryst, empowered by
a lunar kiss, and use this precious time of yours,
to reach for goals and greater shores.

Let go, detach from chains of past and seek a
slimmer, narrow path. Take what you need and
leave behind the old beliefs, no longer mine."

~ Andrew Pacholyk MS L.Ac

The Power of Detachment

When you hear the word, you may think of a Buddhist monk, leaving all his worldly possessions behind and climbing the lonely mountain to live in complete solitude for the rest of his days. Detachment, or non-attachment is basically freedom from "things." These are things our EGO feels are important to us.

Non-attachment is actually a fully engaged connection to our life through the act of being more conscious or mindful about ourselves. It is the self-realization of the truth about reality. Detachment is not about distancing yourself, but more about understanding the true significance of life so that we better connect to it. By learning to understand that your consciousness cannot be affected by things you hold on to, this gives you a better sense of what actually holds you back.

The concept had alluded me for a long time. The understanding that I had to "give up" all that I worked for, seemed unfathomable to me. I know through all my religious studies that Buddha taught "with attachment comes suffering. Relinquish the delusion and ignorance that fuels both the attachment/clinging and the aversion/hatred that makes life so unsatisfying, and you will find peace (Nirvana)."

In his teachings, Jesus expressed to us through the book of Corinthians, "As we look not to the things that are seen but to the things that are unseen. For the things that are seen are transient, but the things that are unseen are eternal."

My own Hindu yoga teacher would often say, "let go the realm of material things, for, in time, they will bring you nothing but dissatisfaction."

Through my meditation practice, I have come to realize that starting with the things I cannot control, are the first things to detach from. For I have no voice in their outcome, therefore, holding on to them has no purpose and can never serve me.

A friend of mine always travels. On her journeys, she must take with her at least 3 suitcases. She drags them through airports, waits for them to come through on airport baggage belts and hustles them through the streets of whatever city she has landed in. She "needs" every bag. One day, her luggage was lost in transit and she arrived to her destination with nothing, but her little carry-on bag and the clothes on her back. For two weeks she waited and waited for her possessions to appear. They never did. It was at that point that she realized how she could get through her journey without all that "baggage" and what was really important, was right in front of her. At least she had clothes on her back and the means to nourish herself. That was all she discovered, was really important.

About a year ago, I decided to convert my entire website, Peacefulmind.com over to word press. This website format has gained great popularity and works much better when viewed on cell phones. One of the "plugins" or programs I chose to include in my site was a dictionary of terms. I had spent a year, filling in the definitions and by the end of that year, I realized that the plugin I chose was slowing down my website, as it was not compatible. I had website designers and experts analyze my site over and over. Every time they did, they came up with the same response. It was the plugin that was slowing my site down to a crawl. Yet, I could not let go of it. I made every excuse in my head that it was something else. I had invested so much time and effort into it, that I became so stubborn, unhappy, and in denial, that it was starting to reverberate back to me ~ and not in a good way. I could imagine it likened to investing time in a relationship or in a job and it not working out. Yet, the Universe (and everyone else I asked), was clearly pointing me to the answer. My ego could not let it go. Finally, I came to the realization, by meditating on detachment, how I could actually benefit by letting it go.

I then started to re-analyzed my life and looked further back into my past. I sensed just how little control or influence I really had over it. I clearly wasn't paying attention to what life meant at all. I was attached to all the outcomes, holding on to what I thought I had control over, and was not letting life "just flow." I was living life attached and because of this, the result was suffering. I was suffering due to my lack of confidence, which was being undermined by what I thought people thought of me. I was fearful of making my own way through life, due to my belief that people expected certain behaviors or responsibilities by those in my circle of family and friends. It was all due to my belief that I attached to these situations, whether they were really true or not!

Now, I always lecture about being true to yourself and finding a belief that serves who you are. By seeking out the truths in your life and what makes you happy, you will always be your intrinsic guide and mentor. I still believe that these ideas ring true today and it has to do with what we attach our minds and emotions to.

Detachment is not about creating distance. I have learned that it is more about understanding the true purpose and what is of value in your life, so we may better connect to its meaning. We must not get bogged down by the things that anchor us to the ground and not allow our spirit to soar. Detachment is about mindfully paying attention to what is really important on your journey.

As always, you have the right to re-evaluate your path along the way. What may have been the center of your Universe a few years ago, has no more material significance or spiritual relevance and can be looked at through a different set of eyes with the power of detachment.

The practice of non-attachment has you look at outcomes that you have no control over and choose to release them.

The practice of non-attachment has you appreciate, love, life, and your relationships even more. Simply by not having your ego expect an outcome, you are finding the selfless person who does not need to control every situation, but rather understand the decisions that are made.

The practice of non-attachment makes you no longer self-centered or selfish, and you become conscious in your awareness of the other person. You no longer self-identify with a needed outcome.

The practice of non-attachment simply means that your happiness is no longer defined by anything outside of you. You, therefore remain free.

Gemstone:
As Winter Slowly Dies

"We take a breath and let it go,
releasing with a sigh,

We reach a point that tips the scales, as
Winter slowly dies.

I've loved and hated, cried and laughed
and sometimes endured pain,

but, through it all, I hope I've found, the
grace through lessons, gained.

I've searched out blindly or intently to
find that, which I seek,

And sometimes I could barely think
about another week…

ahead as days and days go by and
months turn into years.

I know now that within this time, my
efforts, they were clear

Accumulated over time. to make a better
man.

I hope I did enough to move me through
my own lifespan.

So now, let go and leave it all to powers
that will lead,

perhaps the promise of a Spring, is all
we ever need.

~ Andrew Pacholyk MS. L.Ac

Chapter 9

Making it Happen

Life is a culmination of moments we create for ourselves. We have an obligation to follow our hearts. We can no longer suppress our desires, dreams, or spiritual life journeys based on the ideas, wants, and needs of others. It is our birthright to be who we desire to be. If it is those who say they love us, yet hold us back, then they are only loving you with their conditions, not yours.

We must be allowed to fall and fail, to reach out and go forth. We must take the opportunities granted us and create opportunities that are not. The only one standing in our way is ourselves.

Let go of the fear and reservations. Release the doubt and ties that bind you to what brings you down. Walk away from the negative, overwhelming obstructions standing in your way. Be free of anyone or any belief that makes you feel less than who you want to be.

These are the first steps on your personal, spiritual journey.

Stress, as you can now see, has a large emotional component that affects our energies in so many ways. The crucial take-home lesson here is how WE allow it to affect us.

We are not always going to make the right choices or the best decisions in our process of regulating our lives, but as we have seen here, it is the cumulative effects that make the difference in the end. When we are conscious of our bad habits, we can understand where these habits come from, and make a change.

This is tuning into your energy. By doing so on a daily basis, it allows us to make better choices over time that matter, not the choices in each moment. It is important to see how our self-love and forgiveness opens the door to a better outlook and a better outcome. It is also relevant to pay attention to those feelings, emotions, and behaviors that are a detriment to our life-balancing journey.

As you have now read, so much of the energy spent trying to regulate our lives, has nothing to do with what comes at us, but it has everything to do with the "mental energy" surrounding the process and how we choose to handle it.

Learning to regulate everything in your life will be your greatest lessons. Regulating how you eat, how you handle your emotions, how you move, and how you manage your daily life choices. This will add up to who you are.

I hope this book gives you much love and support and that you use it as a workbook. We know every day is different with different challenges. Use this book to bring you through each day. Use it to your advantage. Allow it to help you on your journey to find a balanced mind, a better body, and a spiritual path.

Chart information, emotions, feelings, or simply find words that come up during the day that encourage you or need your attention. I have always found that by doing this, it opens a window to your soulful thoughts. I hope you have the same experiences.

The first way to pay it forward is by writing a review of this book to let others know of the benefits you've got from it. This will not only help others reach their goals, but it is incredibly rewarding for me to know how much work has benefited others, as well as learning any ways I can improve. This way you can help empower others in the way this book has empowered you.

In happiness,

Andrew Pacholyk, MS, L.Ac
Peacefulmind.com

References

I could not have written this book without the great insight of so many. These references have strengthened my beliefs, encouraged my spirit, and have brought me to a higher place in my life. Please find help in these references. Read more, in order to learn. Check back with them often.

1. *Wellness I.Q. Test* by Dr. Robert Ivker, president of the American Holistic Medical Association.

2. *Spirituality and Health* Magazine

3. *Seven Spiritual Truths*: www.holisticlearningcenter.com/truths.html

4. *Spiritual Truths of World Religions*: http://www.bci.org/carlisle/truths.html

5. *"Forgiveness, What Its For?"*, adapted from Larry James's books, "How to Really Love the One You're With: Affirmative Guidelines for a Healthy Love Relationship," "LoveNotes for Lovers: Words That Make Music for Two Hearts Dancing" and "Red Hot LoveNotes for Lovers." Author Larry James presents seminars nationally for singles and couples.

6. Shakespeare's *Mid Summer's Night Dream*

7. Robert Graves, *The White Goddess,* Faber & Faber; 2nd edition (August 23, 1999) ISBN-10: 0571174256

8. *Triangular Theory of Love* is a theory of love developed by Robert Sternberg. Please visit his website; http://www.robertjsternberg.com/love/

9. *The Luck Project*, Dr. Matthew Smith and Dr. Peter Harris

10. Dr. Edwards Taub's *Seven Steps to Self-Healing*, ASIN: 0789445891

11. Very special thank you to: Castleden, Rodney (2012) *The Element Encyclopedia of the Celts*, Harper Collins Publishers Ltd (January 17, 2013) ISBN-10: 000792979X.

12. An extreme debt of gratitude goes to: Nozedar, Adele (2008) *The Element Encyclopedia of Secret Signs and Symbols*, Harper Collins Publishers; UK ed. edition (March 1, 2009) ISBN-10: 000729896X

13. Many thanks to Ellis, Peter Berresford , *Irish Astrology*, http://www.radical-astrology.com/irish/miscellany/ellis.htm

14. *The Tao of Music: Sound Psychology - Using Music to Change Your Life*, by John M. Ortiz, Weiser Books; n edition (October 1, 1997). ISBN-10: 1578630088

15. *The Secret Language of Birthdays: Your Complete Personology Guide for Each Day of the Year*, by Gary Goldschneider, Joost Elffers, Avery; Reprint edition (October 31, 2013) ISBN-10: 0525426884

16. *Wikipedia*: This incredible, online resource is one of the best for almost any type of research. I encourage you to use them often. Once a year, they ask for donations to help with their operating expenses. They are a worthy cause to donate towards.

17. *The Foundations of Chinese Medicine: A Comprehensive Text*, 3e 3rd Edition, by Giovanni Maciocia C.Ac (Nanjing) Churchill Livingstone; 3 edition (July 27, 2015), ISBN-10: 0702052167

18. *The Web That Has No Weaver: Understanding Chinese Medicine* – May 2, 2000, by Ted J. Kaptchuk, McGraw-Hill Education; 2 edition (May 2, 2000), ISBN-10: 0809228408

19. *Healing with Whole Foods: Asian Traditions and Modern Nutrition* (3rd Edition), by Paul Pitchford, North Atlantic Books; 3rd ed. edition (November 5, 2002), ISBN-10: 1556434308

20. Buddhism: https://en.m.wikipedia.org/wiki/Buddhism

21. Hinduism: https://uri.org/kids/world-religions/hindu-beliefs

22. *Medjugorje*, http://www.medjugorje.org

23. *Medjugorje* http://www.medjugorje.ws

24. *Children of Medjugorje*,
http://www.childrenofmedjugorje.com/content/medjugorje-mainmenu-86/5- stones/13-about-medjugorje/28-5-stones

25. *A Conversation with the Visionaries*, by Sego, Kresimir – Medjugorje 2012

26. *Mudjugorje, Pilgram's* by Dodig, Radoslav –Monograph, Holli Ltd 2011

27. *Kundalini Awakening: A Gentle Guide to Chakra Activation and Spiritual Growth, by John Selby, Zachary Selig* – August 1, 1992, Bantam Books (August 1, 1992), ISBN-10: 0553353306

28. *Eastern Body, Western Mind: Psychology and the Chakra System As a Path to the Self,* by Anodea Judith, Celestial Arts; Revised edition (August 1, 2004), ISBN-10: 9781587612251

29. *The Complete Book of Essential Oils and Aromatherapy*, by Valerie Ann Worwood, New World Library; 1st edition (1991), ISBN-10: 0931432820

30. *Love is in the Earth: A Kaleidoscope of Crystals - The Reference Book Describing the Metaphysical Properties of the Mineral Kingdom*, by Melody, Julianne Guilbault (Illustrator), Earth Love Pub House; Updated, 3rd edition (1995), ISBN-10: 0962819034 ~She is the "original" metaphysical artist on the study and practice of crystal healing. Melody, thank you!

31. *Healing with Crystals and Chakra Energies, Sue and Simon Lily, Hermes House, 2003-2004* ~ This wonderful, colorful book has great information and beautiful color illustrations. The Chakra life development stages are from this insightful book.

32. *Radical Healing*, author Rudolph Ballentine, MD, Himalayan Institute Press. This book is a compelling vision of alternative and integrative medicine. In depth and exceptional.

Index

A

awareness, 45, 47, 58, 62, 64, 71, 78, 80, 82, 128, 249–50, 267–68, 294–95, 306–7, 332

Ayurveda, 122, 231, 253

Azurite, 43–44, 261, 306, 328

B

Bach, Johann Sebastian, 161

BAH FAITH, 49

balance, 12, 38, 40–42, 52, 57, 59, 101–4, 106, 111–12, 142–43, 223, 249, 251, 280–85, 306–7

barley, 177, 237

barley grass, 105, 252

basil, 27, 43, 106, 110, 156, 253, 309

bath, 24, 107, 111, 119, 164, 188, 310

beach, 162, 164–65, 170, 173, 188, 278

bean, 105, 253–54, 309

  red kidney, 105, 253, 309

beauty, 48, 55, 66–68, 95, 97, 102, 117, 124, 164, 167, 172, 175, 181, 297, 304

Beethoven, 117, 161

beliefs, 48, 50, 70–71, 79, 85–88, 115, 130, 138–39, 142, 227, 231–33, 285, 287–88, 333–34, 336

belief system, 9, 12, 44, 70, 84–87, 99, 130–31, 138, 142, 199, 227, 232, 291–92

Beltane, 10, 52, 109, 184

bergamot, 26, 41, 91, 178, 254, 257, 309–10, 312

bible, 170, 326–27

bilberry, 112, 185, 188, 258

biorhythms, 52, 282

birds, 160, 182–83

birthday, 53–54, 60, 198, 320, 342

Black Obsidian, 39, 100, 267–68

bladder

  gall, 41, 105

  urinary, 271, 308

Blavatsky, Madame 303

blessings, 6, 30–31, 48, 184, 247, 259–60, 263, 297, 329

blood, 39, 79, 151–52, 154, 164

Bloodstone, 39, 110, 112–13

Blue Quartz, 43, 328

Britain, 313, 316

broccoli, 106, 177, 253
Buddha, 134, 176, 228, 275, 285, 335
Buddhism, 49, 228, 342
burdock root, 112, 185, 188, 308
butterflies, 181, 183

C

cabbage, 253
calming, 79, 102, 119, 151–52, 167–69, 173, 178, 305–6, 331
Cancer, 60, 172, 269, 297–98
candles, 39, 110, 113, 178, 188, 199–200, 256, 268, 314, 318
Capricorn, 60, 235, 237, 269, 271
cardamom, 40–41
Carnelian, 22, 40, 110, 190, 249, 258, 306
catnip, 112, 185, 188, 298
cauliflower, 106, 177, 253–54
cedarwood, 255–56, 261, 312, 317
Celtic, 38, 108, 110, 112, 184-85, 258, 313, 341
cerebral cortex, 55–56, 207
Chakra, 15, 21, 38–45, 51, 118, 235, 249, 279, 281, 297
Chakra centers, 21, 43, 46, 51, 104, 166, 191, 279, 327, 343
chamomile, 26, 43, 112, 176, 178, 185, 187–88
chest, 41–42, 86, 107, 179, 292
Chiastolite, 110, 112–13
Chinese Medicine, 12, 38, 54, 59, 89, 122, 232, 308, 342
chlorophyll, 252
Christ, 111–12, 324–25
Christianity, 49, 108, 110, 314
Christians, 108, 110, 112, 115, 184, 257–58, 262, 313, 318, 326
Christmas, 300, 316–17
chrysanthemum, 156, 261, 314
Chrysocolla, 103, 169, 298
Chrysoprase, 173
church, 48, 52, 73, 191, 226, 289, 322, 326
cinnamon, 156, 255, 257, 309, 314
circle, 53, 59, 116, 119, 130, 132, 197, 201, 230, 269–70, 272, 278, 281, 316, 318
circulation, 151–52, 164, 249
Citrine, 41, 91, 110, 112–13, 118, 156, 306
citronella, 178
clairvoyance, 44, 103, 168

348

D

dance, 4, 11, 13–14, 31–32, 34, 38, 48, 186, 216, 226, 247, 301
dandelion, 91, 106, 112, 185, 253, 309
darkness, 52, 59, 97, 101, 109, 192–93, 240, 244, 268, 271, 307, 318
death, 18, 53–54, 61, 64, 103, 128, 153, 193, 272, 279, 294, 296, 298, 318, 324
depression, 79, 94, 104, 118, 154, 170, 178–79, 248, 250, 267, 288, 306, 310–12
dermatitis, 107, 311
desert, 9, 95, 97–99
detachment, 10, 307, 335–37
dharma, 285
diet, 12, 43, 57, 105, 152, 176, 194, 253, 308
digestion, 171–72, 176, 255, 311
dill, 156, 177, 258, 261
direction, 91, 93, 110, 112, 119, 152, 156, 160, 185, 188, 190, 258, 261, 314, 317
divination, 10, 66, 102, 194–97, 201, 248, 266, 314
Doctrine of Dharma, 285
Doctrine of the Means, 228
dreams, 34–35, 37, 74, 76, 84, 143, 145–46, 169, 171, 198, 213–14, 229–30, 265–66, 268, 339
Dr.Upledger, 230
Dr.Wilhelm Reich, 230

E

earth, 10–11, 39, 50–51, 53, 89, 100, 112, 114, 190, 192, 234–38, 246, 264, 269, 330
Easter, 52, 111–12, 322
Ecuador, 245, 251
Edwards Taub, 47, 341
eggs, 112–13, 253, 308
Egyptians, 115, 119
elder flower, 188
Elffers, Joost, 60, 342
emerald, 42, 172, 237
emotions, 38, 40, 50–51, 53, 56, 122, 171–72, 227–29, 277–78, 294–95, 297–99, 331, 333, 337, 339–40
energy, 18, 38, 45–46, 59–60, 76–79, 83–84, 89–91, 101–2, 104, 154–56, 172–73, 201, 232, 248–51, 289–90

foods, 12, 26, 28, 30, 39, 50, 57, 62, 105, 152, 154, 175–77, 252–54, 258–59, 308

forgiveness, 10, 42, 48, 194, 201–5, 261, 339, 341

frankincense, 43, 45, 317

Freud, Sigmund, 229–30

fruits, 23, 56, 105, 107, 153, 176–77, 179, 253, 259, 309, 311

G

Gabriel, 237

game playing, 196–97

garden, 181–83, 198, 304

garlic, 106, 252–53, 261, 309, 314

Garnet, 156, 174

Gaulish Coligny, 52, 109

Gemini, 60, 90–91, 173, 269

gemstone, 41–43, 65–66, 110–14, 122–23, 157–58, 160–62, 185–87, 189–90, 194–95, 238–39, 260–61, 263–65, 299–300, 316–17, 329–30

geranium, 42, 110, 187, 298, 312

ginger, 106, 156, 252–53, 256, 261, 309, 314, 317

goals, 64–65, 75, 77–78, 80, 84, 121, 124, 143–45, 148, 152, 199, 213–15, 264, 268, 280–81

God, 7, 47–48, 101, 108, 115, 118, 153, 155, 184, 244, 257, 260, 313, 316, 323–24

goddess, 106, 108, 111–12, 115, 155, 260, 316, 331–32

grace, 8, 40, 102, 114, 120, 129, 150, 153, 168, 297, 328–29, 338

Graham, Martha, 14

Grandth, 49

grapefruit, 105, 177, 179, 187, 309, 312

grapes, 105, 179, 253, 262, 298

gratitude, 8, 47, 129, 169, 207, 221, 225, 261–62, 284, 290, 333, 342

gratitude project, 10, 223, 261–62

Gratitude Stone, 252, 261

Graves, Robert, 187, 341

Greeks, 52, 108, 112, 114–15, 155, 180

grief, 294–95, 306

grounding, 39, 99–101, 103, 106, 118, 174, 235, 248–51, 253, 264, 267–69, 276, 307

growth, 39–45, 51, 61–62, 112, 122, 174, 178, 182, 237, 245, 259, 266, 303, 307, 310

guided imagery, 35–36, 68

guilt, 87, 103, 125, 169, 205, 295

H

I

introspection, 69, 240, 271, 316–18
intuition, 9, 41, 44, 58, 60–61, 63–64, 66, 167–68, 170, 173, 193–96, 206, 209, 277, 282
Iolite, 44–45
Ireland, 184, 257–58, 313–14, 316
Iron, 99, 101, 246, 251
Ivker, Robert, 341

J

Jade, 42, 252, 298
James, Larry 203
jasmine, 42, 44, 106, 113, 298
Jasper, 101, 156, 249, 306
jealousy, 174–75
Jerusalem, 108, 184
Jesus, 109, 187, 300, 324, 335
journal, 34, 143, 204–5, 214, 277, 295, 333
journey, 5, 10–11, 47, 61–62, 100, 117, 151–52, 167–68, 192, 194, 209–12, 243, 245, 302, 304, 324–25, 333, 335–39
joy, 33–34, 94, 122, 129–31, 154, 161–62, 164, 173, 175, 178, 182, 188–89, 245, 300, 304
JUDAISM, 49
Jung, Carl, 198, 230
juniper berry, 27, 310, 312, 317

K

Kaptchuk, Ted J., 342
karma, 86, 234, 285
kidneys, 40, 227, 271, 297, 308
kindness, 6, 48, 130–31, 169, 262
knowledge, 10, 45, 49, 60–61, 66, 75, 90, 191, 194, 197, 216, 265–68, 271, 330, 333
Krotona School of Theosophy, 303–4
kundalini, 45, 83, 173, 307, 331
Kunzite, 42, 250
Kyanite, 43, 103

L

M

Mabon, 10, 260, 262, 298

Maciocia Giovanni, 342

magic, 34–35, 82–83, 106, 108, 161, 184, 192, 257, 264–65, 302, 313

Magic Eye Stone, 252

Mahatma Gandhi, 144, 203

manifest, 53, 103, 130, 132, 211, 266, 297, 333

mantra, 19, 86, 120

Marble, 251

Marble Wish Stones, 251

marigold, 156, 261, 314

marjoram, 27, 42, 177, 258, 261, 314

Martin Luther King, 202

massage, 21, 23–25, 179–80, 212, 226, 254–55, 279

Mayan, 115, 246

medicine wheel, 53, 197

meditation, 4, 28–31, 61–62, 79, 100–104, 120–21, 138, 166–68, 173–74,
    191–92, 199, 247–48, 250–51, 268, 331–33

meditation practice, 28, 138, 335

Medjugorje, 319–28, 342–43

Melody, 343

memories, 7, 23, 55–56, 90, 92, 158, 216, 218, 243, 249, 255, 263, 267,
    306, 316

Memorium, 243–44

Mendez, Sylvia, 7, 199

mentors, 9, 13, 16–17, 81, 118, 190, 294–95, 336

mermaids, 165, 167, 344

metaphysics, 15, 128-130, 194-5

Meteorites, 101, 115, 267

Michael, 2, 91, 241

middle way, 234, 285

migraines, 180

milk, 110–11, 253

mind, 12–13, 29–30, 35–36, 44–45, 64, 66, 71, 73–76, 78–79, 83–85, 147–
    52, 154, 200, 226–29, 292

mindfulness, 79, 204, 212, 220, 317

mind games, 76, 217

mind's eye, 35, 166, 195, 200, 210, 222, 279

minerals, 61–62, 102, 164, 172, 190, 236, 327–28, 331

miracle, 319, 324–26, 333

mirror, 51, 62, 64, 69–70, 100, 134, 148, 185, 200, 267–68, 307

N

O

P

77, 307
psychic abilities, 103, 196, 248, 306, 328
psychic power, 91, 297
psychology, 93, 229–30, 343

Q

Qi, 55, 72, 76, 79, 90, 227
Quartz, 42, 104, 110, 112–13, 175, 190–91, 267, 298, 306–7, 317, 331

R

Rainbow Moonstone, 185
Rainbow Obsidian, 185, 187
rebirth, 53, 63, 103, 112–13, 246, 260, 316–17
relax, 3, 20–21, 32–33, 36, 56, 100, 111, 164, 166, 201, 212, 220, 242,
    273, 278–79
relaxation, 36, 94, 103, 164, 167, 173
religions, 37, 47, 114–15, 151, 189, 263, 289, 330
remembrance, 180, 299, 324
renewal, 53, 63–64, 71, 112–13, 133, 156, 260
Rhodochrosite, 42, 156, 174
rhubarb, 106, 253, 309
river, 238, 244, 273, 275
road, 13, 70, 83, 142, 159, 171, 174, 210–11, 213, 287, 321
rocks, 98, 100, 236, 242, 323, 325
role playing, 196–97
Romans, 52, 108, 112, 115, 155, 180, 315
Root Chakra, 39, 101, 103, 235, 249–50, 267–68, 279, 307, 327
rosemary, 27, 41, 110, 180, 187, 258, 261, 311–12, 314
rosewood, 39, 43
Ruby, 39, 42, 156, 175
Ruiz, Tonio, 6, 16, 320, 323–24

S

Sacral Spleen Chakra, 40, 168, 172–73, 249, 327, 297
Sacred Spirit, 110–13, 185–86, 188–89, 243, 258, 260–61, 263, 314, 316–
    17, 319
sage, 21, 26–27, 111, 164, 169, 237, 258, 261, 314
Sagittarius, 60, 154, 156, 269
salt, 100, 164, 177, 237

254–55, 310

skin photosensitive, 107, 311

sleep, 12, 51, 179, 192, 244, 255, 288–89, 297–98

Smoky Quartz, 267

Snow White Quartz, 110, 317, 332

Sodalite, 43–44, 250

solar plexus, 41, 58, 119, 172

Solar Plexus Chakra, 41, 44, 102, 104, 118–20, 167–68, 250

soul, 30, 33, 38, 66, 68, 72, 130, 136, 211, 267–68, 272, 286–87, 292, 303, 307

sour, 57, 105, 152, 175, 179, 252, 308

southeast, 182, 185, 328

spine, 39, 249

spirit medicine, 227, 232

spirituality, 3, 16, 34, 47–48, 50, 62, 84, 90, 102, 110, 151, 153, 191, 226, 230

Spring, 9, 60–61, 63–65, 67, 71, 81, 89, 91, 94–97, 102, 105–6, 109–14, 132, 254, 258

Sternberg, Robert, 132, 135, 341

stomach, 41, 57, 176, 179, 235–36, 249, 255, 311

stones, 18, 20–23, 79, 99–104, 116, 118–20, 167–71, 173–75, 248–52, 261, 267–68, 305–8, 326–28, 331–32, 344

strength, 6, 9, 13–14, 31, 34, 68, 110, 114, 118, 122–23, 141–44, 187–88, 267, 271, 291–92

stress, 32, 35, 102–3, 107, 148–49, 153, 163–64, 168, 170, 173, 178–79, 249–50, 256, 331–32, 339

stretch, 32, 54, 64, 150, 152, 218

success, 9, 15, 55, 61, 66, 123, 142–43, 145–48, 151, 175, 213, 221, 249, 261, 282

Summer, 9–10, 60–61, 89, 122, 137, 148–49, 154, 156, 162–64, 172–73, 175–78, 181, 184–85, 189, 192

sun, 9–10, 51–52, 59, 61, 108, 113–22, 155–56, 162–64, 166–67, 177–79, 187–92, 247–49, 264–65, 302, 333–34

sunburn, 178, 180, 256

Sunday, 108, 115, 244, 258, 320, 324

sunlight, 22–23, 107, 122, 183, 189, 192, 264, 272, 311–12, 318

sunrise, 9, 61, 98, 114–15, 117, 192, 243, 246, 322–23

sunsets, 97, 109, 189–92, 264

Sunstone, 118, 187, 250

sun walk, 120

survival, 39, 89, 152, 276

sweat, 149–50, 242

sweet fennel, 27
symbols, 37, 39–45, 110, 112, 115, 172, 180, 185, 187, 249–50, 252, 258, 261, 314, 317
synchronicity, 93, 195, 198, 207

T

Tao of Music, 93, 343
tarot, 197
taste, 36, 40, 55, 57, 201, 225, 297–98, 308
Taurus, 60, 235, 237, 269
tea tree, 27, 180, 187, 256, 311
teeth, 39, 198–99, 218
Tektites, 267
temple, 48, 108–9, 226
Thanksgiving, 223, 241, 243
theosophy, 303–4
Third Eye Chakra, 41, 44, 103–4, 167, 171, 250, 328
throat, 43, 57, 102–3, 168, 236, 242, 307
Throat Chakra, 43, 103, 168–69, 173, 250, 306, 328
Thunderegg, 101
thyme, 27, 187, 258, 261, 298, 314
Tiger's Eye, 41, 45, 119, 306
toes, 29, 165–66, 238
tomatoes, 177
tongue, 154–55, 199, 297
tourmaline, 104, 185, 331
Traditional Chinese Medicine (TCM), 12, 52, 227, 231, 255
trees, 28, 80, 106, 178–79, 255, 289, 317
triangular theory of love, 132, 135, 341
trust, 31, 34, 42, 50, 66, 76, 101, 107, 136, 168, 174, 189, 195–96, 275–76, 283
truth, 43, 45, 66, 69, 74, 78, 87–88, 102–3, 195, 197, 228, 300–301, 303, 333, 335–36
Turquoise, 22, 43, 298
twilight, 10, 183, 264, 298

V

valleys, 10, 61, 100, 185, 210, 302, 304–5, 323
Van Itallie, Jean-Claude, 4, 6, 118, 120, 216
violet, 45–46, 112, 185, 317

361

Resources

Crystals and Stones

https://www.peacefulmind.com/crystals

Huge selection of high quality crystals, stones, crystal jewelry, crystal pouches, pendulums and specialty gifts at fair market prices.

Herbs, Incense & Teas

https://www.peacefulmind.com/herbs-and-teas

Fresh, organic herbs, teas, vitamins, supplements and specialty herbs, and highly scented hand-rolled incense sticks, cones and raw herbal resins.

Essential Oils

https://www.peacefulmind.com/essential-oils

Andrew's own line of organic essential oils sourced from all over the world! Angel's Mist essential oils are 100% pure therapeutic grade oils used in any aromatherapy remedy or solution.

Metaphysics & Energy Medicine

https://www.peacefulmind.com/metaphysics

Healing spiritual and emotional tools including Chakra gifts, Aura Kits, themed gifts including Mermaids, Elements, Seasons, Dreams, Spirit gifts

Candle Therapy

https://www.peacefulmind.com/candle-therapy

Beautifully, hand-crafted, highly scented candles created with love. 3-in-1 candles with exceptional scents, lovely charms and educational references wrapped around these healing tools of light!

Certification Home Study Courses

https://www.peacefulmind.com/courses

Since, 1998, Peacefulmind.com makes it possible for anyone to study energy medicine at home, on your time! Endorsed by the National Association of Holistic Wellness, we have certified thousands of students and launched the careers of practitioners all over the world. We continue to lead the way in providing the best and most up-to-date information and exciting new courses!

Made in the USA
Monee, IL
20 December 2022

23148049R00203